F. Scott Fitzgerald on Authorship

"... writing has been my chief interest in life, and I am in every sense a professional."

Edited by Matthew J. Bruccoli
With Judith S. Baughman

D1416728

UNIVERSITY OF SOUTH CAROLINA PRESS

© 1996 University of South Carolina

Published in Columbia, South Carolina, by the
University of South Carolina Press

Manufactured in the United States of America

00 99 98 97 96   5 4 3 2 1

Library of Congress Cataloging-in-Publication Data

Fitzgerald, F. Scott (Francis Scott), 1896–1940.
    F. Scott Fitzgerald on authorship / edited by Matthew J. Bruccoli,
with Judith S. Baughman.
        p. cm.
    Includes bibliographical references and index.
    ISBN 1-57003-146-0
    1. Fitzgerald, F. Scott (Francis Scott), 1896-1940—Authorship.
    2. Fitzgerald, F. Scott (Francis Scott), 1896-1940—Interviews.
    3. American literature—20th century—History and criticism—Theory,
etc. 4. English literature—20th century—History and criticism—
Theory, etc. 5. Authors and publishers—United States—
History—20th century. 6. Books—Reviews. 7. Authorship.
I. Bruccoli, Matthew Joseph, 1931– . II. Baughman, Judith.
III. Title.
PS3511I9.Z464 1996
813'.52—dc20   96-10076

For Scottie

Contents

Editorial Note

The texts of published essays, articles, and reviews by F. Scott Fitzgerald have been silently emended. Excerpts from his letters and notebooks are printed here as written by Fitzgerald. People, titles, and events referred to by Fitzgerald are usually identified only on first appearance, but in certain instances supplementary notes have been provided.

Robert W. Trogdon and Park Bucker ably assisted in the research for this volume. Catherine Fry and the staff of the University of South Carolina Press performed their customary miracles.

Necessary permissions were provided by Henry Dunow, Harold Ober Associates; Lydia Zelaya, Simon & Schuster; and Daniel J. Allman, New Directions.

The Man of Letters as Professional

Civilians hold these notions about writers and writing to be self-evident: that it is easy; that there is a trick to it; that writers earn fortunes but that they don't write for money. These assumptions have impeded the proper assessment of F. Scott Fitzgerald as a professional author and distorted his reputation as a man of letters. The professors and the Fitzgerald groupies have collaborated to create an irresponsible writer who sold out to *The Saturday Evening Post*.

Fitzgerald provides a laboratory case for the profession-of-authorship approach to American literary history as formulated by William Charvat in studying the careers of Hawthorne, Melville, and Emerson:

> The terms of professional writing are these: that it provides a living for the author, like any other job; that it is a main and prolonged, rather than intermittent or sporadic, resource for the writer; that it is produced with the hope of extended sale in the open market, like any article of commerce; and that it is written with reference to buyers' tastes and reading habits. The problem of the professional writer is not identical with that of the literary artist; *but when a literary artist is also a professional writer, he cannot solve the problems of the one function without reference to the other.*[1]

Freud stated that writers write for fame, money, and the love of beautiful women. Dr. Johnson—who combined Grub Street assignments with high scholarship—declared "No man but a blockhead ever wrote except for money." The compulsion to write is concomitant with the compulsion to eat and drink.

Much has been written about Fitzgerald and money—as a subject in his fiction and as a determining factor in his career. The popular notion that he squandered his genius on lavishly paid hackwork persists with the legends of his orgiastic irresponsibility. In actuality Fitzgerald functioned for twenty years as a professional writer and as a literary artist—but he did not have two separate careers. He had one career to which everything he wrote connected.

Willa Cather—who should have known better—expressed this lofty position: "Writing ought either to be the manufacture of stories for which there is a market demand—a business as safe and commendable as making soap or breakfast foods—or it should be an art, which is always a search for something for which there is no market demand, something new and untried, when the values are intrinsic and have nothing to do with standardized values."[2] The key word in her pronouncement is *ought*. Geniuses ought not to be concerned with money. Serious writers ought to be able to write what they want to write. But professional writers write for publication. Otherwise they are hobbyists.

During their college days Fitzgerald dumbfounded Edmund Wilson by announcing, "I want to be one of the greatest writers who ever lived, don't you?"[3] He meant it. Moreover, Fitzgerald believed that writers should receive financial rewards commensurate with the quality of their work. He never expected to starve for his art.

One of the enduring myths attached to Fitzgerald is that he made and squandered fortunes. He was extravagant, but he did not earn vast sums from his magazine work or from his books. His total income from 1919 through 1936, before he went to Hollywood, was $374,922.58 (after his agent's commissions) according to his *Ledger:* an average of $20,829.03 over eighteen years.[†]

Many writers think of themselves as good businessmen, and most of them are bad at it. Fitzgerald employed an agent, Harold Ober, for his magazine work but dealt directly with Maxwell Perkins at Scribners for his books. Ober had a good business relationship with the *Post* and was able to negotiate steady raises in Fitzgerald's story payments. Over the years Ober's role altered from that of literary representative to banker as he advanced Fitzgerald the price of written but not-yet-sold stories—and then the price of stories in progress. From 1927 to mid-1937 Fitzgerald lived from story to story.

The Fitzgerald/Ober correspondence establishes that Ober's function was to sell the stories; he provided no editorial advice until the late Thirties, when Fitzgerald's stories became hard to place. The *Post* editorial archives are lamentably lost, but the skimpy surviving evidence indicates that Fitzgerald had almost no direct contact with the magazine's editors. A few editorial recommendations about material were relayed to Fitzgerald by Ober. It was not until after *Tender Is the Night*, when Fitzgerald's money problems became acute, that he unwisely attempted to interpose in transactions with the *Post*. Fitzgerald dealt directly with editor Arnold Gingrich at

---

† The buying power of Fitzgerald's dollars is discussed elsewhere in this introduction; but a rough indication of his affluence is provided by the fact that members of the House of Representatives and the Senate were paid $10,000 per year during the Twenties.

Esquire during the Thirties, receiving $200 to $300—the magazine's going rate—for the "Crack-Up" essays and the "short-shorts." Ober did not take a commission on these sales.

More is known about the professional life of Fitzgerald than about that of any other major American author because so much of the evidence has been preserved. The year-by-year autobiographical, financial, and bibliographical records he kept in his business ledger include his every sale in the literary market place. The *Ledger* supplements the evidence provided by Fitzgerald's correspondence with Ober[4] and with Perkins at Scribners.[5] Fitzgerald became a full-time professional before his twenty-fourth birthday when Perkins accepted *This Side of Paradise* on 18 September 1919. Six weeks later Fitzgerald wrote his first letter to his agent asking him to place "Head and Shoulders"—which the *Post* took for $400.

When it became clear to Fitzgerald after *The Beautiful and Damned* that his novels would not support his family's habits of living and spending, he tried to strike it rich by writing a hit play. *The Vegetable* died during its out-of-town try-out in 1923. Thereafter Fitzgerald wrote short stories to buy time for novels in the expectation that his novels would both free him from the need to write stories and establish his permanent literary stature. Fitzgerald's novels were commercial work of a higher order than his magazine stories. He expected them to be critical successes and best-sellers.

The Great Gatsby was written on the $14,700 proceeds from nine stories; but after *Gatsby* the magazine money was often spent before Fitzgerald received it. The composition of *Tender Is the Night* stretched over eight years as he interrupted work on the novel to write stories to pay bills—many of which were for his wife's psychiatric treatment. Fitzgerald's 160 stories during twenty-two years may have required as much writing time as his five novels. Moreover, during his lifetime Fitzgerald was more widely read as a magazine story writer than as a novelist. Although the prominent treatment of his stories in the *Post* and other magazines promoted the recognition of Fitzgerald's name, it does not appear that this exposure significantly increased the sales of his novels. The two novels that sold best pre-dated his peak activity as a *Post* contributor. Fitzgerald never wrote what is now called a blockbuster. *This Side of Paradise* (1920) made the *Publishers' Weekly* monthly best-seller list twice, reaching number four; *The Beautiful and Damned* (1922) appeared three times, reaching number six. *The Great Gatsby* never made the best-seller list and did not break 24,000 copies in 1925. *Tender Is the Night* was number ten for April 1934, but did not sell 15,000 copies that year. In 1929 his royalties on seven books totalled $31.77; and eight *Post* stories brought him $31,000.

The magazines provided most of Fitzgerald's income before he went to work for the movies in 1937: $241,453 for 116 stories. Four short-story collections with royalties of $12,400 increased his cumulative income from short stories to more than $253,800, as against about $41,000 in royalties from four novels.† Between 1919 and 1929 Fitzgerald's *Saturday Evening Post* story price rose from $400 to $4,000. It is impossible to convert 1929 dollars into 1996 dollars, but if the inflation multipliers of eight or ten are used, then a $4,000 Fitzgerald story would be worth between $32,000 and $40,000 in diluted dollars.††

The *Post* and the other "slick" magazines (so called because they were printed on glossy paper to accommodate advertising art) paid well because pre-television Americans had a large appetite for magazine fiction. In addition to the penny-a-word pulp-paper magazines or dime novels (for which Fitzgerald did not write) there was an array of slicks that competed with the *Post* for fiction. Fitzgerald appeared in *Collier's, Red Book, Ladies Home Journal, McCall's, Metropolitan,* and *Hearst's International. The Saturday Evening Post,* with a circulation of 2,750,000, was the most prosperous slick and the most generous to its writers. During the Twenties the *Post's* circulation and advertising revenues enabled it to provide between 200 and 300 pages each week for a nickel.◊ The hebdomadal mixture of fiction and nonfiction included from six to nine short stories and two or three serialized novels. The 13 July 1929 issue, led by Fitzgerald's "Majesty"—a story about an American girl who makes a king out of a European weakling—had stories by Brooke Hanlon, Almet Jenks, E. Phillips Oppenheim, Octavus Roy Cohen, and Clarence Budington Kelland. The serials were by Gilbert Seldes, Harry Leon Wilson, and Henry C. Rowland. These by-lines are no longer recognized, but in their time Oppenheim (*The Magnificent Impersonation*), Kelland (*Scattergood Baines*), and Wilson (*Ruggles of Red Gap*) were prodigiously popular. The issue's five articles included three by Sir Cecil Spring-Rice, Christopher Morley, and Struthers Burt.

Fitzgerald's magazine stories were highly competitive hackwork. His fellow-hacks—as defined by *Post* publication—included William Faulkner, Thomas Wolfe, John P. Marquand,◊◊ Sir Arthur Conan Doyle, Joseph Hergesheimer, Donn Byrne, Sinclair Lewis, P. G. Wodehouse, Stewart Edward White, Edgar Wallace, Thomas Beer, Earl Derr Biggers, and Don Marquis. Before he won the Nobel Prize in 1951, Faulkner was forced to

---

† This figure is approximate because it is impossible to untangle the advances and loans for *Tender Is the Night.*

†† Magazine-fiction rates have not increased since Fitzgerald's time. The *Post's* $4,000 fee represented about eighty cents per word. The top short-story rate in 1996 is one dollar per word, paid by *The New Yorker* and *Esquire; Playboy* pays between $3,000 and $3,500 for a story.

◊ In 1996 it is a 96-page monthly selling for $2.95 and bears no resemblance to Fitzgerald's *Post.*

◊◊ Marquand out-published Fitzgerald in the *Post;* between 1921 and 1939, eighty-three Marquand stories appeared there, plus fourteen serials—including *The Late George Apley.*

supplement his novel royalties. He sold fifty-six magazine stories, sixteen of which appeared in the *Post*. He worked for the movies, and there were years when he spent more time in Hollywood than in Yoknapatawpha County. He probably outdrank Fitzgerald. Yet Faulkner was respected as a genius who made necessary accommodations for the sake of his art, whereas Fitzgerald was typed as a casualty of materialism and dissipation.

The circumstance that two of Fitzgerald's masterpieces—"May Day" (1920) and "The Diamond as Big as the Ritz" (1922)—appeared in the low-paying *Smart Set* (circulation of 22,000) raises futile speculation about the stories he might have written if literary magazines had paid as well as the mass-circulation slicks. Fitzgerald wrote stories to meet market requirements—a matter of material and plot. But he had one style: style, Lionel Trilling observed, is "where eventually all a writer's qualities have their truest existence."[6] The writing in some stories is rushed and flashy, but it unmistakably purveys Fitzgerald's tone and sensibility. The superb "Diamond as Big as the Ritz" was written for the commercial market, and the rejection of this story by half a dozen slicks elicited Fitzgerald's 1922 declaration to his agent: "I am rather discouraged that a cheap story like The Popular Girl [*Saturday Evening Post*, 11 and 18 February 1922] written in one week while the baby was being born brings $1500.00 + a genuinely imaginative thing into which I put three weeks real entheusiasm like The Diamond in the Sky brings not a thing. But, by God + Lorimer,† I'm going to make a fortune yet."[7]

At the beginning of his career Fitzgerald was exuberant about the money and exposure generated by his stories. In 1925, following publication of *Gatsby*, he wrote to H. L. Mencken with a characteristic compound of confession and self-judgment: "My trash for the Post grows worse and worse as there is less and less heart in it. . . . I never really 'wrote down' until after the failure of the Vegetable and that was to make this book possible."[8] The tailoring required for *Post* publication is touched on in a letter wherein Fitzgerald argues that he was in effect a *Post* employee. Having tax problems in 1932, he hoped for a ruling that his earnings from the *Post* be treated as earned income. He asked Ober to provide a document for the Collector of Internal Revenue attesting:

> (3.) That you had never considered me a free lance author but that on the contrary my sales were arranged long in advance and that it has been understood for years among editors that my stories were written specificly for the Post by definate arrangment and that I was what is known as a "Post Author."

---

† George Horace Lorimer, the editor of *The Saturday Evening Post*.

(4.) Moreover that they conform to Post specifications as to length and avoidance of certain themes so that for instance they could not have been published in <u>Liberty</u> which insisted on stories not over 5000 words, + would have been inacceptable to womens magazines since they were told from the male angle. That when I contracted with another magazine such as <u>College Humor</u> the stories were different in tone + theme, half as long, signed in conjunction with my wife. That the <u>Post</u> made it plain that they wanted to be offered all my work of the kind agreed apon; that they always specified that no work of mine should appear in several competing magazines. That during the years 1929 and 1930 no story of mine was rejected by the Post. . . .[9]

The *College Humor* connection requires clarification. During 1929–1930 this magazine published five "Girl" stories by Zelda Fitzgerald with the proviso that Fitzgerald be by-lined as co-author. The stories were written by her with some polishing by him. The magazine was buying his name for $500 per story. Ober sold one of the stories in the series, "The Millionaire's Girl," to the *Post* for $4,000 as Fitzgerald's solo work.

The greatest change in literary finances between the Twenties and the Nineties involves subsidiary rights. Civilians read current newspaper reports about five-million-dollar book deals and assume that publishing has always been a jackpot business for authors. The newspapers usually fail to make clear that most of the millions derive from sub-rights (everything except hard-cover publication) in what has become known as "literary property." In the Twenties the standard Scribners contract for Fitzgerald's books disposed of sub-rights in one gentlemanly sentence because these rights were not lucrative: "It is further agreed that the profits arising from any publication of said work, during the period covered by this agreement, in other than book form shall be divided equally between said Publishers and said Author." Now a book contract devotes a page or pages to reprint, book-club, movie, television, audio, dramatic, and electronic rights. Publishers refer disparagingly to a book as making only a "publishing profit"—that is, from the sale of copies of a publisher's own edition, without ancillary income.

Fitzgerald received no income from paperback rights because there were no paperbacks. There were no book clubs before 1925, and they paid chicken feed during their early years. Fitzgerald's foreign rights were negligible, and he did not have a British readership during his lifetime. Serial rights for *The Beautiful and Damned* brought $7,000 from *Metropolitan Magazine*, and *Scribner's Magazine* paid $10,000 for serializing *Tender Is the Night*. Movie rights to stories brought relatively modest amounts: $2,500 for "Head and Shoulders," $2,500 for *The Beautiful and Damned*, $10,000 for *This Side of Paradise*. The most subsidiary income for a Fitzgerald property derived from

The Great Gatsby: about $15,000 from the play by Owen Davis; $18,000 for the movie rights; and $1,000 for second serial rights. Apart from occasional windfalls Fitzgerald lived on the sales of his stories and the dwindling royalties from his books until he went on the Metro-Goldwyn-Mayer payroll in 1937. From 1926 to 1933 the royalties on his three novels averaged $2,860 per year.

Like many American writers of varying talents, Fitzgerald regarded Hollywood as an emergency financial resource. When *The Great Gatsby* failed to sell he wrote Perkins:

> In all events I have a book of good stories for the fall. Now I shall write some cheap ones until I've accumulated enough for my next novel. When that is finished and published I'll wait and see. If it will support me with no more intervals of trash I'll go on as a novelist. If not I'm going to quit, come home, go to Hollywood and learn the movie business. I can't reduce our scale of living and I can't stand this financial insecurity. Anyhow there's no point in trying to be an artist if you can't do your best.[10]

His first two Hollywood trips were failures. In 1927 he was paid $3,500 to write an original screen story titled "Lipstick," which was rejected. In 1931 he was paid $6,000 to write a screenplay for *Red-Headed Woman,* which was also rejected. His final California sojourn during 1937–1940 brought him $91,000 for eighteen months at M-G-M and one screen credit for *Three Comrades.* Fitzgerald was unsuccessful as a screenwriter because he resisted collaboration and because the movies could not film the style and voice of his prose.

Satisfying the requirements of the slicks was hard work; it took a lot of fuel to boil the pot. Scholars frequently cite Fitzgerald's denigration of himself as an "old whore" in a 1929 letter to Hemingway:

> Your analysis of my inability to get my serious work done is too kind in that it leaves out dissipation, but among acts of God it is possible that the 5 yrs between my leaving the army + finishing *Gatsby* 1919–1924 which included 3 novels, about 50 popular stories + a play + numerous articles + movies may have taken all I had to say too early, adding that all the time we were living at top speed in the gayest worlds we could find. This <u>au fond</u> is what really worries me—tho the trouble may be my inability to leave anything once started—I have worked for 2 months over a popular short story that was foredoomed to being torn up when completed. . . . Here's a last flicker of the old cheap pride:—the *Post* now pays the old whore $4000. a screw.

These commentators often omit the next sentence of the passage: "But now its because she's mastered the 40 positions—in her youth one was enough."[11] This complaint makes the point that Fitzgerald's magazine stories required technique and craftsmanship, that early ebullience had given way to mature technique. Hemingway's response clearly identifies the function of Fitzgerald's stories in his working life:

> I wish there was some way that your economic existence would depend on this novel [*Tender Is the Night*] or on novels rather than on the damned stories. Because that is one thing that drives you and gives you an outlet too—the damned stories—
>
> . . . .
>
> (They never raise an old whore's price—she may know the 850 positions—they cut her price all the same—so either you aren't old or not a whore or both). The stories aren't whoring They're just bad judgement—You could have and can make enough to live on writing novels.[12]

Fitzgerald could not live on his novels. Neither could Hemingway in 1929; his second wife had a wealthy and generous family.

Fitzgerald's denunciations of his stories became more vociferous during the years when he was stalled on the novel that became *Tender Is the Night* and he began to function as a supplier of *Post* series stories: the eight Basil Duke Lee stories (1928–1929) and the five Josephine Perry stories (1930–1931). When Ober advised him to make a book out of the Basil stories in 1930, Fitzgerald's response made a firm distinction between reader response to his stories and his novels:

> I could have published four lowsy, half baked books in the last five years + people would have thought I was at least a worthy young man not drinking myself to pieces in the south seas—but I'd be dead as Michael Arlen, Bromfield, Tom Boyd, Callaghan + the others who think they can trick the world with the hurried and the second rate. These <u>Post</u> stories <u>in</u> the <u>Post</u> are at least not any spot on me—they're honest and if their <u>form</u> is stereotyped people know what to expect when they pick up the <u>Post</u>. The novel is another thing—if, after four years I published the Basil Lee stories as a book I might as well get tickets for Hollywood immediately.[13]

There was a close—even symbiotic—relationship between Fitzgerald's magazine fiction and his novels because the stories often functioned as tryouts for subjects and themes that were more complexly developed in novels. Thus the cluster of *Gatsby*-related stories: "Winter Dreams," "The Sensible Thing," "Absolution" (cut from an early draft of *Gatsby*), "Dice, Brassknuckles & Guitar," and "The Diamond as Big as the Ritz." Fitzgerald did not have a different style for magazine work. A good writer writes the only way he can write. The writing in the stories is sometimes self-indulgent, the story plots are often too gimmicky, and there is a reliance on intrusive philosophizing; but the style, tone, voice, and rhythm of the prose are authentic Fitzgerald. He was unable to improve on certain passages that were later required for a novel. It therefore became obligatory for Fitzgerald to maintain a system to prevent himself from using the same passage in a collected story and in a novel—which he considered dishonest. When he classified a story as not worth reprinting in one of his four story collections, he "stripped" passages and phrases for possible use in novels. If material in a story chosen for a collection had been recycled in a novel, he revised the story to remove repetition. During the eight-year evolution of *Tender* he borrowed material from the novel drafts for use in stories.[14] When Perkins advised him not to be overconcerned about duplication of passages in *Taps at Reveille* and *Tender,* citing Hemingway's repetitions, Fitzgerald responded firmly:

> The fact that Ernest has let himself repeat here and there a phrase would be no possible justification for my doing the same. Each of us has his own virtues and one of mine happens to be a great sense of exactitude about my work. He might be able to afford a lapse in that line where I wouldn't be and after all I have got to be the final judge of what is appropriate in these cases. . . .
>
> Besides, it is not only the question of the repetitions but there are certain other stories in the collection that I couldn't possibly think of letting go out in their current form. I fully realize that this may be a very serious inconvenience to you but for me to undertake anything like that at this moment would just mean sudden death and nothing less than that.[15]

Writing about Fitzgerald after his death, James Gould Cozzens observed that "writing short stories is living on your capital if you are naturally a novelist—you can get through in a few years all the subjects, even if you have a lot, that you could have written books on."[16] One of the reasons Fitzgerald resented his stories is that they depleted his literary and emotional capital. In 1935 when he was having difficulty writing marketable stories, Fitzgerald explained to his agent that "all my stories are concieved like novels, require a special emotion, a special experience—so that my readers, if such there be, know that each time it'll be something new, not in form but in substance (it'd be far better for me if I could do pattern stories but the pencil just goes dead on me. . . .)"[17]

Largely as a consequence of his reputation as a bad speller, compounded by the factual errors in his published work, Fitzgerald has been classified as a literary ignoramus—as someone who wrote brilliantly without knowing what he was doing. A natural. This condescending view is corrected by his letters, notebooks, book reviews, and articles—which establish that Fitzgerald reached usable conclusions about the craft of writing, the discipline of authorship, and the obligations of literature. Fitzgerald wrote perceptively and eloquently when he was analyzing his own work. "Our April Letter," a prose poem in his *Notebooks*, expresses Fitzgerald's sense of his exhausted creative capital: "I have asked a lot of my emotions—one hundred and twenty stories, The price was high, right up with Kipling, because there was one little drop of something not blood, not a tear, not my seed, but me more intimately than these, in every story, it was the extra I had."[18]

There was a time when the appellation "man of letters" would have seemed inappropriate for Fitzgerald; but the evidence of his career establishes that he functioned as a literary personage—not just a literary personality. In 1945 Lionel Trilling provided one of the earliest and best assessments of Fitzgerald as a man of letters:

> It is hard to overestimate the benefit which came to Fitzgerald from his having consciously placed himself in the line of the great. . . . To read Fitzgerald's letters to his daughter . . . and to catch the tone in which he speaks about the literature of the past, or to read the notebooks he faithfully kept . . . and to perceive how continuously he thought about literature, is to have some clue to the secret of the continuing power of Fitzgerald's work.[19]

Fitzgerald's conduct as a literary figure was exemplary. He encouraged younger writers and recruited writers—including Hemingway—for Scribners. He did not regard writing as competitive and did not resent the success of other writers. He had firm critical standards and, for example, regarded John Steinbeck's work as bogus. Other writers respected Fitzgerald's literary intelligence—sometimes almost involuntarily. John Dos Passos recalled, "When he talked about writing his mind, which seemed to me full of preposterous notions about most things, became clear and hard as a diamond. . . . about writing he was a born professional. Everything he said was worth listening to."[20]

From 1920, when he wisecracked that "An author ought to write for the youth of his own generation, the critics of the next, and the schoolmasters of ever afterward,"[21] Fitzgerald was concerned about his permanent stature as a literary figure. Yet it often seemed that he was almost deliberately damaging his literary stature by trading permanent fame for notoriety. Fitzgerald lacked the ruthlessness that normally fosters great literary reputations. He was incapable of sacrificing everything and everybody to his writing—as did Hemingway, Faulkner, and Wolfe. The posthumous Fitzgerald revival was a triumph of genius over misfortune—testimony to the enduring force of words on paper. Although the reviewers of his time—except for Gilbert Seldes—did not recognize him as a great writer, other writers understood how important Fitzgerald's writing was. T. S. Eliot orphically pronounced that *Gatsby* was "the first step that American fiction has taken since Henry James."[22] Dos Passos stated of *The Last Tycoon*: "Even in their unfinished state these fragments, I believe, are of sufficient dimensions to raise the level of American fiction to follow in some such way as Marlowe's blank verse line raised the whole level of Elizabethan verse."[23]

Fitzgerald did not play the game of careerism, except by writing. Although he sought the friendship of writers, he belonged to no self-promoting literary-critical groups. During the Thirties he eschewed the mandatory mea culpas and fashionable Marxist conversions by which other writers protected themselves. The condescending obituaries in 1940 indicate that Fitzgerald was generally classified as a failure, a writer who had sold out to the slicks and the movies. Inevitably, F. Scott Fitzgerald provided the best epitaph on the mechanism of his professional work and his literary achievements. Writing to his daughter, Scottie, he declared: "I am not a great man, but sometimes I think the impersonal and objective quality of my talent, and the sacrifices of it, in pieces, to preserve its essential value has some sort of epic grandeur."[24] A professional's life is lived most fully in terms of his vocation.

M.J.B.
19 March 1996

1. William Charvat, *The Profession of Authorship in America, 1800–1870*, edited by Matthew J. Bruccoli (Columbus: Ohio State University Press, 1968), p. [3].

2. "On the Art of Fiction," *On Writing* (New York: Knopf, 1949), p. 103.

3. Wilson, "Thoughts on Being Bibliographed," *Princeton University Library Chronicle*, 5 (February 1944), p. 54.

4. *As Ever, Scott Fitz—: Letters Between F. Scott Fitzgerald and His Literary Agent Harold Ober, 1919–1940*, edited by Bruccoli and Jennifer McCabe Atkinson (Philadelphia & New York: Lippincott, 1972).

5. *Dear Scott/Dear Max: The Fitzgerald-Perkins Correspondence*, edited by John Kuehl and Jackson R. Bryer (New York: Scribners, 1971).

6. *The Liberal Imagination* (New York: Viking, 1950), p. 344.

7. 7 February 1922. *F. Scott Fitzgerald: A Life in Letters*, ed. Matthew J. Bruccoli with the assistance of Judith S. Baughman (New York: Scribners, 1994), p. 54.

8. 4 May 1925. *Life in Letters*, p.111

9. Received 23 April 1932. *Life in Letters*, p. 215.

10. C. 24 April 1925. *Life in Letters*, p. 107.

11. 19 September 1929. *Life in Letters*, p. 169.

12. 13 September 1929. Bruccoli, *Fitzgerald and Hemingway: A Dangerous Friendship* (New York: Carroll & Graf, 1994), pp. 135–136.

13. Received 13 May 1930. *Life in Letters*, pp. 182–183.

14. See George Anderson, "Appendix D: F. Scott Fitzgerald's Use of Story Strippings in *Tender Is the Night*," *Reader's Companion to F. Scott Fitzgerald's Tender Is the Night*,

edited by Bruccoli with Baughman (Columbia: University of South Carolina Press, 1996), pp. 213–261.

15. 24 August 1934. *Dear Scott/Dear Max*, p. 207.

16. To Bertha Wood Cozzens, 22 December 1940. Princeton University Library.

17. Received 2 July 1935. *Life in Letters*, p. 284.

18. "Our April Letter," *The Notebooks of F. Scott Fitzgerald*, edited by Bruccoli (New York & London: Harcourt Brace Jovanovich/Bruccoli Clark, 1978), p. 131.

19. *The Liberal Imagination*, p. 243.

20. *The Best Times: An Informal Memoir* (New York: New American Library, 1968), p. 146.

21. "The Author's Apology," *F. Scott Fitzgerald In His Own Time: A Miscellany*, edited by Bruccoli and Bryer (Kent, Ohio: Kent State University Press, 1971), p. 164.

22. *The Crack-Up*, ed. Edmund Wilson (New York: New Directions, 1945), p. 310.

23. *The Crack-Up*, p. 343.

24. 31 October 1939. *Life in Letters*, p. 419.

Untitled Review of
David Blaize by E. F. Benson

Of late years there have been really good boys' stories, with the boy treated from a subjective point of view neither cynically nor sentimentally. In the class belong *The Varmint*,[1] *Youth's Encounter*,[2] *Seventeen*,[3] and perhaps a new book, *David Blaize*, by E. F. Benson, author of *Dodo*. Benson, by the way, is one of the famous Benson trilogy with Arthur C. Benson and the late Monsignor Robert Hugh Benson.[4] The book carries the English hero through his last year at a "private" school and through three forms at an English public school, presumably Eton under the name of Marchester.

Frank Maddox, David's first and last hero, is the strongest personality in the book, David being rather a peg on which the author hangs virtues and adventures. The book starts well and until three-quarters the way through is very interesting. Then follows a long and, to an American, dry and unintelligible account of a cricket match in which, by careful sounding, we fathom that the hero and his idol Frank Maddox, in the orthodox Ralph Henry Barbour[5] manner, win the day for the school.

Mr. Benson's indebtedness to Compton Mackenzie and Kipling[6] is very great. Swinburne[7] introduces David to literature as he did Michael in *Youth's Encounter*, and the disagreement of David with the prefects is very like certain chapters in Stalky's[8] career. The one incident which forms the background of the book is foreign to anything in our preparatory schools and, although handled with an overemphasized delicacy, seems rather unnecessary and unhealthy from our point of view.

One of the great charms of the book lies in the chapters where Frank first lights upon David near the old cathedral and where David is visiting Frank at the seashore. The chapter on David's love affair is poorly written and seems a half-hearted attempt to make him seem well-rounded. The last melodramatic incident, the injury and recovery of the hero, is well done but does not go for unity. The first two-thirds of the book is immensely entertaining, the last third disappointing.

(David Blaize, *by E. F. Benson, The George Doran Company, New York. $1.35 net*).

—*F.S.F.*

The Nassau Literary Magazine, 72 (February 1917), 343–344.

1. A 1910 prep-school novel by Owen Johnson (1878–1952).
2. The American title for the first volume of *Sinister Street* (1913–1914), the two-volume novel by English writer Compton Mackenzie (1883–1972). This novel, set in an English public school and Oxford University, influenced the writing of *This Side of Paradise*.

3. 1916 novel by Booth Tarkington (1869–1946) about adolescent infatuation.

4. *Dodo* was published in 1893. The Bensons, extremely prolific writers, were sons of E. W. Benson (1829–1896), Archbishop of Canterbury. A. C. Benson (1862–1925) was a poet and diarist; E. F. Benson (1867–1940) is best remembered for his "Lucia" novels; fiction writer Robert Hugh Benson (1871–1914) was ordained by the Anglican Church in 1895 but converted to Roman Catholicism in 1903.

5. Barbour (1870–1944) was a prolific author of boys' books, often about football.

6. Rudyard Kipling (1865–1936), English fiction writer and poet now best known for his stories set in India.

7. Algernon Charles Swinburne (1837–1909), English poet, whose work was admired by Fitzgerald at Princeton.

8. Stalky was the hero of *Stalky & Co.* (1899), stories by Kipling about English school boys.

Untitled Review of
The Celt and the World by Shane Leslie

After his most entertaining *End of a Chapter*, Mr. Leslie[1] has written what I think will be a more lasting book. *The Celt and the World* is a sort of bible of Irish patriotism. Mr. Leslie has endeavored to trace a race, the Breton, Scotch, Welsh, and Irish Celt, through its spiritual crises, and he emphasizes most strongly the trait that Synge, Yeats and Lady Gregory[2] have made so much of in their plays, the Celt's inveterate mysticism. The theme is worked out in an era-long contrast between Celt and Teuton, and the book becomes ever ironical when it deals of the ethical values of the latter race. "Great is the Teuton indeed," it says, "Luther in religion, Bessemer in steel, Nietzsche in philosophy, Rockefeller in oil—Cromwell and Bismarck in war." What a wonderful list of names! Could anyone but an Irishman have linked them in such damning significance?

In the chapter on the conversion of the Celt to Christianity, is traced the great missionary achievements of the Celtic priests and philosophers, Dungal, Fergal, Abelard, Duns Scotus and Ereugena. At the end of the book that no less passionate and mystical, although unfortunate, incident of Pearse, Plunkett and the Irish Republic is given sympathetic but just treatment.[3]

To an Irishman the whole book is fascinating. It gives one an intense desire to see Ireland free at last to work out her own destiny under Home Rule. It gives one the idea that she would do it directly under the eyes of God and with so much purity and so many mistakes. It arouses a fascination with the mystical lore and legend of the island which "can save others, but herself she cannot save."[4] The whole book is colored with an unworldliness, and an atmosphere of the futility of man's ambitions. As Mr. Leslie says in the foreword to *The End of a Chapter* (I quote inexactly) we have seen the suicide of the Aryan race, "the end of one era and the beginning of another to which no Gods have as yet been rash enough to give their names."

The Celt and the World is a rather pessimistic book: not with the dreary pessimism of Strindberg and Sudermann,[5] but with the pessimism which might have inspired "What doth it profit a man if he gaineth the whole world and loseth his own soul." It is worth remarking that it ends with a foreboding prophecy of a Japanese-American war in the future. The book should be especially interesting to anyone who has enjoyed *Riders to the Sea* or *The Hour-Glass*.[6] He will read an engrossing view of a much discussed race and decide that the Irishman has used heaven as a continued referendum for his ideals, as he has used earth as a perennial recall for his ambitions.

(The Celt and the World, *by Shane Leslie, New York; Charles Scribner's Sons.*)

—*F.S.F.*

The Nassau Literary Magazine, 73 (May 1917), 104–105.

1. *The End of a Chapter* was published in 1917. Shane Leslie (1885–1971) was an Anglo-Irish writer who encouraged the young Fitzgerald's literary ambitions.

2. Dramatist John Millington Synge (1871–1909), poet and dramatist William Butler Yeats (1865–1939), and dramatist Lady Augusta Gregory (1852–1932)—prominent figures in the Irish literary renaissance.

3. Irish Republicans Patrick Pearse (1879–1916) and Joseph Plunkett (1887–1916) were leaders of the April 1916 Easter Rebellion against English forces in Dublin. Both were executed in May 1916.

4. Fitzgerald echoes *Matthew* 27:42: "He saved others; himself he cannot save," words of those reviling Christ at his crucifixion.

5. Swedish dramatist August Strindberg (1849–1912) and German dramatist Hermann Sudermann (1857–1928).

6. Play by Synge first produced in 1904 and play by Yeats first produced in 1903.

Untitled Review of
Verses in Peace and War by Shane Leslie

Mr. Leslie, after starting out as a sort of Irish Chesterton,[1] now produces a diminutive volume of poetry under the title of *Verses in Peace and War*. In this poetical era of titles like *Men, Women and Ghosts* and *Sword Blades and Poppy Seed*,[2] Mr. Leslie is liable to be out-advertised by that dashing soubrette of American rhyming, Miss Amy Lowell, but if one desires poetry instead of the more popular antics of the School of Boston Bards and Hearst Reviewers,[3] let him sit down for an hour with Mr. Leslie's little book. At first, one gets the impression of rather light verse but soon finds that it is the touch rather than the verse which is light. The same undercurrent of sadness which runs through Mr. Leslie's prose is evident in his poetry and gives it a most rare and haunting depth. In the series, "Epitaphs for Aviators," two are particularly apt. The one on Lieutenant Hamel:

> Nor rugged earth, nor untamed sky,
> Gave him his death to die,
> But gentlest of the Holy Three;
> The long grey liquid sea.

And the one on Lieutenant Chavez:

> One flying past the Alps to see
>   What lay behind their crest—
> Behind the snows found Italy;
>   Beyond the mountains—rest.

There is a savor of the Greek in his poem "The Hurdlers," dedicated to two of England's representatives in the last Olympian games, since killed in Flanders. The lines:

> Oh, how are the beautiful broken
>   And how are the swiftest made slow—

sound as if they'd scan as well in Greek as in English. The lighter poems, such as "Nightmare" and "Rubies," are immensely well done as are the Irish poems "The Two Mothers" and "A Ballad of China Tea," but the brightest gem of the coffer is the poem "The Dead Friend," beginning:

> I drew him then unto my knees
>   My friend who was dead,

And I set my live lips over his,
And my heart to his head.

Mr. Leslie has a most distinct gift, and the only pity is that his book is so small. Poets are really so very rare that it seems almost unfair for them to become essayists. Despite Mr. Taine,[4] in the whole range from Homer's *Odyssey* to Masters's idiocy,[5] there has been but one Shakespeare, and every lost name leaves a gap that it, and it only, could have filled.

(Verses in Peace and War *by Shane Leslie; Scribner's.*)

—*F. S. F.*

The Nassau Literary Magazine, 73 (June 1917), 152–153.

1. English man of letters G. K. Chesterton (1874–1936) was, like Shane Leslie, a Catholic convert.

2. *Men, Women and Ghosts* (1916) and *Sword Blades and Poppy Seed* (1914) were verse volumes by poet Amy Lowell (1874–1925).

3. Fitzgerald is playing on the title of the satirical poem *English Bards, and Scotch Reviewers* (1809) by Lord Byron (1788–1824).

4. Hippolyte Taine (1828–1893), French literary critic.

5. Poet Edgar Lee Masters (1868–1950), author of *Spoon River Anthology* (1915).

Untitled Review of
God, the Invisible King by H. G. Wells

The fad of rediscovering God has reached Mr. Wells.[1] Started by Tolstoy (who has since backed his case by fathering a brand new revolution)[2] it has reached most of the Clever People, including Bernard Shaw, who tried to startle us last year with his preface to *Androcles and the Lion.*[3] But Mr. Wells has added very little. Like Victor Hugo,[4] he has nothing but genius and is not of the slightest practical help. Neither a pacifist nor a crusader, he has been wise enough to keep God out of the war, which is only what the sanest people have been doing all along; if any war was ever made on earth, it is this one.

If there is anything older than the old story, it is the new twist. Mr. Wells supplies this by neatly dividing God into a Creator and a Redeemer. On the whole we should welcome *God, the Invisible King* as an entertaining addition to our supply of fiction for light summer reading.

(God, the Invisible King *by H. G. Wells; MacMillan Co.*)

—*F. S. F.*

The Nassau Literary Magazine, 73 (June 1917), 153.

1. English writer H. G. Wells (1866–1946), whose "quest novels" influenced the writing of *This Side of Paradise.*

2. Around 1876 Russian novelist Count Leo Tolstoy (1828–1910) embraced a form of Christianity that involved renouncing his wealth. Fitzgerald suggests that his action inspired the Russian Revolution of 1917.

3. In his preface to *Androcles and the Lion* (1916), Shaw portrayed Christ and Christianity as revolutionary, practical, and unlikely to be embraced by people in influential positions.

4. French novelist and poet (1802–1885) best known as the author of the 1831 novel *Notre-Dame de Paris* (*The Hunchback of Notre Dame*).

To: Maxwell Perkins[1]
18 September 1919

Of course I was delighted to get your letter and I've been in a sort of trance all day; not that I doubted you'd take it but at last I have something to show people. It has enough advertisement in St. Paul already to sell several thousand copies + I think Princeton will buy it (I've been a periodical, local Great-Expections for some time in both places.)

Terms etc I leave to you but one thing I can't relinquish without at least a slight struggle. Would it be utterly impossible for you to publish the book Xmas—or say by February? I have so many things dependent on its success—including of course a girl[2]—not that I expect it to make me a fortune but it will have a psychological effect on me and all my surroundings and besides open up new fields. I'm in that stage where every month counts frantically and seems a cudgel in a fight for happiness against time. Will you let me know more exactly how that difference in time of publication influences the sale + what you mean by "early Spring"?

. . . .

F. Scott Fitzgerald: A Life in Letters, edited by Matthew J. Bruccoli with the assistance of Judith S. Baughman (New York: Scribners, 1994), p. 32.

1. Editor Maxwell Perkins (1884–1947) had accepted Fitzgerald's first novel, *This Side of Paradise*, for publication by Scribners.
2. Fitzgerald and Zelda Sayre were married on 3 April 1920, eight days after the publication of *This Side of Paradise*.

To: Harold Ober[1]
8 January 1920

You could have knocked me over with a feather when you told me you had sold Myra[2]—I never was so heartily sick of a story before I finished it as I was of that one.

Enclosed is a new version of <u>Barbara</u>, called <u>Bernice Bobs Her Hair</u>[3] to distinguish it from Mary Rineheart's[4] "Bab" stories in the <u>Post</u>. I think I've managed to inject a snappy climax into it. Now this story went to several Magazines this summer—Scribners, Woman's H. Companion + the Post but it was in an entirely different, <u>absolutely unrecognizable</u> form, <u>single-spaced</u> and none of 'em kept it more than three days except Scribner, who wrote a personal letter on it.

Is there any money in collections of short stories?

This Post money comes in very handy—my idea is to gosouth—probably New Orleans and write my second novel.[5] Now my novels, at least my first one, are not like my short stories at all, they are rather cynical and pessimistic—and therefore I doubt if as a whole they'd stand much chance of being published serially in any of the uplift magazines at least until my first novel + these Post stories appear and I get some sort of a reputation.

Now I published three incidents of my first novel in <u>Smart Set</u> last summer + my idea in the new one is to sell such parts as might go as units separately to different magazines, as I write them, because it'll take ten weeks to write it + I don't want to run out of money. There will be one long thing which might make a novellette for the Post called The <u>Diary of a Popular Girl</u>,[6] half a dozen cynical incidents that might do for <u>Smart Set</u> + perhaps a story or two for <u>Scribners</u> or <u>Harpers</u>. How about it—do you think this is a wise plan—or do you think a story like C. G. Norris' <u>Salt</u>[7] or Cabells <u>Jurgen</u>[8] or Driesers <u>Jenny Gerhard</u>[9] would have one chance in a million to be sold serially? I'm asking you for an opinion about this beforehand because it will have an influence on my plans.

. . . .

F. Scott Fitzgerald: A Life in Letters, p. 36.

1. Harold Ober (1881–1959), Fitzgerald's literary agent, was at this time associated with the Paul Revere Reynolds agency. In 1929 he left Reynolds to found an agency under his own name; Fitzgerald remained Ober's client until they had a falling out in July 1939.
2. "Myra Meets the Family," *The Saturday Evening Post* (20 March 1920).
3. *The Saturday Evening Post* (1 May 1920).
4. Popular fiction writer Mary Roberts Rinehart (1876–1958).

5. Fitzgerald resided in New Orleans during January and February 1920.

6. This novelette was not written.

7. *Salt* (1918) by Charles G. Norris (1881–1945) realistically portrayed the struggles of a young man coming of age in the pre-World War I era.

8. James Branch Cabell (1879–1958) published his "romance" *Jurgen* in 1919. It was acquitted of obscenity in a 1922 court case.

9. A novel whose heroine is abused by family, lovers, and fate, *Jennie Gerhardt* by Theodore Dreiser (1871–1945) appeared in 1911.

Harold Ober, Fitzgerald's literary agent.

"An Interview with
F. Scott Fitzgerald"

In 1920, a few weeks after the publication of "This Side of Paradise," F. Scott Fitzgerald suggested to John William Rogers, then book advertising manager of Scribners, that he might write an interview with himself for use in publicizing his book. A few days later Fitzgerald handed him a rough pencil draft. The interview was not used, however, because, as Mr. Rogers recalls, "Fitzgerald was just one more young man with a promising first novel. An interview giving impressions of him and his literary opinions was of very little interest to anybody." Recently Mr. Rogers came across Fitzgerald's manuscript, which had been filed away for nearly forty years, and made it available to SR [The Saturday Review]. The manuscript, printed here exactly as the twenty-four-year-old Fitzgerald wrote it, has been given by Mr. Rogers to the Dallas Public Library.

With the distinct intention of taking Mr. Fitzgerald by surprise I ascended to the twenty-first floor of the Biltmore[1] and knocked in the best waiter-manner at the door. On entering my first impression was one of confusion—a sort of rummage sale confusion. A young man was standing in the center of the room turning an absent glance first at one side of the room and then at the other.

"I'm looking for my hat," he said dazedly, "How do you do. Come on in and sit down on the bed."

The author of *This Side of Paradise* is sturdy, broad shouldered and just above medium height. He has blond hair with the suggestion of a wave and alert green eyes—the mélange somewhat Nordic—and good looking too, which was disconcerting as I had somehow expected a thin nose and spectacles.

We had preliminaries—but I will omit the preliminaries. They consisted in searching for things cigarettes, a blue tie with white dots, an ash tray. But as he was obviously quite willing to talk, and seemed quite receptive to my questions we launched off directly on his ideas of literature.

"How long did it take to write your book?" I began.

"To write it—three months, to concieve it—three minutes. To collect the data in it—all my life. The idea of writing it occurred to me on the First of last July. It was sort of a substitute form of dissipation."[2]

"What are your plans now?" I asked him.

He gave a long sigh and shrugged his shoulders.

"I'll be darned if I know. The scope and depth and breadth of my writings lie in the laps of the Gods. If knowledge comes naturally, through interest, as Shaw learned his political economy or as Wells devoured modern science—why, that'll be slick. On study itself—that is in 'reading up' a subject—I haven't ant-hill moving faith. Knowledge must cry out to be known—cry out that only I can know it and then I'll swim in it to satiety as I've swum in—in many things."

"Please be frank."

"Well, you know if you've read my book. I've swum in various seas of adolescent egotism. But what I meant was that if big things never grip me—well, it simply means I'm not cut out to be big. This conscious struggle to find bigness outside, to substitute bigness of theme for bigness of perception, to create an objective *Magnum Opus* such as the *Ring in the Book*[3]—well, all that's the antithesis of my literary aims.

"Another thing," he continued, "My idea is always to reach my generation. The wise writer, I think, writes for the youth of his own generation, the critic of the next and the schoolmasters of ever afterward.[4] Granted the ability to improve what he imitates in the way of style, to choose from his own interpretation of the experiences around him what constitutes material, and we get the first-water genius."

"Do you expect to be—to be—well, part of the great literary tradition?" I asked, timidly.

He became excited. He smiled radiantly. I saw he had an answer for this. "There's no great literary tradition," he burst out. "There's only the tradition of the eventual death of every literary tradition. The wise literary son kills his own father."

After this he began entheusiasticly on style.

"By style, I mean color," he said. "I want to be able to do anything with words: handle slashing, flaming descriptions like Wells, and use the paradox with the clarity of Samuel Butler,[5] the breadth of Bernard Shaw and the wit of Oscar Wilde,[6] I want to do the wide sultry heavens of Conrad,[7] the rolled-gold sundowns and crazy-quilt skies of Hichens[8] and Kipling as well as the pastelle dawns and twilights of Chesterton. All that is by way of example. As a matter of fact I am a professed literary thief, hot after the best methods of every writer in my generation."

The interview terminated about then. Four young men with philistine faces and conservative ties appeared, and looking at each other exchanged broad winks. Mr. Fitzgerald faltered and seemed to lose his stride.

"Most of my friends are—are like those," he whispered as he showed me to the door. "I don't care for literary people much—they make me nervous."

It was really rather a good interview, wasn't it!

Saturday Review, 43 (5 November 1960), 26, 56. Although the *Saturday Review* stated in 1960 that this self-interview was never used, it was partly published in Heywood Broun's "Books" column as Carleton R. Davis's interview with Fitzgerald, *New York Tribune*, 7 May 1920, p. 14. Fitzgerald's misspellings and punctuation have not been emended here. M.J.B.

1. The Biltmore Hotel in Manhattan.

2. Enforcement of Prohibition began on 1 July 1919.

3. *The Ring and the Book*, a long poem by Robert Browning (1812–1889), was published in 1868–1869.

4. Fitzgerald used this statement—and the one about the gestation and composition of the novel—in "The Author's Apology," a signed leaf inserted in copies of *This Side of Paradise* distributed at the May 1920 meeting of the American Booksellers Association.

5. (1835–1902), English writer best known for his posthumously published novel *The Way of All Flesh* (1903).

6. (1854–1900), British wit and playwright, author of *The Importance of Being Earnest* (1895). Fitzgerald took one of the epigraphs for *This Side of Paradise* from Wilde's novel *The Picture of Dorian Gray* (1891).

7. Born in Russia of Polish parents, English novelist Joseph Conrad (1857–1924) was best known for his sea novels, including *Lord Jim* (1900).

8. English novelist Robert Hichens (1864–1950) was known for his lush style.

This statement by Fitzgerald was inserted in copies of *This Side of Paradise* distributed at a meeting of the American Booksellers Association (Bruccoli Collection, Thomas Cooper Library, University of South Carolina).

"Contemporary Writers and Their Work, a Series of Autobiographical Letters —F. Scott Fitzgerald"

The idea of "The Ice Palace" (*Saturday Evening Post*, May 22d), grew out of a conversation with a girl out in St. Paul, Minnesota, my home. We were riding home from a moving picture show late one November night.

"Here comes winter," she said, as a scattering of confetti- like snow blew along the street.

I thought immediately of the winters I had known there, their bleakness and dreariness and seemingly infinite length, and then we began talking about life in Sweden.

"I wonder," I said casually, "if the Swedes aren't melancholy on account of the cold—if this climate doesn't make people rather hard and chill—" and then I stopped, for I had scented a story.

I played with the idea for two weeks without writing a line. I felt I could work out a tale about some person or group of persons of Anglo-Saxon birth living for generations in a very cold climate. I already had one atmosphere detail—the first wisps of snow weaving like advance-guard ghosts up the street.

At the end of two weeks I was in Montgomery, Alabama, and while out walking with a girl I wandered into a graveyard. She told me I could never understand how she felt about the Confederate graves, and I told her I understood so well that I could put it on paper. Next day on my way back to St. Paul it came to me that it was all one story—the contrast between Alabama and Minnesota. When I reached home I had

(1) The idea of this contrast.

(2) The natural sequence of the girl visiting in the north.

(3) The idea that some phase of the cold should prey on her mind.

(4) That this phase should be an ice palace—I had had the idea of using an ice palace in a story since several months before when my mother told me about one they had in St. Paul in the eighties.

(5) A detail about snow in the vestibule of a railway train.

When I reached St. Paul I intrigued my family into telling me all they remembered about the ice palace. At the public library I found a rough sketch of it that had appeared in a newspaper of the period. Then I went carefully through my notebook for any incident or character that might do—I always do this when I am ready to start a story—but I don't believe that in this case I found anything except a conversation I had once had with a girl as to whether people were feline or canine.

Then I began. I did an atmospheric sketch of the girl's life in Alabama.

This was part one. I did the graveyard scene and also used it to begin the love interest and hint at her dislike of cold. This was part two. Then I began part three which was to be her arrival in the northern city, but in the middle I grew bored with it and skipped to the beginning of the ice palace scene, a part I was wild to do. I did the scene where the couple were approaching the palace in a sleigh, and of a sudden I began to get the picture of an ice labyrinth so I left the description of the palace and turned at once to the girl lost in the labyrinth. Parts one and two had taken two days. The ice palace and labyrinth part (part five) and the last scene (part six) which brought back the Alabama motif were finished the third day. So there I had my beginning and end which are the easiest and most enjoyable for me to write, and the climax, which is the most exciting and stimulating to work out. It took me three days to do parts three and four, the least satisfactory parts of the story, and while doing them I was bored and uncertain, constantly re- writing, adding and cutting and revising—and in the end didn't care particularly for them.

That's the whole story. It unintentionally illustrates my theory that, except in a certain sort of naturalistic realism, what you enjoy writing is liable to be much better reading than what you labor over.

The Editor, 53 (Second July Number 1920), 121–122.

"Who's Who—and Why"

The history of my life is the history of the struggle between an over-whelming urge to write and a combination of circumstances bent on keeping me from it.

When I lived in St. Paul and was about twelve I wrote all through every class in school in the back of my geography book and first year Latin and on the margins of themes and declensions and mathematics problems. Two years later a family congress decided that the only way to force me to study was to send me to boarding school.[1] This was a mistake. It took my mind off my writing. I decided to play football, to smoke, to go to college, to do all sorts of irrelevant things that had nothing to do with the real business of life, which, of course, was the proper mixture of description and dialogue in the short story.

But in school I went off on a new tack. I saw a musical comedy called *The Quaker Girl*,[2] and from that day forth my desk bulged with Gilbert & Sullivan[3] librettos and dozens of notebooks containing the germs of dozens of musical comedies.

Near the end of my last year at school I came across a new musical-comedy score lying on top of the piano. It was a show called *His Honor the Sultan*, and the title furnished the information that it had been presented by the Triangle Club[4] of Princeton University.

That was enough for me. From then on the university question was settled. I was bound for Princeton.

I spent my entire Freshman year writing an operetta for the Triangle Club. To do this I failed in algebra, trigonometry, coördinate geometry and hygiene. But the Triangle Club accepted my show, and by tutoring all through a stuffy August I managed to come back a Sophomore and act in it as a chorus girl.[5] A little after this came a hiatus. My health broke down and I left college one December to spend the rest of the year recuperating in the West. Almost my final memory before I left was of writing a last lyric on that year's Triangle production while in bed in the infirmary with a high fever.

The next year, 1916–17, found me back in college, but by this time I had decided that poetry was the only thing worth while, so with my head ringing with the meters of Swinburne and the matters of Rupert Brooke[6] I spent the spring doing sonnets, ballads and rondels into the small hours. I had read somewhere that every great poet had written great poetry before he was twenty-one. I had only a year and, besides, war was impending. I must publish a book of startling verse before I was engulfed.

By autumn I was in an infantry officers' training camp at Fort Leavenworth,[7] with poetry in the discard and a brand-new ambition—I was writing an immortal novel. Every evening, concealing my pad behind *Small Problems for Infantry*[8], I wrote paragraph after paragraph on a somewhat edited history of me and my imagination. The outline of twenty-two chapters, four of them in verse, was made, two chapters were completed; and then I was detected and the game was up. I could write no more during study period.

This was a distinct complication. I had only three months to live—in those days all infantry officers thought they had only three months to live—and I had left no mark on the world. But such consuming ambition was not to be thwarted by a mere war. Every Saturday at one o'clock when the week's work was over I hurried to the Officers' Club, and there, in a corner of a roomful of smoke, conversation and rattling newspapers, I wrote a one-hundred-and-twenty-thousand-word novel on the consecutive week-ends of three months. There was no revising; there was no time for it. As I finished each chapter I sent it to a typist in Princeton.

Meanwhile I lived in its smeary pencil pages. The drills, marches, and *Small Problems for Infantry* were a shadowy dream. My whole heart was concentrated upon my book.

I went to my regiment happy. I had written a novel. The war could now go on. I forgot paragraphs and pentameters, similes and syllogisms. I got to be a first lieutenant, got my orders overseas—and then the publishers wrote me that though *The Romantic Egotist*[9] was the most original manuscript they had received for years they couldn't publish it. It was crude and reached no conclusion.

It was six months after this that I arrived in New York and presented my card to the office boys of seven city editors asking to be taken on as a reporter. I had just turned twenty-two, the war was over, and I was going to trail murderers by day and do short stories by night. But the newspapers didn't need me. They sent their office boys out to tell me they didn't need me. They decided definitely and irrevocably by the sound of my name on a calling card that I was absolutely unfitted to be a reporter.

Instead I became an advertising man at ninety dollars a month, writing the slogans that while away the weary hours in rural trolley cars.[10] After hours I wrote stories—from March to June. There were nineteen altogether; the quickest written in an hour and a half, the slowest in three days. No one bought them, no one sent personal letters. I had one hundred and twenty-two rejection slips pinned in a frieze about my room. I wrote movies. I wrote song lyrics. I wrote complicated advertising schemes. I wrote poems. I wrote sketches. I wrote jokes. Near the end of June I sold one story for thirty dollars.[11]

On the Fourth of July, utterly disgusted with myself and all the editors, I went home to St. Paul and informed family and friends that I had given up my position and had come home to write a novel. They nodded politely, changed the subject and spoke of me very gently. But this time I knew what

I was doing. I had a novel to write at last, and all through two hot months I wrote and revised and compiled and boiled down. On September fifteenth *This Side of Paradise* was accepted by special delivery.

In the next two months I wrote eight stories and sold nine. The ninth was accepted by the same magazine that had rejected it four months before. Then, in November, I sold my first story to the editors of *The Saturday Evening Post*.[12] By February I had sold them half a dozen. Then my novel came out. Then I got married. Now I spend my time wondering how it happened.

In the words of the immortal Julius Cæsar: "That's all there is; there isn't any more."[13]

The Saturday Evening Post, 193 (18 September 1920), 42, 61.

1. Fitzgerald attended Newman, a Catholic prep school in Hackensack, N.J., during 1911–1913.

2. An English musical comedy by James T. Tanner, Lionel Monckton, Adrian Ross, and Percy Greenbank, *The Quaker Girl* opened at the Park Theatre in New York City on 23 October 1911. It starred Ina Claire and Clifton Crawford.

3. William Schwenck Gilbert (1836–1911) and Arthur Sullivan (1842–1900) wrote the lyrics and music for a series of very successful operettas in the late nineteenth century.

4. Undergraduate organization that presented an original musical comedy each year. *His Honor the Sultan* was the 1909 Triangle show.

5. Fitzgerald wrote three Triangle Club shows: *Fie! Fie! Fi-Fi!* (1914), *The Evil Eye* (1915), and *Safety First* (1916). There is no evidence that he was permitted to perform in any of his Triangle shows.

6. English poet (1887–1915) who died in World War I; Fitzgerald drew the title of *This Side of Paradise* from Brooke's "Tiare Tahiti" (1914): "Well this side of Paradise! . . . / There's little comfort in the wise."

7. In Kansas.

8. This 1917 textbook by Alfred William Bjornstad was used in officer training classes.

9. This novel was rewritten as *This Side of Paradise*.

10. Fitzgerald wrote advertising slogans for the Barron Collier agency in New York. One of his creations was "We keep you clean in Muscatine."

11. "Babes in the Woods," *The Smart Set* (September 1919).

12. "Head and Shoulders" appeared in the 21 February 1920 issue.

13. Actress Ethel Barrymore (1879–1959) was famous for making this statement after her encores.

To: Robert D. Clark[1]
9 February 1921

Your letter riled me to such an extent that I'm answering immediatly. Who are all these "real people" who "create business and politics"? and of whose approval I should be so covetous? Do you mean grafters who keep sugar in their ware houses so that people have to go without or the cheapjacks who by bribery and high-school sentiment manage to controll elections. I can't pick up a paper here without finding that some of these "real people" who will not be satisfied only with "a brilliant mind" (I quote you) have just gone up to Sing Sing for a stay—Brindell and Hegerman, two pillars of society, went this morning.

Who in hell ever respected Shelley, Whitman, Poe, O. Henry, Verlaine, Swinburne, Villon,[2] Shakespeare ect when they were alive. Shelley + Swinburne were fired from college; Verlaine + O Henry were in jail. The rest were drunkards or wasters and told generally by the merchants and petty politicians and jitney messiahs of their day that real people wouldn't stand it And the merchants and messiahs, the shrewd + the dull, are dust—and the others live on.

Just occasionally a man like Shaw who was called an immoralist 50 times worse than me back in the 90ties, lives on long enough so that the world grows up to him. What he believed in 1890 was heresy then—by by now its almost respectable. It seems to me I've let myself be dominated by "authorities" for too long—the headmaster of Newman, S.P.A,[3] Princeton, my regiment, my business boss—who knew no more than me, in fact I should say these 5 were all distinctly my mental inferiors. And that's all that counts! The Rosseaus,[4] Marxes,[5] Tolstois—men of thought, mind you, "impractical" men, "idealist" have done more to decide the food you eat and the things you think + do than all the millions of Roosevelts and Rockerfellars that strut for 20 yrs. or so mouthing such phrases as 100% American (which means 99% village idiot), and die with a little pleasing flattery to the silly and cruel old God they've set up in their hearts.

A letter

Stratford-on-Avon
June 8th 1595

Dear Will:

Your family here are much ashamed that you could write such a bawdy play as Troilius and Cressida. All the real people here (Mr. Beef, the butcher and Mr. Skunk, the village undertaker) say they will not be satisfied with a brilliant mind and a pleasant manner. If you really want to ammount to

something you've got be respected for yourself as well as your work
Affectionately
Your Mother, Mrs. Shakespeare

. . . .

F. Scott Fitzgerald: A Life in Letters, pp. 45–46.

1. Clark, a boyhood friend in St. Paul, had written Fitzgerald a disapproving letter about *This Side of Paradise*.
2. English Romantic poet Percy Bysshe Shelley (1792–1822), American poets Walt Whitman (1819–1892) and Edgar Allan Poe (1809–1849), American fiction writer William Sydney Porter (O. Henry, 1862–1910), and French poets Paul Verlaine (1844–1896) and François Villon (1431–?).
3. St. Paul Academy.
4. French philosopher Jean-Jacques Rousseau (1712–1778).
5. German political philosopher Karl Marx (1818–1883), author of *Das Kapital*, the basic text for Communism.

Public Letter to Thomas Boyd

Dear Boyd:[1] It seems to me that the overworked art-form at present in America is the "history of a young man." Frank Norris began it with *Vandover and the Brute*,[2] then came Stephen French Whitman with *Predestined*[3] and of late my own book and Floyd Dell's *Moon-Calf*.[4] In addition I understand that Stephen Benét has also delved into his past.[5] This writing of a young man's novel consists chiefly in dumping all your youthful adventures into the readers' lap with a profound air of importance, keeping carefully within the formulas of Wells and James Joyce.[6] It seems to me that when accomplished by a man without distinction of style it reaches the depth of banality as in the case of *Moon-Calf*.

Up to this year the literary people of any pretensions—Mencken, Cabell, Wharton, Dreiser, Hergesheimer, Cather and Charles Norris[7]—have been more or less banded together in the fight against intolerance and stupidity, but I think that a split is due. On the romantic side Cabell, I suppose, would maintain that life has a certain glamour that reporting—especially this reporting of a small Midwestern town—cannot convey to paper. On the realistic side Dreiser would probably maintain that romanticism tends immediately to deteriorate to the Zane Grey-Rupert Hughes[8] level, as it has in the case of Tarkington,[9] fundamentally a brilliant writer.

It is encouraging to notice that the number of pleasant sheep, i.e., people who think they're absorbing culture if they read Blasco Ibanez,[10] H. G. Wells and Henry Van Dyke[11]—are being rounded into shape. This class, which makes up the so- called upper class in every American city, will read what they're told and now that at last we have a few brilliant men like Mencken at the head of American letters, these amiable sheep will pretend to appreciate the appreciable of their own country instead of rushing to cold churches to hear noble but intelligible lords, and meeting once a week to read papers on the aforementioned Blasco Ibanez. Even the stupidest people are reading *Main Street*,[12] and pretending they thought so all the time. I wonder how many people in St. Paul ever read *The Titan*[13] or *Salt* or even *McTeague*.[14] All this would seem to encourage insincerity of taste. But if it does it would at least have paid Dreiser for his early struggles at the time when sucn cheapjacks as Robert Chambers[15] were being hailed as the "Balzacs of America."

—*F. Scott Fitzgerald*

St. Paul Daily News, 20 February 1921, Feature Section, p. 8. Reprinted as "The Credo of F. Scott Fitzgerald," *Chicago Daily News*, 9 March 1921, and as "How the Upper Class Is Being Saved by 'Men Like Mencken,'" *Baltimore Sun*, 22 March 1921.

1. Thomas Boyd was book-review editor for the *St. Paul Daily News* when Fitzgerald met him in 1921. Fitzgerald recommended Boyd's novel *Through the Wheat* to Perkins, and Scribners published it in 1923.

2. This novel by Norris (1870–1902) was posthumously published in 1914.

3. Whitman (1880–1948) published *Predestined* in 1910.

4. *Moon-Calf* by Dell (1887–1969) appeared in 1920.

5. *The Beginning of Wisdom* by Stephen Vincent Benét (1898–1943) was published in 1921.

6. Irish novelist James Joyce (1882–1941) published *A Portrait of the Artist as a Young Man* in 1916.

7. Critic H. L. Mencken (1880–1956), novelist James Branch Cabell (1879–1958), novelist Edith Wharton (1862–1937), novelist Theodore Dreiser (1871–1945), novelist Joseph Hergesheimer (1880–1954), novelist Willa Cather (1873–1947), and novelist Charles G. Norris (1881–1945).

8. Grey (1872–1939) was a prolific best-selling Western writer; Hughes (1872–1956) was a popular novelist and magazine contributor.

9. Tarkington twice won the Pulitzer Prize—for *The Magnificent Ambersons* (1918) and *Alice Adams* (1921).

10. Vicente Blasco Ibáñez (1867–1928), Spanish novelist whose works, such as *The Four Horsemen of the Apocalypse* (1916; English trans., 1918), were popular in English translation.

11. (1852–1933), Princeton professor and respected essayist.

12. A best-selling 1920 novel by Sinclair Lewis (1885–1951), it satirized midwestern small-town life.

13. 1914 novel by Theodore Dreiser.

14. 1899 classic naturalistic novel by Frank Norris.

15. Robert W. Chambers (1865–1933), popular fiction writer whom Fitzgerald had parodied as Robert W. Shameless in *The Nassau Literary Magazine* (December 1916).

"The Baltimore Anti-Christ"
by F. Scott Fitzgerald

The incomparable Mencken will, I fear, meet the fate of Aristides.[1] He will be exiled because one is tired of hearing his praises sung. In at least three contemporary novels he is mentioned as though he were dead as Voltaire[2] and as secure as Shaw with what he would term "a polite bow." His style is imitated by four-fifths of the younger critics; moreover, he has demolished his enemies and set up his own gods in the literary supplements.

Of the essays in the new book the best is the autopsy on the still damp bones of Roosevelt.[3] In the hands of Mencken Roosevelt becomes almost a figure of Greek tragedy; more, he becomes alive and loses some of that stuffiness that of late has become attached to all 100% Americans. Not only is the essay most illuminating but its style is a return to Mencken's best manner, the style of *Prefaces*,[4] with the soft pedal on his amazing chord of adjectives and a tendency to invent new similes instead of refurbishing his amusing but somewhat overworked old ones.

Except for the section on American aristocracy there is little new in the first essay "The National Letters": an abundance of wit and a dozen ideas that within the past year and under his own deft hand have become bromides. The Knights of Pythias,[5] Right Thinkers, On Building Universities, Methodists, as well as the corps of journeyman critics and popular novelists come in for their usual bumping, this varied with unexpected tolerance toward *The Saturday Evening Post* and even a half grudging mention of Booth Tarkington. Better than any of this comment, valid and vastly entertaining as it is, would be a second Book of Prefaces say on Edith Wharton, Cabell, Woodrow Wilson[6]—and Mencken himself. But the section of the essay devoted to the Cultural Background rises to brilliant analysis. Here again he is thinking slowly, he is on comparatively fresh ground, he brings the force of his clarity and invention to bear on the subject—passes beyond his function as a critic of the arts and becomes a reversed Cato[7] of a civilization.

In "The Sahara of Bozart"[8] the dam breaks, devastating Georgia, Carolina, Mississippi, and Company. The first trickle of this overflow appeared in the preface to *The American Credo;*[9] here it reaches such a state of invective that one pictures all the region south of Mason-Dixon to be peopled by moron Catilines.[10] The ending is gentle—too gentle, the gentleness of ennui.

To continue in the grand manner of a catalogue: "The Divine Afflatus" deals with the question of inspiration and the lack of it, an old and sad problem to the man who has done creative work. "Examination of a Popular

Virtue" runs to eight pages of whimsical excellence—a consideration of in-gratitude decided at length with absurd but mellow justice. "Exeunt Omnes," which concerns the menace of death, I choose to compare with a previous "Discussion" of the same subject in *A Book of Burlesques*.[11] The comparison is only in that the former piece, which I am told Mencken fatuously considers one of his best, is a hacked out, glued together bit of foolery, as good, say, as an early essay of Mark Twain's, while this "Exeunt Omnes," which follows it by several years, is smooth, brilliant, apparently jointless. To my best recollection it is the most microscopical examination of this particular mote on the sun that I have ever come across.

Follows a four paragraph exposition of the platitude that much music loving is an affectation and further paragraphs depreciating opera as a form. As to the "Music of Tomorrow" the present reviewer's ignorance must keep him silent, but in "Tempo di Valse" Mencken, the modern, becomes Victorian by insisting that what people are tired of is more exciting than what they have just learned to do. If his idea of modern dancing is derived from watching men who learned it circa thirty-five, toiling interminably around the jostled four square feet of a cabaret, he is justified; but I see no reason why the "Bouncing Shimmee" efficiently performed is not as amusing and as graceful and cer-tainly as difficult as any waltz ever attempted. The section continues with the condemnation of a musician named Hadley,[12] an ingenious attempt to preserve a portrait of Dreiser, and a satisfactory devastation of the acting profession.

In "The Cult of Hope" he defends his and "Dr. Nathan's"[13] attitude to-ward constructive criticism—most entertainingly—but the next section "The Dry Millennium," patchworked from the Répétition Générale,[14] consists of general repetitions of theses in his previous books. "An Appendix on a Tender Theme" contains his more recent speculations on women, eked out with pas-sages from *The Smart Set*.

An excellent book! Like Max Beerbohm,[15] Mencken's work is inevitably distinguished. But now and then one wonders—granted that, solidly, book by book, he has built up a literary reputation most to be envied of any American, granted also that he has done more for the national letters than any man alive—one is yet inclined to regret a success so complete. What will he do now? The very writers to the press about the blue sabbath[16] hurl the bricks of the build-ings he has demolished into the still smoking ruins. He is, say, forty; how of the next twenty years? Will he find new gods to dethrone, some eternal "yokelry" still callous enough to pose as intelligentsia before the Menckenian pen fingers? Or will he strut among the ruins, a man beaten by his own suc-cess, as futile, in the end, as one of those Conrad characters that so tremen-dously enthrall him?

Prejudices, Second Series. By H. L. Mencken. Alfred A. Knopf.
The Bookman, 53 (March 1921), 79–81.

1. Greek general (550–468 B.C.), who was known as "The Just."
2. François Marie Arouet de Voltaire (1694–1778), French author best known for his philosophical tale, *Candide* (1759).
3. Theodore Roosevelt (1858–1919), twenty-sixth president of the United States.
4. *A Book of Prefaces* (1917).
5. Fraternal organization.
6. (1856–1924), twenty-eighth president of the United States.
7. Dionysias Cato—name assigned to a fourth-century volume of Latin precepts; its author is unknown.
8. One of Mencken's most celebrated essays; its title refers to the American South— i.e., the Sahara of the Beaux Arts.
9. 1920 volume by Mencken and George Jean Nathan (1882–1958); it is subtitled *A Contribution toward the Interpretation of the National Mind.*
10. Catiline (108–62 B.C.) was a Roman conspirator.
11. 1916, revised 1920; volume by Mencken.
12. Henry K. Hadley (1871–1937), composer of "In Bohemia: A Concert Overture for Full Orchestra" (1912).
13. Mencken and Nathan applied honorifics to each other.
14. A department in *The Smart Set*, a magazine edited by Mencken and Nathan.
15. (1872–1956), English parodist.
16. So-called blue laws banned public entertainments on Sunday.

"*Three Soldiers*"
A Review by F. Scott Fitzgerald

With the exception of a couple of tracts by Upton Sinclair,[1] carefully disguised as novels but none the less ignored by the righteous booksellers of America, *Three Soldiers* by a young Harvard man named John Dos Passos[2] is the first war book by an American which is worthy of serious notice. Even *The Red Badge of Courage*[3] is pale beside it. Laying *Three Soldiers* down I am filled with that nameless emotion that only a piece of work created in supreme detachment can arouse. This book will not be read in the West. *Main Street* was too much of a strain. I doubt if the "cultured" public of the Middle Border will ever again risk a serious American novel, unless it is heavily baited with romantic love.

No, *Three Soldiers* will never compete with *The Sheik*[4] or with those salacious sermons whereby Dr. Crafts[5] gives biological thrills to the wives of prominent butchers and undertakers, nor will it ever do aught but frighten the caravanserie of one- hundred-and-twenty-proof Americans, dollar-a-year men,[6] and slaughter-crazy old maids who waited in line at the book stores to buy and read the war masterpiece of the Spanish Zane Grey, the one that is now being played in the movies by a pretty young man with machine oil on his hair.[7]

To a dozen or so hereabouts who require more seemly recreation I heartily recommend *Three Soldiers*. The whole gorgeous farce of 1917–1918 will be laid before him. He will hear the Y.M.C.A. men[8] with their high-pitched voices and their set condescending smiles, saying, "That's great, boys. I would like to be with you only my eyes are weak. * * * Remember that your women folk are praying for you this minute. * * * I've heard the great heart of America beat. * * * O boys! Never forget that you are in a great Christian cause."

He will hear such stuff as that, and he will see these same obnoxious prigs charging twenty cents for a cup of chocolate and making shrill, preposterous speeches full of pompous ministers' slang. He will see the Military Police (the M.P.'s) ferociously "beating up" privates for failure to salute an officer.

He will see filth and pain, cruelty and hysteria and panic, in one long three-year nightmare, and he will know that the war brought the use of these things not to some other man or to some other man's son, but to himself and to his OWN son, that same healthy young animal who came home two years ago bragging robustly of the things he did in France.

Dan Fuselli, from California, petty, stupid and ambitious, is the first soldier. His miserable disappointments, his intrigues, his amiable and esurient humanities are traced from the camp where he gets his "training" to postwar Paris where, considerably weakened in his original cheap but sufficing fibre, he has become a mess-cook.

The second soldier, Chrisfield, a half-savage, southern-moraled boy from

Indiana, murders his fancied oppressor—not because of any considerable wrong, but simply as the reaction of his temperament to military discipline—and is A.W.O.L. in Paris at the end.

These two inarticulate persons are woven in the pattern with a third, a musician, who is in love with the mellifluous rhythms of Flaubert.[9]

It is with this John Andrews, the principal protagonist of the story, that John Dos Passos allows himself to break his almost Flaubertian detachment and begin to Britling-ize[10] the war. This is immediately perceptible in his style, which becomes falsely significant and strewn with tell-tale dots. But the author recovers his balance in a page or two and flies on to the end in full control of the machine.

This is all very careful work. There is none of that uncorrelated detail, that clumsy juggling with huge masses of material which shows in all but one or two pieces of American realism. The author is not oppressed by the panic-stricken necessity of using all his data at once lest some other prophet of the new revelation uses it before him. He is an artist—John Dos Passos. His book could wait five years or ten or twenty. I am inclined to think that he is the best of all the younger men on this side.

The deficiency in his conception of John Andrews is this: John Andrews is a little too much the ultimate ineffectual, the Henry-Adams-in-his-youth[11] sort of character. This sort of young man has been previously sketched many times—usually when an author finds need of a mouthpiece and yet does not wish to write about an author.

With almost painstaking precaution the character is inevitably made a painter or a musician, as though intelligence did not exist outside the arts. Not that Andrews' puppet-ness is frequent. Nor is it ever clothed in aught but sophistication and vitality and grace; nevertheless the gray ghosts of Wells's heroes and those of Wells's imitators seem to file by along the margin, reminding one that such a profound and gifted man as John Dos Passos should never enlist in Wells's faithful but aenemic platoon along with Walpole,[12] Floyd Dell and Mencken's late victim, Ernest Poole.[13] The only successful Wellsian is Wells. Let us slay Wells, James Joyce and Anatole France[14] that the creation of literature may continue.

In closing I will make an invidious comparison: Several weeks ago a publisher sent me a book by a well-known popular writer, who has evidently decided that there is better pay of late in becoming a deep thinker or, to quote the incomparable Mencken, "a spouter of great causes." The publishers informed me that the book was to be issued in October, that in their opinion it was the best manuscript novel that had ever come to them, and ended by asking me to let them know what I thought of it. I read it. It was a desperate attempt to do what John Dos Passos has done. It abounded with Fergus Falls[15] mysticism and undigested Haeckel,[16] and its typical scene was the heroic dying Poilu[17] crying "Jesu!" to the self-sacrificing Red Cross worker! It reached some sort of decision—that Life was an Earnest Matter or something! When it was not absurd it was so obvious as to be painful. On every page the sawdust leaked out of the characters. If anyone wishes to cultivate the rudiments of literary taste let him read *The Wasted Generation* by Owen Johnson and *Three Soldiers* by John Dos Passos side by side. If he can realize the difference he is among the saved. He will walk with the angels in Paradise.

F. SCOTT FITZGERALD.

St. Paul Daily News, 25 September 1921, Feature Section, p. 6.

1. (1878–1968), prolific author of reform novels.
2. (1896–1970); his *Manhattan Transfer* appeared in 1925 and his *U.S.A.* trilogy between 1930 and 1936.
3. 1895 novel by Stephen Crane (1871–1900) about the American Civil War.
4. Edith Maude Hull's best-selling 1921 novel about desert love. During the year of the novel's publication, Famous Players produced a silent-film adaptation directed by George Melford (1889–1961) and starring Rudolph Valentino (1895–1926).
5. Wilbur F. Crafts (1850–1922), religious writer and prohibitionist.
6. Businessmen who volunteered their services during World War I.
7. Valentino had the lead role in the movie version of Blasco Ibáñez's *The Four Horsemen of the Apocalypse* (Paramount, 1921).
8. The Y.M.C.A. workers were disliked by soldiers in World War I.
9. French novelist Gustave Flaubert (1821–1880), author of *Madame Bovary* (1857).
10. Reference to H. G. Wells's *Mr. Britling Sees It Through* (1916), a stiff-upper-lip novel about England during World War I.
11. Adams (1838–1918) was a historian and novelist whose best-known work was *The Education of Henry Adams* (1907).
12. Hugh Walpole (1884–1941), popular British novelist whose *Mr. Perrin and Mr. Traill* (1910) treated schoolmasters and whose *Jeremy* (1919) was an education novel.
13. Novelist (1880–1950) who wrote books expressing his socialist convictions. *His Family* (1918) won the first Pulitzer Prize for fiction.
14. (1844–1924), French man of letters who won the Nobel Prize for literature in 1921.
15. Location of the Minnesota insane asylum.
16. Ernst Haeckel (1834–1919), German naturalist and philosopher.
17. French soldier.

"Three Cities"

By F. Scott Fitzgerald
Author of This Side of Paradise, Flappers and Philosophers[1]

It began in Paris, that impression—fleeting, chiefly literary, unprofound—that the world was growing darker. We carefully reconstructed an old theory and, blonde both of us, cast supercilious Nordic glances at the play of the dark children around us. We had left America less than one half of one per cent American, but the pernicious and sentimental sap was destined to rise again within us. We boiled with ancient indignations toward the French. We sat in front of Anatole France's house for an hour in hope of seeing the old gentleman come out—but we thought simultaneously that when he dies, the France of flame and glory dies with him. We drove in the Bois de Boulogne—thinking of France as a spoiled and revengeful child which, having kept Europe in a turmoil for two hundred years, has spent the last forty demanding assistance in its battles, that the continent may be kept as much like a bloody sewer as possible.

In Brentano's[2] near the Café de la Paix, I picked up Dreiser's suppressed "*Genius*"[3] for three dollars. With the exception of *The Titan* I liked it best among his five novels, in spite of the preposterous Christian Science episode near the end. We stayed in Paris long enough to finish it.

Italy, which is to the English what France is to the Americans, was in a pleasant humor. As a French comedy writer remarked we inevitably detest our benefactors, so I was glad to see that Italy was casting off four years of unhealthy suppressed desires. In Florence you could hardly blame a squad of Italian soldiers for knocking down an Omaha lady who was unwilling to give up her compartment to a Colonel. Why, the impudent woman could not speak Italian! So the *Carabinieri*[4] can hardly be blamed for being incensed. And as for knocking her around a little—well, boys will be boys. The American ambassadorial tradition in Rome having for some time been in the direct line of sentimental American literature, I do not doubt that even they found some compensating sweetness in the natures of the naughty *Bersaglieri*.[5]

We were in Rome two weeks. You can see the fascination of the place. We stayed two weeks even though we could have left in two days—that is we *could* have left if we had not run out of money. I met John Carter, the author of "These Wild Young People,"[6] in the street one day and he cashed me a check for a thousand lira. We spent this on ointment. The ointment trust thrives in Rome. All the guests at the two best hotels are afflicted with what the proprietors call "mosquitos too small for screens." We do not call them that in America.

John Carter lent us *Alice Adams* and we read it aloud to each other under the shadow of Caesar's house. If it had not been for Alice we should have collapsed and died in Rome as so many less fortunate literary people have done. *Alice Adams* more than atones for the childish heroics of *Ramsey Milholland* and for the farcical spiritualism in *The Magnificent Ambersons*. After having made three brave attempts to struggle through *Moon-Calf* it was paradise to read someone who knows how to write.

By bribing the ticket agent with one thousand lira to cheat some old general out of his compartment—the offer was the agent's, not ours—we managed to leave Italy.

"Vous avez quelque chose pour déclarer?" asked the border customs officials early next morning (only they asked it in better French).

I awoke with a horrible effort from a dream of Italian beggars.

"Oui!" I shrieked, *"Je veux déclare que je suis très, très heureux a partir d'Italie!"* I could understand at last why the French loved France. They have seen Italy.

We had been to Oxford before—after Italy we went back there arriving gorgeously at twilight when the place was fully peopled for us by the ghosts of ghosts—the characters, romantic, absurd or melancholy, of *Sinister Street*, *Zuleika Dobson*[7] and *Jude the Obscure*.[8] But something was wrong now—something that would never be right again. Here was Rome—here on the High[9] were the shadows of the Via Appia.[10] In how many years would our descendants approach this ruin with supercilious eyes to buy postcards from men of a short, inferior race—a race that once were Englishmen. How soon—for money follows the rich lands and the healthy stock, and art follows begging after money. Your time will come, New York, fifty years, sixty. Apollo's head is peering crazily, in new colors that our generation will never live to know, over the tip of the next century.

Brentano's Book Chat, 1 (September–October 1921), 15, 28.

1. Fitzgerald's first collection of short stories was published on 10 September 1920.

2. Paris bookstore.

3. *The "Genius"* (1915).

4. Members of the Italian national police force.

5. Members of a crack Italian infantry regiment.

6. An article by John F. Carter, Jr. (1897–1967), it appeared in the September 1920 *Atlantic Monthly*.

7. Max Beerbohm's 1911 fantasy set at Oxford University.

8. 1895 novel by British author Thomas Hardy (1840–1928).

9. High Street, Oxford.

10. The Appian Way, road connecting Rome with Capua.

"Poor Old Marriage"
By F. Scott Fitzgerald

Although not one of the first I was certainly one of the most enthusiastic readers of Charles Norris's *Salt*—I sat up until five in the morning to finish it, stung into alertness by the booming repetition of his title phrase at the beginning of each section. In the dawn I wrote him an excited letter of praise. To me it was utterly new. I had never read Zola[1] or Frank Norris or Dreiser—in fact the realism which now walks Fifth Avenue was then hiding dismally in Tenth Street basements.[2] No one of my English professors in college ever suggested to his class that books were being written in America. Poor souls, they were as ignorant as I—possibly more so. But since then Brigadier General Mencken has marshaled the critics in aquiescent column of squads for the campaign against Philistia.

In the glow of this crusade I read *Brass* and suffered a distinct disappointment. Although it is a more difficult form than *Salt* and is just as well, perhaps more gracefully, constructed, the parallel marriages are by no means so deftly handled as the ones in Arnold Bennett's *Whom God Hath Joined*.[3] It is a cold book throughout and it left me unmoved. Mr. Norris has an inexhaustible theme and he elaborates on it intelligently and painstakingly— but, it seems to me, without passion and without pain. There is not a line in it that compares with Griffith Adams's[4] broken cry of emotion, "Why, I love you my girl, better than any other God damned person in the world!"

There was a fine delicacy in Frank Norris's work which does not exist in his brother's. Frank Norris had his realistic tricks—in *McTeague*, for instance, where the pictures are almost invariably given authenticity by an appeal to the sense of smell or of hearing rather than by the commoner form of word painting—but he seldom strengthens his dose from smelling salts to emetics. *Brass*, on the contrary, becomes at times merely the shocker— the harrowing description of Leila's feet could only be redeemed by a little humor, of which none is forthcoming. Early in the book one finds the following sentence: "He inflated his chest . . . pounding with shut fists the hard surface of his breast, alternately digging his finger-tips into the firm flesh about the nipples."

Here he has missed his mark entirely. I gather from the context that he has intended to express the tremendous virility of his hero in the early morning. Not questioning the accuracy of the details in themselves, it is none the less obvious that he has chosen entirely the *wrong* details. He has given a glimpse not into Philip's virility but into the Bronx zoo.

Save for the pseudo-Shavian[5] discussion on marriage near the end Mr. Norris manages to avoid propaganda and panacea. Some of the scenes are excellent—Philip's first courtship, his reunion with Marjorie after their first separation, his final meeting with her. Marjorie and Philip's mother are the best characters in the book, despite the care wasted on Mrs. Grotenberg. Leila is too much a series of tricks—she is not in a class with Rissie in *Salt*.

Had this novel appeared three years ago it would have seemed more important than it does at present. It is a decent, competent, serious piece of work—but excite me it simply doesn't. A novel interests me on one of two counts: either it is something entirely new and fresh and profoundly felt, as, for instance, *The Red Badge of Courage* or *Salt*, or else it is a tour de force by a man of exceptional talent, a Mark Twain or a Tarkington. A great book is both these things—*Brass*, I regret to say, is neither.

Brass, A Novel of Marriage. By Charles G. Norris. E. P. Dutton and Co.

The Bookman, 54 (November 1921), 253–254.

1. Émile Zola (1840–1902), French novelist who founded the Naturalist literary movement.

2. Many of New York's most expensive shops are located on Fifth Avenue; Tenth Street crosses Greenwich Village, the bohemian section of Manhattan.

3. 1906 novel by English fiction writer Arnold Bennett (1867–1931).

4. The hero of Norris's *Salt*.

5. Reference to Irish dramatist George Bernard Shaw, whose plays contained sometimes long-winded discussions of marriage.

"Reminiscences of Donald Stewart"[1]

By F. Scott Fitzgerald

(In the Manner of. . . . .)

Sitting surrounded by my children and fortified by many tons of coal at $20 a ton against the northern winter, it pleases me to look back upon the days of my youth. Back and back, as the flames flicker, I seem to gaze upon those very first moments of my literary career, and the years give up a certain name to be pondered upon—the name of a companion of my youth, now, like me, a white-beard grown old in the service of letters—his name, Donald Ogden Stewart.

How well do I remember our first meeting! It was at a dinner of Sidney Strong's at the University Club.[2] Donald Ogden Stewart said:

"How do you do?"

And quick as a flash I answered.

"Very well thank you."

With these first words we seemed to understand that there was a kinship between us. We were not monkeys, but MEN. There was no doubt about it. We could talk, we could laugh, we could shimmee—

Ah, the old days! Those quaint old fashioned dances like the shimmee— How different from the rough boisterous steps I see performed by the youngsters of today. But I depart from the subject; the old man's mind is feeble and it wanders.

The first thing he said to me, I think, was: "Let's commit a burglary!"

Oh, the simple hearts of those days, the pleasures!

Then he wanted us to break the windows of an undertaker just established on Summit Ave.[3] I remember the smile of amusement that this quaint old idea aroused. But that was Don—innocent, trying always to see things for the best. After that, I remember him at a party. He caused to be thrown on a white screen, upside down, a picture of a religious revival in South Africa, and in his naive and gullible way he thought, he believed, mind you, that this was the photograph of the reunion of a certain family well known in St. Paul. He believed it! And of course everybody was laughing at him. Nobody believed it was that family. Why, the people in the picture were upside down. It was absurd.

Then at another party he pretended that he was a ventriloquist. That's what he told everybody. And anybody who was at the party could see that he was not. All it took was common sense to see that he wasn't. The doll that he was supposed to have in his lap was not a doll. It was a real fellow. How he thought he'd get away with it, I don't know. Everybody that came knew it wasn't a doll even when it moved its mouth and head. So they gave poor Don the laugh as usual and made a guy of him. He felt pretty cheap after that.

How cheerful was St. Paul while he was here. He made all the women feel beautiful and all the men feel witty. He went to the opening of a "one-building university" down in southern Minnesota, enrolled as a freshman, made the football team and was initiated into the Delta Omicron Psi fraternity. Then his vacation was over, and he came back to St. Paul to his position—putting up telephone wires or tearing them down or something.

When the snow came he would throw snowballs against my window about midnight, and we would stroll out Summit Ave. wondering if we had the nerve to call on Father Barron[4] and start a small-hours discussion as to the ascetic ideals of the 13th century or whether, after all, we hadn't better break the undertaker's window to assert the sacrosanctity of Summit Ave. against the invasions of mortuary commerce.

Sometimes, when the snow-covered boulevard was deserted, we would give his favorite Colgate college cheer—"Comes out like a ribbon, lies flat on the brush"[5]—or he would speculate as to how he could inject his synthetic gin of humor into an imitation vermouth party that promised to be awfully dull.

It's not the same town without him—so say many of us. A scandal is only a scandal, but he could turn a Sunday School picnic into a public holiday. But we were all young then. And as I look around at my white-haired compatriots I wonder that the old days have gone. Ah, that was away back before the arms conference, when Fatty Arbuckle[6] was still respectable, when bobbed hair was considered daring. Sic transit. The author of *A Parody Outline of History*[7] and I are old men. I realize at last that our work is behind us and our day is done.

St. Paul Daily News, 11 December 1921, City Life Section, p. 6.

1. Donald Ogden Stewart (1894–1980), American humorist whose friendship with Fitzgerald began in St. Paul before the publication of *This Side of Paradise*.
2. In St. Paul, Minnesota.
3. The principal residential street in St. Paul.
4. Joseph Barron, a priest who was Fitzgerald's friend in St. Paul.
5. This joke depends on confusing Colgate College with Colgate toothpaste.
6. Movie comedian Roscoe "Fatty" Arbuckle (1887–1933) was banned from the movies after he was tried for—but acquitted of—rape.
7. (1921).

Dust-jacket Statement
for John Cournos's *Babel*

Babel is a beautifully written story. . . . The author's graphic atmospheres in London and Paris and New York are flawless. . . . Its love affair is the love affair of hundreds of thousands of people, one of the most real and human love episodes in recent fiction.

Babel (New York: Boni & Liveright, 1922).

To: Harold Ober
5 February 1922

. . . .

I am rather discouraged that a cheap story like <u>The Popular Girl</u>[1] written in one week while the baby was being born[2] brings $1500.00 + a genuinely imaginative thing into which I put three weeks real entheusiasm like <u>The Diamond in the Sky</u>[3] brings not a thing. But, by God + Lorimer,[4] I'm going to make a fortune yet.

. . . .

F. Scott Fitzgerald: A Life in Letters, p. 54.

1. *The Saturday Evening Post* published this long story in two parts (11 and 18 February 1922).
2. The Fitzgeralds' daughter, Scottie, was born 26 October 1921.
3. "The Diamond as Big as the Ritz" was declined by several slick magazines before publication in the June 1922 *Smart Set*, which paid $300 for it.
4. George Horace Lorimer (1867–1937), editor-in-chief of *The Saturday Evening Post*.

To: Edmund Wilson[1]
6 February 1922

I read your letter in a chastened mood. My whole point was that you read the book a long time ago in its informal condition, before its final revision and before your own critisisms had strained out some of the broken cork—that, therefore, while as a critic seeing the book for the first time you would, of course, have to speak the truth whether it hurt me financially or not, still that this case was somewhat different and that a pre-publication review which contained private information destined (in my opinion) to hurt the sale of my book, was something of which I had a legitimate right to complain. My specification of "financial" injury is simply a private remark to you—it would be absurd for me to pretend to be indifferent to money, and very few men with a family they care for can be. Besides, you know that in these two novels I have not suppressed anything with the idea of making money by the suppression but I think I am quite justified in asking you to suppress a detail of my private life—and it seems to me that a financial reason is as good as any, rather better in fact, according to Samuel Butler, than to spare my family.

. . . .

F. Scott Fitzgerald: A Life in Letters, p. 55.

1. Edmund Wilson (1895–1972), literary critic and Fitzgerald's Princeton friend, wrote an article about him for *The Bookman* (March 1922). When Fitzgerald read the article before its publication, he asked that references to his drinking and his army experiences be cut.

"Aldous Huxley's *Crome Yellow*"
Reviewed by F. Scott Fitzgerald

Now this man is a wit. He is the grandson of the famous Huxley[1] who, besides being one of the two great scientists of his time, wrote clear and beautiful prose—better prose than Stevenson[2] could ever master.

This is young Huxley's third book—his first one, *Limbo*, was a collection of sketches; his second, *Leda*, which I have never read, contained one long poem and, I believe, a few lyrics.[3]

To begin with, Huxley, though he is more like Max Beerbohm than any other living writer (an ambiguity which I shall let stand, as it works either way), belongs as distinctly to the present day as does Beerbohm to the '90's. He has an utterly ruthless habit of building up an elaborate and sometimes almost romantic structure and then blowing it down with something too ironic to be called satire and too scornful to be called irony. And yet he is quite willing to withhold this withering breath from certain fabulous enormities of his own fancy—and thus we have in *Crome Yellow* the really exquisite fable of the two little dwarfs which is almost, if not quite, as well done as the milkmaid incident in Beerbohm's *Zuleika Dobson*.

In fact I have wanted a book such as *Crome Yellow* for some time. It is what I thought I was getting when I began Norman Douglas's *South Wind*.[4] It is something less serious, less humorous, and yet infinitely wittier than either *Jurgen* or *The Revolt of the Angels*.[5] It is—but by telling you all the books it resembles I will get you no nearer to knowing whether or not you will want to buy it.

Crome Yellow is a loosely knit (but not loosely written) satirical novel concerning the gay doings of an house party at an English country place known as Crome. The book is yellow within and without—and I do not mean yellow in the slangy sense. A sort of yellow haze of mellow laughter plays over it. The people are now like great awkward canaries trying to swim in saffron pools, now like bright yellow leaves blown along a rusty path under a yellow sky. Placid, impoignant, Nordic, the satire scorns to burn deeper than a pale yellow sun, but only glints with a desperate golden mockery upon the fair hair of the strollers on the law; upon those caught by dawn in the towers; upon those climbing into the hearse at the last—beaten by the spirit of yellow mockery.

This is the sort of book that will infuriate those who take anything seriously, even themselves. This is a book that mocks at mockery. This is the highest point so far attained by Anglo-Saxon sophistication. It is written by a man who has responded, I imagine, much more to the lyric loves of lovers long dust than to the contemporary seductions of contemporary British flappers. His protagonist—what a word for Denis, the mocked-at mocker—is lifted from his own book, *Limbo*. So is Mr. Scoogan, but I don't care. Neither do I care that it "fails to mirror life;" that it is "not a novel"— these things will be said of it, never fear. I find Huxley, after Beerbohm, the wittiest man now writing in English.

The scene where Denis was unable to carry Anne amused me beyond measure.

And listen to this, when Huxley confesses to a but second-hand knowledge of the human heart:

"In living people one is dealing with unknown and unknowable qualities. One can only hope to find out anything about them by a long series of the most disagreeable and boring human contacts, involving a terrible expense of time. It is the same with current events; how can I find out anything about them except by devoting years of the most exhausting first-hand studies, involving once more an endless number of the most unpleasant contacts? No, give me the past. It does not change; it is all there in black and white, and you can get to know about it comfortably and decorously, and, above all, privately—by reading."

Huxley is just 30, I believe. He is said to know more about French, German, Latin and medieval Italian literature than any man alive. I refuse to make the fatuous remark that he should know less about books and more about people. I wish to heaven that Christopher Morley[6] would read him and find that the kittenish need not transgress upon the whimsical.

I expect the following addenda to appear on the green jacket of "Crome Yellow" at any moment:

"Drop everything and read 'Crome Yellow.'"

—H-yw-d Br-n.[7]

"Places Huxley definitely in the first rank of American (sic!) novelists."

—General Chorus

(The "sic" is mine. It is not harsh as in "sic 'im!" but silent as in "sick room.")

"It may be I'm old—it may be I'm mellow,
But I cannot fall for Huxley's "Crome Yellow."

—F.P.A.[8]

"Exquisite. Places Huxley among the few snobs of English literature."

—G-tr-de Ath-r-t-n.[9]

(*Crome Yellow*, by Aldous Huxley. George H. Doran Co. $2.)

St. Paul Daily News, 26 February 1922, Feature Section, p. 6.

1. Thomas Henry Huxley (1825–1895), English biologist and leading writer on evolution.

2. Scottish novelist and essayist Robert Louis Stevenson (1850–1894).

3. *Limbo* (1920) and *Leda* (1920) were the first two books by Huxley (1894–1963) to be published in the United States.

4. 1917 satirical novel; Douglas (1868–1952) was an English novelist and travel writer who spent much of his life in Italy.

5. 1914 satirical novel by Anatole France.

6. (1890–1957), American man of letters who at that time wrote essays about literary subjects.

7. Heywood Broun had written an unfavorable notice of *This Side of Paradise*.

8. Newspaper columnist Franklin P. Adams (1881–1960).

9. American novelist Gertrude Atherton (1857–1948).

"Literary Libels—
Francis Scott Key Fitzgerald"
Thomas A. Boyd

When I came to St. Paul I was interested most in meeting people who could tell me of the intimate side of Fitzgerald. Being charmed with *This Side of Paradise* and with the remarkable promise it evinced, I wanted to know something of the person who wrote it other than that which was appearing in the literary supplements and magazines. From numerous opinions of him given by people who know him and his family, I conjectured that in some way he had ruffled the composure of his fellow townsmen. It might have been, I thought, that he refused to pronounce the name of the city of his birth in the provincial way. But he had done something, I was sure.

One of his friends of an earlier day, replying to a question I had asked, told me: "Yes. I know Scott very well. He is an awful snob." Another reported that at the present time he was sequestered in a New York apartment with $10,000 sunk in liquor and that he was bent on drinking it before he did anything else.

Still another related the story of how in New York Fitzgerald became bored with his guests and called the fire department. When the firemen arrived and asked where the fire was Scott pounded his stomach and dramatically announced: "The fire is right here. Inside me."

One or two admitted that "Scottie was a great boy" but further than that they would not pledge themselves. That all of these cheerfully thrown handsful of mud could be true I doubted. Further I was a little put out with my informants because, I reflected, I could have imagined more lurid stories than those myself.

Then one day someone told me that Fitzgerald was coming to St. Paul to spend the winter. He was to take a house at White Bear[1] until the weather got cold and then he was to move into the city. Eager to meet him I awaited the opportunity with a great deal of interest.

But when the time came it was on one of those torrid days of late summertime when the collar around one's neck becomes a wriggling snake with a hot sticky belly.

Thoroughly disgusted, I was all for calling it a day when a close acquaintance walked into the office and said, "Scott Fitzgerald is out at White Bear. Let's go out and see him." Had the day been less stifling I would have been more impressed. As it was I managed only to answer that as no place in the world could be hotter than the office where I then was I would be glad to drive out with him to meet Mr. Fitzgerald.

We were soon on our way, and as we rode past the small pumpkin-planted farms the various rumors that I had heard concerning Fitzgerald came to my mind. I judged that if they were true he would appear rather dissipated. No one could drink a thousand bottles of liquor in one year without having a red nose and blue-veined face. Not even Anton Dvorak.[2] Nor could anyone, because he was bored with his guests, telephone a hurry call to the fire department and not show that he was a peculiar person. These thoughts, and others of more marvelous fabric, engaged me as we plowed through the necessary 10 miles of white smoky dust to reach White Bear.

"Now that we are here how are we going to find the house," my friend wanted to know, and I was about to tell him that we might ask at the yacht club, when a Ford laundry delivery truck coughed past. We hailed the driver and explained our difficulty. "You wish to be directed to the home of Mr. Scott Fitzgerald the novelist," he answered in a high voice. "Well, if you'll just follow behind me I will take you there because I am delivering some laundry to them." We thanked him and drew our car in rear of his, and in this way we reached a modestly proportioned house whose color, setting and architecture was admirably suited for a summer home.

Grasping a bottle of synthetic gin[3] firmly around the neck I preceded my friend out of the car and up the path to the house. A voice answering the bell announced: "I'll be down in a minute." It was a strong boyish voice that could not have ascended from a liquor-parched throat. Another literary legend punctured.

Out on the enclosed porch, with the bottle of gin resting on a table beside us, we waited for the appearance of Mr. Fitzgerald. In a few minutes he came and, on seeing us, exclaimed to me: "Why, I thought you'd be wearing a frock coat and a long white beard."

I scanned him closely. His eyes were blue and clear; his jaw was squared at the end which perceptibly protruded; his nose was straight and his mouth, though sensitive looking, was regular in outline. His hair which was corn-colored, was wavy. His were the features that the average American mind never fails to associate with beauty. But there was a quality in the eye with which the average mind is unfamiliar.

"I thought you would be a baby with rouged lips, so I too am disappointed," I told him.

We resumed our seats while he visited the kitchen, returning in a few minutes with lemons, oranges and cracked ice. I was surprised that he only brought two glasses. "I suppose that's synthetic gin you've got there. Will you have lemon or orange." We named our choice and while squeezing the juice of an orange into a glass turned and said: "You like Mencken, don't you?"

"That would be like saying that I like the law of gravity," I replied, "but I suppose I would say yes."

"Speaking of Mencken," I resumed, "I thought I saw a Baltimore forefinger in *This Side of Paradise*. There is hardly a good book these days without it."

"Well!" he replied, "I don't think *Main Street* would have been written if Mencken hadn't been born. There are pages in that book that read just like the Répétition Générale, but that isn't true with *This Side of Paradise*. It was not until after I had got the proofs of my book back from the publishers that I learned of Mencken. I happened across the *Smart Set* one day and I thought 'Here's a man whose name I ought to know. I guess I'll stick it in the proof sheets.' But I've met Mencken since then and I'm glad I put his name in. Have you ever met?"

I sorrowfully replied that I had not, but that I meant to some day.

"Gee, he's great. He's the one man in America for whom I have a complete respect."

"But what is he like," I wanted to know.

"Well, he's like a good natured beer-drinking German whom you would imagine liking to sit around in his stocking feet."

"I can conceive of him being good-natured and liking to drink beer, if it is good beer, but somehow the shoeless feet won't fit in. I suppose it's because he plays the piano or else I have the orthodox complex. But he certainly has made many things possible for the younger generation."

"Yes, you bet he has. He even helped boost Floyd Dell's *Moon-Calf* into success. There's a book which certainly touches the depths of banality. He hasn't even a pretense of style and his manner of dumping youthful history into the reader's lap with such a profound air of importance is simply disgusting. No, for once Mencken made a mistake."

At the time I was a Dell enthusiast so I took Fitzgerald's criticism with a gulp. I had nothing on the subject to offer in return, and the conversation was as self-conscious as a fish out of water; my mind grasped at the first thought that entered my head.

"Sandburg," I said. "What do you think of Sandburg?"[4]

And again my choice was horrific.

"Sandburg is probably an intelligent fellow. But to say that he is a poet is rot. The great city of Chicago felt a literary awakening and they looked around for a verse writer to call great, Sandburg was the only one in sight and immediately the legend of the great poet of the proletariat was built up to fit the shoulders of Sandburg."

But this time my position was not untenable.

"But, I don't agree with you there," I said. "Sandburg is a great poet. There are only two or three great poets in America and surely Sandburg is one of them."

"But he doesn't write any great lines. Tell me one of his verses that stick in your memory like Keats's "Ode on a Grecian Urn?"[5]

"Well, there's 'Five Towns on the B. and O.'"

"All right, say it."

And I tried and failed. It may have been the fourth synthetic gin and orange juice concoction but my tongue would go no further than: "Hungry smoky shanties hanging to the slope."

"See there, you can't do it. And what kind of a poet is a man who can't make lines to stick in your head. Why even Vachel Lindsay—"[6]

And he started off a verse from the "Chinese Nightingale."

"From that point of view probably you're right, but Sandburg works otherwise. He makes his poems so that in their entirety they are ravishing. They are a complete thing in themselves. You see in them lyricism. The whole drama of the human race unfolds when he recites one of his verses."

"Why he's not half as lyrical as the feet of Charlie Chaplin."[7]

"Well, if you're going to drag in Charlie Chaplin's pathetic feet, I can't discuss Sandburg with you any more. I should like to see Chaplin because I admire his work so much, but I detest the whole caboodle of the movies outside of him. Consequently, I am seldom aware when a picture of his is showing in town."

"But you might as well protest against a Cunarder[8] or the income tax as to protest against the movies," said Fitzgerald. "The movies are here to stay."

"Yes, I suppose they are, but then so is *Uncle Tom's Cabin*.[9] By the way, what do you think of Ben Hecht[10] as a writer."

"Oh, I like the things of his that I've seen very much. I'm looking forward to his novel that's coming out this fall. *Erik Dorn*, I think is the name of it."

"*Erik Dorn*, yes. So am I looking out for it. I remember seeing one of Hecht's plays shown at a ragamuffin theater in Chicago. It was about a hungry bum who was spending the night on the sidewalk. Toward morning as he was passing a plate-glass window in a store he saw his reflection and exclaimed: 'Well, I'm a cock-eyed son-of-a-gun, if it ain't Jesus.' I thought it was good."

"That's funny. I've no doubt that Hecht will do wonders in fiction, but the author whose book I want to see most is John Dos Passos."

"Oh yes, I heard about his book. It's called *Three Soldiers*,[11] isn't it?"

"That's it, and I've a hunch that it will be one of the best, if not the best book of the year," Fitzgerald said enthusiastically.

Three months later that proved to be a very wise prediction.

"I've got Charles Norris's new novel[12] in the house. John Farrar of the *Bookman* sent it to me for review. Have you seen it?"

I replied that I had read the book and that I thought it very good.

"Well, the question of marriage is a rather important one and for one to write a novel, or what Norris would call an interpretative novel, of marriage, in which the author fails to take sides either for or against marriage and divorce is quite an achievement. And then Norris makes his characters into real human beings. That's more than many fictionists do."

"Maybe you're right. But I can't see much in it. The grouping isn't clever and he has loaded his book with too many characters. It's too much like a brief."

"Norris can take care of himself. Tell me about your new novel. I've read the first installment of it in the *Metropolitan*."[13]

"It's something after the manner of *Linda Condon*.[14] Hergesheimer tried to show the effect on a woman after her once- legitimate beauty had passed. That is what I am trying to do with Gloria."

"But that isn't all, is it?"

"No, that isn't all, but you wait and read it." He disappeared into the house and returned with the manuscript of *The Beautiful and Damned*.[15] "Here it is."

It was written on ordinary sized paper and not typed. The pencil scrawl was in large letters and altogether it must have been two-feet thick. This thing must be almost 200,000 words, I thought. After I had finished reading the first chapter (He writes legibly), I remarked that the manuscript was not very much like the printed story in the *Metropolitan*.

"Look here," I said, "this is much better than the *Metropolitan* version. There were some excellent descriptive passages entirely left out in the part that I read."

"Well," he looked in rather a funny way, "they bought the rights to do anything they like with it when they paid for it."

"Of course it will appear as it was originally written when it comes out in book form, won't it?"

"Surely it will, I only hope—" and then he was silent.

"But good lord, if I were you I'd go around telling people that the original story was different from the *Metropolitan* story. Why, that *Metropolitan* story," I confessed, "was nothing but cheap sensationalism without any coherence at all."

As he offered no remark on the subject I turned the conversation. "What started you writing?"

"I've written ever since I can remember. I wrote short stories in school here, I wrote plays and poetry in prep school, and I wrote plays and short stories for the Triangle and the 'Lit' at Princeton. But Hugh Walpole was the man who started me writing novels. One day I picked up one of his books while riding on a train from New York to Washington. After I had read about 100 pages I thought that 'if this fellow can get away with it as an author I can too.' His books seemed to me to be as bad as possible. The principal thing he did was to make unessentials seem important, but he was one of the near best-sellers. After that I dug in and wrote my first book."

"Well, you are probably right about Walpole and you may be right about Floyd Dell, but I think you're wrong about Charlie Norris and I know you're wrong about Sandburg. The trouble is you don't get Sandburg. It's the same way with Sherwood Anderson.[16] Now that Anderson has been boosted so long by really intelligent persons the pretenders are beginning to praise him and ascribe motives to his work of which I know he never dreamed. There's something to Sandburg, a lot. I wish I could tell you about it, but it's not clear enough in my mind."

"I sure wish I could see it. If the man even wrote as well as Vachel Lindsay—you can remember Lindsay's stuff. 'Booth led boldly with a big brass drum.'"[17]

"But that's only cheap alliteration and it comes from a howling Methodist Y.M.C.A. proselyte to right-living. You can't seriously consider him."

But just then another automobile horn sounded from the gravel path and we prepared to leave. St. Paul already was paying homage to success! The sight of the large automobile stopping in front of the Fitzgerald home was an inspirational sight, I reflected. People will go 10 miles to warm themselves in the warm rays thrown off by his glory. Oh, well, it were better that the singer of beauty be honored even at the cost of annihilation of the decalogue rather than that it be left to its own devices.

The Fitzgerald family gave up the summer place rather early and removed to one of the new apartment hotels here. After that we saw each other daily. Scott was at that time beginning a comedy for the stage[18] and he felt that his work would be less interrupted if he rented an office in a down-town business building. His new novel *The Beautiful and Damned* had appeared in its last installment in a popular magazine, and Fitzgerald had suggested that I should not read it until I could read the entire book.

He had been hard at work rewriting parts of the original story and changing it to advantage so that it would be ready for publication in book form by March 3. He had also written three or four short stories. Two of them he sold to popular magazines and the price he got for one, he told me, was $1,500. And then he worked nearly every day on his play. And yet people with the utmost seriousness report stories of Fitzgerald's abandoned carousals that, to hear them tell it, happened every day.

Enthusiasm runs high in the nature of Fitzgerald. He is even enthusiastic in his dislikes and certainly he is whole-hearted over the things that he enjoys. To be with him for an hour is to have the blood in one's veins thawed and made fluent. His bright humor is as infectious as smallpox and as devastating to gloom. He has humor all right, someone may remark, but it is never shown when he is made the butt of it. Of course, it isn't. He is not enough of a dissimulator for that. What person honestly does enjoy being made the butt of a joke? I have searched far but the man still remains a bird of paradise. Some persons, when a joke is made at their expense, will smile, but the mouth will droop in one corner, like a courageous prize-fighter who has been struck on the nose. No, the entire psychology of the joke is against one's smiling at one's own expense. Where is the "sudden glory" of which Max Eastman[19] speaks? How can one appreciate the "cracker" when it knocks out three of his front teeth?

At this time a man passed through St. Paul who had, years ago, written three or four good books, but since had almost completely stopped writing to devote his time to drink.

One day after we left him and were walking up the street Scott remarked:

"There goes one of the last survivors of the 'booze and inspiration' school. Bret Harte[20] was one of the earliest ones and it was all right in his day, but the old school of writers who learned to drink and to write while reporting for a newspaper is dying out. Do you remember that story of how Harte, visiting Mark Twain in California, said one night that he had to write a story and get it to the publisher the next afternoon?"

I replied that I might have heard it but if I had I must have forgotten.

"Well, Bret Harte came to Mark Twain's home one afternoon for a visit, and after he had been there a few hours he said that he had to write a story that night because he had promised the publishers of a magazine that he would have it for them in the morning. So Twain suggested that Harte could use his study, but Harte said, 'I've got plenty of time. Let's talk a while.'

"They killed most of the afternoon talking and after dinner Twain again suggested that Harte go up to his study and start to work. But again Harte was not ready. 'There's no rush. Let's talk a while longer.'

"After a while it got to be 1 o'clock, and Twain, becoming sleepy, told Harte that he was going to bed and asked him whether he wanted anything before he started to work.

"'Well,' said Harte. 'If you'll have a fire made in the study and a quart of whiskey sent up I'll be all right.'

"So Twain went to bed and Harte to the study. About 5 o'clock in the morning a servant was called, and another fire was made in the room and another bottle of whiskey was brought in. At 9 o'clock Harte came downstairs to breakfast with the story of 6,000 words, completed.

"But that gang is not to be met any more. I can't think of how he could have done it. For me, narcotics are deadening to work. I can understand any one drinking coffee to get a stimulating effect, but whiskey—oh, no."

"*This Side of Paradise* doesn't read as if it were written on coffee," I remarked.

"And it wasn't. You'll laugh, but it was written on Coca Cola. Coca Cola bubbles up and fizzes inside enough to keep me awake."

Imagine Amory Blaine being born of a Coca Cola mother! But it is exuberant and sparkling enough to have been, at that.

Fitzgerald's apartment was perhaps 20 minutes walk from his office, and when there was not too much snow on the ground, he would walk rather than take the street car. From this, many people got the idea that he positively refused to ride on the street car, and many of them began to uphold him in what they considered another of his eccentricities.

His writing is never thought out. He creates his characters, and they are likely to lead him into almost any situation. His phrasing is done in the same way. It is rare that he searches for a word. Most of the time words come to his mind and then spill themselves in a riotous frenzy of song and color all over the page. Some days he writes as many as 7,000 or 8,000 words; and then, with a small *Roget's Thesaurus*, he carefully goes over his work, substituting synonyms for any unusual words that appear more than once in seven or eight consecutive pages. Bernard Shaw has said that no one should write until he can supply at least five synonyms for any word that comes into his mind. Mr. Shaw says that he is able to do that, but it is not an entirely wild speculation to venture that if anyone entered the Shaw study sometimes he might see a well thumbed *Thesaurus* lying around.

Fitzgerald is extraordinarily curious. To that quality in him is due the responsibility for a number of the legends that have been built up around him. To illustrate:

We had gone into a cigar store to roll dice[21] for a package of cigarettes. Fitzgerald rolled the dice first and the highest combination that turned was three of sixes. I must have been standing on a four-leafed clover because when I threw the dice I was apportioned four treys. But Fitzgerald did not notice. A blind man, feeling his way along with walking stick, had come in the door and Fitzgerald was watching him as if he were a unique fact. "You lose," I called. "I've got four treys," but he did not hear. So I paid the cigar man for both packages, and we went out into the street. I noticed that Fitzgerald was acting queerly as we stepped on the sidewalk. He seemed quite unsteady on his feet and, as I looked up, I saw that he had closed his eyes. Silently, I watched him walk down the crowded street, feeling his way along by tapping against the sides of the buildings with his walking stick. A young woman, passing in company with a man, exclaimed, "Oh look at that poor boy. How sad it must be to be blind." But Fitzgerald walked on, his eyes shut. He had almost experienced the sensations of a blind man for an entire block on a crowded street when, unluckily, two middle aged women passed us by and passing, one said to the other: "Oh look at that." And then Fitzgerald opened his eyes.

I told you he was curious. When he discovered that the woman's ejaculation had been caused by the sight of a bargain window in a department store he was furious.

"It's perhaps just as well that no one recognized you else you would be reported to have blind staggers." I said to him.

"Didn't I walk very well—as well as the blind man?" His voice was truculent.

"No, you didn't. It is remarkable that you didn't knock your brains out. There were a number of times when I started to take hold of your arm to keep some passerby from knocking you down."

At that he seemed rather downcast, but he almost immediately cheered up, thinking, no doubt, that he could sell his experiences to some popular magazine.

St. Paul Daily News, 5 March 1922, 12 March 1922, 19 March 1922, City Life Sections, p. 6. This text omits material from the original. M.J.B.

1. White Bear Lake, at Dellwood, Minnesota, where the Fitzgeralds rented a house during summer 1921.

2. Antonín Dvořák (1841–1904), Czech composer.

3. During Prohibition so-called bathtub gin was made by adding flavoring to alcohol.

4. Chicago poet Carl Sandburg (1878–1967).

5. "Ode on a Grecian Urn" by English poet John Keats (1795–1921) was published in 1820.

6. Vachel Lindsay (1879–1931) wrote strongly rhythmic poems, such as "The Congo" (collected 1914). "The Chinese Nightingale" was collected in 1917.

7. (1889–1977), legendary movie comedian.

8. Ocean liner operated by the Cunard Line.

9. 1852 abolitionist novel by Harriet Beecher Stowe (1811–1896).

10. (1894–1964), prolific writer who became a highly successful dramatist and screenwriter.

11. See Fitzgerald's 25 September 1921 review of *Three Soldiers* in this volume.

12. See Fitzgerald's November 1921 review of *Salt* in this volume.

13. *The Beautiful and Damned* was serialized in *Metropolitan Magazine* (September 1921–March 1922) before book publication.

14. Joseph Hergesheimer's 1919 novel.

15. Fitzgerald's second novel was published in March 1922.

16. Writer (1876–1941) best known for his short-story collection *Winesburg, Ohio* (1919).

17. From the poem "General William Booth Enters into Heaven" (1913).

18. *The Vegetable* failed during its 1923 try-out in Atlantic City, N.J.

19. Radical critic and editor (1883–1969).

20. Local-color writer (1836–1902), author of "The Luck of Roaring Camp" (1868).

21. In the 1920s it was the custom for men to gamble for their purchases in tobacco shops.

"What I Was Advised to Do—and Didn't"

By F. Scott Fitzgerald

Author of The Beautiful and Damned, *etc.*

"Good morning, Mr. Fitzgerald," said the man with horn- rimmed spectacles, "I was asked to come down to the copy department and speak to you about writing. I understand that you received $30 for a story.[1] Now I have had five stories in the *Saturday Evening Post* during the last ten years and I know the game from A to Z. There's nothing in it. It's all right for picking up a little spare cash, but as for making a living at it, it won't do. You're dreaming. It would take ten years before you'd even begin to get a start. In the meanwhile, you'd starve. Take my advice, give up writing and stay at your job."

I didn't!

Philadelphia Public Ledger, 22 April 1922, p. 11.

1. When Fitzgerald made his first story sale ("Babes in the Woods" to *The Smart Set* in 1919), he was employed by the Barron Collier advertising agency.

"Tarkington's *Gentle Julia*"
A Review by F. Scott Fitzgerald

Tarkington's latest consists of half a dozen excellent short stories sandwiched in between half a dozen mediocre short stories and made into an almost structureless novel on the order of *Seventeen*. But it has not *Seventeen's* unity of theme nor has it a dominant character to hold it together like the Penrod books.[1] In fact, the book could be called after little Florence as well as after her popular older cousin, Julia. Nevertheless, in parts it is enormously amusing.

The stories which make up the narrative were written over a period of ten years. They concern Herbert, age 14; his cousin Florence, age 13, and their cousin Julia, age 19—and Julia's beaux, in particular one unbelievably calfish one named Noble Dill. From much interior evidence I doubt whether they were originally intended to form a continuous story at all. For instance, the Julia who is cross and peremptory with Florence in the early chapters is scarcely the gentle Julia who cannot bear to hurt a simple suitor's feelings in the last—and in addition the book jumps around from character to character in a way that is occasionally annoying, as it proceeds from the lack of any unity of design. Add to this that Tarkington seems a bit tired. He has used material throughout the book practically identical with material he has used before. The dance is the dance of *Seventeen*, though not so fresh and amusing. The little girl, Jane, grown up, is legitimately new but the little boy repeats the experiences of Hedrick in *The Flirt*[2]—it is held over his head by a shrewd female that he has made love to a little girl, he lives in torture for awhile, and finally when the secret is exposed he becomes the victim of his public school.

All the above sounds somewhat discouraging, as if Tarkington, our best humorist since Mark Twain, had turned stale in mid-career. This is not the case. Parts of the book—the whole scene of the walk, for example, and the astounding abuse of Florence's poem by the amateur printers—are as funny as anything he has ever done. Even the inferior parts of the book are swiftly moving and easily readable. When Noble Dill flicked his cigaret into the cellar I howled with glee. When Florence waved her hand at her mother and assured her that it was "all right," I found that I was walking with the party in a state of almost delirious merriment. In fact, the only part of the book which actively bored me was the incident of the bugs—which had the flavor of Katzenjammer humor.[3] I expected this incident to be bad because Edward J. O'Brien,[4] the world's greatest admirer of mediocre short stories, once gave it a star when it appeared in story form under the title of "The Three Foological Wishes."

71

The book is prefaced by a short paragraph in which Mr. Tarkington defends, for some curious Freudian reasons, his right to make cheerful books in the face of the recent realism. But no one questions it and the greatest whoopers for *Three Soldiers* and *Main Street* and *My Ántonia*⁵ has admitted and admired the sheer magic of *Seventeen*. We simply reserve the right to believe that when Mr. Tarkington becomes mock-sociological and symbolical about smoke as in *The Turmoil*,⁶ he is navigating out of his depth and invading the field of such old-maids' favorites as Winston Churchill.⁷ His ideas, such as they are, are always expressed best in terms of his characters as in the case of *Alice Adams* and parts of *The Flirt*. Mr. Tarkington is not a thoughtful man nor one profoundly interested in life as a whole, and when his ideas can not be so expressed they are seldom worth expressing. *Ramsey Milholland*, one of the most wretched and absurd novels ever written, showed this. So did the spiritualistic climax of *The Magnificent Ambersons*.

It is a pity that the man who writes better prose than any other living American was brought up in a generation that considered it a crime to tell the truth.

But read *Gentle Julia*—it will give you a merry evening. With all its fault it is the best piece of light amusement from an American this past year.

St. Paul Daily News, 7 May 1922, Feature Section, p. 6.

1. Penrod Schofield was the twelve-year-old hero of three novels by Tarkington.

2. 1913 novel by Tarkington.

3. The Katzenjammer Kids—Hans and Fritz—were the subjects of a very popular comic strip that found its humor in practical jokes.

4. Editor of annual *Best Short Stories* collections.

5. 1918 novel by Willa Cather.

6. 1915 novel by Tarkington.

7. American novelist Winston Churchill (1871–1947); he was not related to the British statesman.

"Homage to the Victorians"
By F. Scott Fitzgerald

The Oppidan. By Shane Leslie. Charles Scribner's Sons.

Now, Shane Leslie is the son of an Anglo-Irish baronet. He is an old Etonian[1] and he is chamberlain to the Pope. He is half a mystic, and he is entirely a cousin of the utilitarian Winston Churchill.[2] In him there is a stronger sense of old England, I mean a sense not of its worth or blame, but of its *being*, than is possessed by any one living, possibly excepting Lytton Strachey.[3]

It is almost impossible to review a book of his and resist the temptation to tell anecdotes of him—how a hair-pin fell from heaven, for instance, and plumped into the King of Spain's tea, of a certain sentimental haircut, of the fact that he has been the hero of two successful modern novels—but with such precious material I can be no more than tantalizing, for it belongs to his biographer, not to me.

He first came into my life as the most romantic figure I had ever known. He had sat at the feet of Tolstoy, he had gone swimming with Rupert Brooke, he had been a young Englishman of the governing classes when the sense of being one must have been, as Compton Mackenzie says, like the sense of being a Roman citizen.

Also, he was a convert to the church of my youth, and he and another,[4] since dead, made of that church a dazzling, golden thing, dispelling its oppressive mugginess and giving the succession of days upon gray days, passing under its plaintive ritual, the romantic glamour of an adolescent dream.

He had written a book then. It had a sale—not the sale it deserved. *The End of the Chapter,* it was; and bought by the snap- eyed ladies who follow with Freudian tenseness the missteps of the great. They missed its quality of low, haunting melancholy, of great age, of a faith and of a social tradition that with the years could not but have taken on a certain mellow despair— apparent perhaps only to the most sensitive but by them realized with a sensuous poignancy.

Well, he has written another book—with a wretched, puzzling title, *The Oppidan,* which to an American means nothing, but to Leslie an intriguing distinction, that has endured since Henry VIII. An Oppidan is an Etonian who either lives in college or doesn't—I am not quite sure which—and what does it matter, for the book is all of Eton. Once, years ago I picked up a novel called *Gray Youth,*[5] and I stared fascinated at that perfect title. I have never read it nor heard tell of it—I'm sure it was worthless—but what two words! And that is what Leslie's new book should be named—a tale of that gray, gray cocoon, where the English-butterfly sheds its cocoon. It should have been called *Gray Youth*. Once in it and you are carried back to the time of Shelley, or day-long fights with occasionally tragic, nay, fatal culminations, of Wellington's playing fields,[6] of intolerable bullyings and abominable raggings. And even more intimately we are shown Eton of the late 90s, and the last magnificence of the Victorian age is spread in front of us, a play done before shadowed tapestries of the past.

The book interested me enormously. Mr. Leslie has a sharp eye for the manners of his age. If he does not plumb the motives of his people or his creations with the keen analysis of Strachey, it is because he refers finer judgments to the court of the Celtic deity which he has accepted for his own—and where the inscrutability of men is relinquished beyond analysis, to fade into that more immense inscrutability in which all final answers and judgments lie.

Those who are interested in the great patchwork quilt picture of Victorian England, which is being gradually pieced together from the memories of survivors and the satire of their commentators, will enjoy *The Oppidan*.

New York Tribune, 14 May 1922, Sect. 4, p. 6.

1. A graduate of Eton, one of England's most prestigious public (i.e., private) schools.
2. By 1922 British statesman Winston Churchill (1874–1965) had already earned a formidable reputation as a political leader and historian.
3. English biographer (1880–1932), author of *Eminent Victorians* (1918).
4. Monsignor Cyril Sigourney Webster Fay, who had befriended Fitzgerald during his prep-school and college years.
5. 1914 novel by Oliver Onions (1873–1961).
6. The Duke of Wellington (1769–1852) remarked that the Battle of Waterloo was won on the playing fields of Eton.

To: Maxwell Perkins
c. 20 June 1922

. . . .

Don't forget that I want another proof of the Table of Contents.[1] There's been one addition to the first section and one substitution in the 3d. Its damn good now, far superior to Flappers + the title, jacket + other books ought to sell at least 10,000 copies and I hope 15,000. You can see from the ms. how I've changed the stories. I cut out my last Metropolitan story[2] not because it wasn't technically excellent but simply because it lacked vitality. The only story about which I'm in doubt is The Camel's Back. But I've decided to use it—it has some excellent comedy + was in one O. Henry Collection[3]—though of course that's against it. Here are some suggested blurbs.

1. Contains the famous "Porcelain and Pink Story"—the bath-tub classic—as well as "The Curious Case of Benjamin Button" and nine other tales. In the book Mr. F. has developed his gifts as a satiric humorist to a point rivalled by few if any living American writers. The lazy meanderings of a brilliant and powerful imagination.

2. TALES OF THE JAZZ AGE
Satyre upon a Saxaphone by the most brilliant of the younger novelists. He sets down "My Last Flappers" and then proceeds in section two to fresher and more fantastic fields. You may like or dislike his work but it will never bore you.

3. TALES OF THE JAZZ AGE
Have you met "Mr. Icky" and followed the ghastly career of "Benjamin Button"? A medly of Bath-tubs, diamond mountains, Fitzgerald Flappers and Jellybeans.
Ten acts of lustrous farce—and one other.

That's probably pretty much bunk but I'm all for advertising it as a cheerful book and not as "eleven of Mr. Fitzgerald's best stories by the y.a.[4] of T.S.O.P."

. . . .

F. Scott Fitzgerald: A Life in Letters, pp. 59–60.

1. Fitzgerald wrote an annotated contents list for his second story collection, *Tales of the Jazz Age*.
2. "Two for a Cent" (April 1922).
3. "The Camel's Back" appeared in *The Saturday Evening Post* (24 April 1920) and was reprinted in *O. Henry Prize Stories of 1920* (1921).
4. Young author.

"A Rugged Novel"

The Love Legend. By Woodward Boyd.[1] New York:
Charles Scribner's Sons. 1922.

Reviewed by F. Scott Fitzgerald

This is a rugged, uneven, and sometimes beautiful novel which concerns four girls, sisters, of Chicago's middle class. These girls believed
in——Listen:

"Ward Harris, at twenty, wore a virginal look like golden rain infil-
trated through the stuff of a morning meadow; a look that came from her
trust in the love legend, in which she had put all the capital of her youthful
hopes, since her mother's whispered story of the prince who was to come
and change the world with a magic kiss."

That sentence, a lovely, ill-constructed sentence, opens the book. Ward
was the Mary of the family—her three sisters were Marthas. Ward believed
in the love legend which "like hope, is deathless." One sister, Sari, who
wanted a career on the stage, became absorbed in the business of life, the
business of poverty, the business of children. Another sister wanted to be a
writer. She had a story accepted by a "Mr. Hopkins," whom I suspect of
being a composite Mencken and Nathan. In one of the few artificial scenes
in the novel she discovers she cannot marry a fool. She goes on writing.
Nita, less intelligent than the others but more shrewd, marries well in the
Far West, and, because of this, incurs the faint hostility of the author.

And Ward goes on believing in the love legend, which, like hope, is
deathless.

This novel is enormously amusing. The incidental portraits, the Jewish
family into which Sari marries, for example, and the environment of the
man "Oz," whom Ward loves, are excellent. They're convincing and they're
intensely of Chicago—couldn't have existed anywhere else. Easily the best
picture of Chicago since *Sister Carrie.*[2] All done in little circles and eddies
and glimpses with no mooning about the heart or voice or "clangor" or
smell of the city. Suddenly you're there. Suddenly you realize that all these
people you are reading about—possibly excepting Ward—talk with slightly
raised voices and are enormously self- confident.

The book is obviously by a woman, but her methods of achieving an
effect are entirely masculine—even the defects in the book are masculine
defects—intellectual curiosity in what amounts to a riot, solid blocks of
strong words fitted into consecutive pages like bricks, a lack of selective
delicacy, and, sometimes, a deliberately blunted perception. Read the scene
where Cecil goes to work in the machine shop and try to think what other

women writers could have written it.

This is not a perfect first novel—but it is honest, well written, if raggedy, and thoroughly alive. Compare it, for instance, with *Dancers in the Dark*[3] as a portrait of young people and the modern young mind. Of course, this is hardly fair because *Dancers in the Dark* is merely a jazzed-up version of the juvenile sweetbooks—and the characters are merely puppets who have read flapper editorials. The characters in *The Love Legend* are real in conception, and where the author fails to get her effects it is because of inexpertness and uncertainty rather than because of dishonesty or "faking."

The book is formless. In first novels this is permissible, perhaps even to be encouraged, as the lack of a pattern gives the young novelist more of a chance to assert his or her individuality, which is the principal thing. The title is excellent and covers the novel adequately as it jumps from character to character. The only one of the girls I liked was Ward—the other three I detested. A good book—put it upon the shelf with *Babbitt*[4] and *The Bright Shawl*[5] and watch and pray for more such entertainment this autumn.

The Literary Review of the New York Evening Post,
28 October 1922, pp. 143–144.

1. Woodward Boyd was the pen name of Peggy Boyd (1898–1965), who was married to Thomas Boyd. Fitzgerald had recommended *The Love Legend* to Maxwell Perkins at Scribners.
2. Theodore Dreiser's 1900 novel.
3. This 1922 novel by Dorothy Speare (1898–1951) was set at a women's college.
4. Sinclair Lewis's 1922 novel about a midwestern businessman.
5. Joseph Hergesheimer's 1922 historical romance set in the West Indies.

"How I Would Sell My Book
If I Were a Bookseller"

By F. Scott Fitzgerald

I believe that a book by a well-known author should be given a full-window display—I don't believe a mixed-window display of four books for four days is nearly as effective as that of one book for one day. To attract attention it might be a coy idea to set all the books upside down and to have a man with large spectacles sitting in the midst of them, frantically engrossed in the perusal of a copy. He should have his eyes wide with rapt attention and his left hand on his heart.

Seriously, the above title puzzles me. If I were a bookseller I should probably push the most popular book of the season, whether it was trash or not.

The vogue of books like mine depends almost entirely on the stupendous critical power at present wielded by H. L. Mencken. And it is his influence at second hand that is particularly important. Such men as Weaver[1] in *The Brooklyn Eagle*, Bishop[2] in *Vanity Fair*, Boyd in the *St. Paul News*, and dozens of others show the liberal tendencies which Mencken has popularized.

The growing demand for likely American books is almost directly created by these men, who give no room to trash in their columns and, city by city, are making the work of living writers acceptable to the wavering and uncertain "better public."

I did not know *This Side of Paradise* was a flapper book until George Jean Nathan, who had read parts of it before publication, told me it was. However, I do not consider any of my heroines typical of the average bob-skirted "Dulcy"[3] who trips through the Biltmore lobby at tea time. My heroine is what the flapper would like to *think* she is—the actual flapper is a much duller and grayer proposition. I tried to set down different aspects of an individual—I was accused of creating a type.

I think that if I were a bookseller with a real interest in better books I would announce the new good books as the publisher announced them to me and take orders from customers in advance.

"See here," I would say; "this is a novel by Fitzgerald; you know, the fella who started all that business about flappers. I understand that his new one is terribly sensational (the word 'damn' is in the title). Let me put you down for one."

And this would be approximately true. I am not in love with sensationalism, but I must plead guilty to it in this instance. And I feel quite sure that, though my books may annoy many, they will bore no one.

Bookseller and Stationer, 18 (15 January 1923), 8.

1. Poet and book-reviewer John V. A. Weaver (1893–1938).
2. Fitzgerald's Princeton classmate John Peale Bishop (1892–1944).
3. The title character in the 1921 play by Marc Connelly (1890–1980) and George S. Kaufman (1889–1961).

"The Defeat of Art"

The Boy Grew Older, by Heywood Broun.
G. P. Putnam's Sons. New York. $2.00.

By no less an authority than that of our leading humorist, Heywood Broun[1] has been pronounced the best all-around newspaper man in America. And he is. He can report a football game, a play, a literary dinner, a prize-fight, scandal, murder, his own domestic interests, his moods, the konduct of the klan[2] and the greatness of Charlie Chaplin with the same skill and the same unfailing personality.

"Now," says Heywood Broun, "every scribbler in Christendom is writing an immortal novel while I continue my ephemeral output. I shall crystallize some of this so-called personality of mine into a novel and preserve it against the short memory of man."

The result is called *The Boy Grew Older.*

Before I talk of this novel I want to list Heywood Broun's most obvious insufficiencies. His literary taste, when it is not playing safe, is pretty likely to be ill-considered, faintly philistine, and often downright absurd. He seems to have no background whatsoever except a fairly close reading of fashionable contemporary novels by British and American novelists. He seems unacquainted with anything that was written before 1900, possibly excepting the English units required for entering Harvard.

This lack is, in an American novelist, a positive advantage insofar as it puts no limit on the width of his appeal. There is nothing in *The Boy Grew Older* to puzzle a movie director or a scenario writer. It is a book free from either the mark or the pretense of erudition.

Once upon a time, in the early days of the American literary revival, Mr. Broun mistook the fact that *Moon-Calf,* by Floyd Dell, was a seriously attempted novel for the fact it was a successful piece of work. "Drop everything and read *Moon-Calf,*" said Mr. Broun to the public. "Drop everything and read Henry James,"[3] said the *Dial*[4] to Mr. Dell. But the public trusts Heywood Broun, and because of his shove, *Moon-Calf* dragged in the wake of *Main Street* to a sale of 30,000 copies or more.

So when I began to read *The Boy Grew Older* I feared that, in the *Moon-Calf* tradition, it would be thick with dots and bestrewn with quotations from Tennyson, Eddie Guest[5] and the early poetic efforts of Mr. Broun. On the contrary it is a competently written, highly interesting and somewhat sketchy story which concerns the soul of a newspaper man named Peter Neale. And the book is about Peter chiefly—about a simple and rather fine man who has somewhat the same devotion to his profession that Mark Twain has to his piloting or Joseph Conrad to the sea.[6] What does it matter if Peter Neale's gorgeously ethical newspaper world is imaginary? By such books and such men as the author of *The Boy Grew Older* such an idealized concept is made a reality. After Kipling, every private in the British army tried to be like *Soldiers Three*.[7]

With a boyish hatred of emotional sloppiness Mr. Broun has utterly failed to visualize for us the affair with Maria. When she leaves Peter I was sorry. But not sorry that she was gone—not with the feeling that something young and beautiful had ceased to be—I was only sorry Peter was wounded.

Peter gets drunk. In the best "cafe fight" I have ever read about, Peter is slugged with a bottle. He meets another woman. Mr. Broun hesitates for a moment whether to be correctly the Harvard man and public "good egg" or whether to make Peter's second affair human and vital and earthy and alive. Somewhere on a dark staircase the question disappears and never emerges from its obscurity.

The boy grows older. The reality he possessed as a portrait of Heywood III fades out when he grows older than his model. At Harvard he plays in 1915 in a football game that took place in 1921.[8] He comes to New York and works for a while under an excellent pen portrait of a famous liberal editor. He has a voice, so his mother takes him away and leaves Peter to his work and to his rather fine concept of honor and to his memories—which, if the incidents had been just a little more emotionally visualized when they occurred, would have made the book more moving at the close.

But Heywood Broun can write. If he will forget himself and let go, his personality will color almost every line he chooses to set down. He is a real talent that even the daily grind of newspaper work cannot dull. His second book is decidedly worth waiting for.

—**F. Scott Fitzgerald**

St. Paul Daily News (21 January 1923), Feature Section, p. 6.

1. At the time of Fitzgerald's review Broun (1888–1939) was a columnist for the *New York World*.

2. The Ku Klux Klan used a written language called klonversation in which *k* was substituted for *c*.

3. American fiction writer (1843–1916).

4. Literary magazine.

5. Popular poet Edgar A. Guest (1881–1959).

6. Samuel Langhorne Clemens (Mark Twain) had been a Mississippi River pilot in his youth; Joseph Conrad had been a ship's captain.

7. Rudyard Kipling's 1890 novel set in India.

8. Fitzgerald apparently is in error. On p. 56 of the novel, the hero is cut from both the varsity and freshman football teams when he first goes to Harvard; but on p. 58, he pitches a baseball game against Yale and wins by score of 2 to 0.

"Minnesota's Capital in the Rôle of Main Street"

By F. Scott Fitzgerald

Along comes another of those annoying novels of American manners, one of those ponderous steel scaffoldings upon which the palaces of literature may presently arise. It is something native and universal, clumsy in its handling of an enormous quantity of material; something which can be called a document but can in no sense be dismissed as such.

Grace Flandrau's *Being Respectable*[1]—the book of the winter and in all probability of the spring, too—is superior to Sinclair Lewis's *Babbitt* in many ways, but inferior in that it deals with too many characters. The characters are complete and excellently motivated in themselves, but there is no one Babbitt or Nostromo[2] to draw together the entire novel. It is a satirical arraignment of the upper class of a middlewestern city—in this case St. Paul, Minnesota—as *Babbitt*, speaking generally, was concerned with the upper middle class of Minneapolis. Poor Minnesota! Sauk Center, Minneapolis, and St. Paul have been flayed in turn by the state's own sons and daughters. I feel that I ought to take up the matter of Duluth and make the thing complete.

Now St. Paul, altho a bloodbrother of Indianapolis, Minneapolis, Kansas City, Milwaukee and Co., feels itself a little superior to the others. It is a "three generation" town, while the others boast but two. In the fifties the climate of St. Paul was reputed exceptionally healthy. Consequently there arrived an element from the East who had both money and fashionable education. These Easterners mingled with the rising German and Irish stock, whose second generation left the cobbler's last, forgot the steerage, and became passionately "swell" on its own account. But the pace was set by the tubercular Easterners. Hence the particular social complacency of St. Paul.

Being Respectable starts with a typical family of today—the sort of family that Tarkington sketched brilliantly but superficially in the first part of *The Magnificent Ambersons*. There is the retired father, a product of the gilded eighties, with his business morality and his utter lack of any ideas except the shop-worn and conventional illusions current in his youth. His son, Charles, is the typical healthy vegetable which Yale University turns out by the hundred every year. The younger daughter, Deborah, is a character frequently met with in recent fiction—and also in life—ever since Shaw shocked the English- speaking world with his emancipated woman of 1900. In her very Carol-Kennicotting[3] against the surrounding conventions Deborah is the most conventional character of all. Her conversations (which, of course, consist of the author's own favorite ideas) are the least important part of the book. The unforgetable part is the great gallery of dumb-bells of which the elder sister, Louisa, is Number One.

Louisa is a woman completely engrossed in St. Paul's passionate imitation of Chicago imitating New York imitating London. Every once in a while some woman's imitation becomes ineffective. The woman "gets in wrong and drops out." The society itself, however, goes on in its distorted and not a little ridiculous fashion. It is a society from which there is no escape. On one side there is nothing but the "common fast set," and just below are the thousand Babbitts, who from time to time furnish recruits to society itself.

Louisa is the real protagonist of the book—Louisa and her young married crowd. They are portraits to the life, differing by less than a hair from each other and from the women on whom they are modeled. They are set down here in all their energy, their dullness, their fear, their boredom—forty well-drest automatons moving with deft, unpleasant gestures through their own private anemic and exclusive Vanity Fair.[4] It is a fine accomplishment to have captured them so—with sophistication, satire, occasional bitterness, and a pervading irony.

A thoroughly interesting and capable novel. The writing is solid throughout, and sometimes beautiful. Like Sinclair Lewis and Woodward Boyd, the author has little sense of selection—seems to have poured the whole story out in a flood. The book lacks the careful balance of *Three Soldiers*, and it is not nearly so successful in handling its three or four protagonists. It skips from character to character in a way that is often annoying. But there it is, the newest and in some ways the best of those amazing documents which are (as Mencken might say) by H. G. Wells out of Theodore Dreiser, and which yet are utterly national and of today. And, when our Conrad or Joyce or Anatole France comes, such books as this will have cleared his way. Out of these enormous and often muddy lakes of sincere and sophisticated observation will flow the clear stream—if there is to be a clear stream at all.

Incidentally, the remarkable portrait of Valeria is the best single instance of artistic power in the book. The entire personality and charm of the woman is conveyed at second-hand. We have scarcely a glimpse of her, and she says only one line throughout. Yet the portrait is vivid and complete.

The Literary Digest International Book Review, 1 (March 1923), 35–36.

1. Flandrau (d. 1971) was a St. Paul novelist.
2. The title character in Joseph Conrad's 1904 novel.
3. Carol Kennicott is the protagonist of Sinclair Lewis's *Main Street*.
4. Reference to the 1848 satiric novel by English fiction writer William Makepeace Thackeray (1811–1863). Thackeray in turn drew his title—and his conception of the worthlessness of human desires—from "Vanity Fair," a setting in *The Pilgrim's Progress* (1678), a religous allegory by John Bunyan (1628–1688).

"Sherwood Anderson on the Marriage Question"

A Review by F. Scott Fitzgerald

Many Marriages.
By Sherwood Anderson. B. W. Huebach, Inc.

In the last century literary reputations took some time to solidify. Not Tennyson's or Dickens's[1]—despite their superficial radicalism such men flowed with the current of popular thought. Not Wilde's or De Musset's,[2] whose personal scandals made them almost legendary figures in their own lifetimes. But the reputations of Hardy, Butler, Flaubert and Conrad were slow growths. These men swam up stream and were destined to have an almost intolerable influence upon succeeding generations.

First they were esoteric with a group of personal claqueurs. Later they came into a dim rippling vogue. Their contemporaries "tried to read *one* of their books" and were puzzled and suspicious. Finally some academic critic would learn from his betters that they were "the thing" and shout the news aloud with a profound air of discovery, arguing from interior evidence that the author in question was really in full accord with Florence Nightingale[3] and Gen. Booth.[4] And the author, old and battered and with a dozen imitators among the younger men, was finally granted a period of wide recognition.

The cultural world is closer knit now. In the last five years we have seen solidify the reputations of two first class men—James Joyce and Sherwood Anderson.

Many Marriages seems to me the fullblown flower of Anderson's personality. It is good enough for Lee Wilson Dodd[5] to write a kittenish parody for "The Conning Tower."[6] On the strength of *Many Marriages* you can decide whether Anderson is a neurotic or whether you are one and Anderson a man singularly free of all inhibitions. The noble fool who has dominated tragedy from Don Quixote to Lord Jim[7] is not a character in *Many Marriages*. If there is nobility in the book it is a nobility Anderson has created as surely as Rousseau created his own natural man. The genius conceives a cosmos with such transcendental force that it supersedes, in certain sensitive minds, the cosmos of which they have been previously aware. The new cosmos instantly approximates ultimate reality as closely as did the last. It is a bromide to say that the critic can only describe the force of his reaction to any specific work of art.

I read in the paper every day that, without the slightest warning, some apparently solid and settled business man has eloped with his stenographer.

This is the central event of *Many Marriages*. But in the glow of an unexhaustible ecstasy and wonder, what is known as a "vulgar intrigue" becomes a transaction of profound and mystical importance.

The book is the story of two moments—two marriages. Between midnight and dawn a naked man walks up and down before a statue of the Virgin and speaks of his first marriage to his daughter. It was a marriage made in a moment of half mystical, half physical union and later destroyed in the moment of its consummation.

When the man has finished talking he goes away to his second marriage and the woman of his first marriage kills herself out of a little brown bottle.

The method is Anderson's accustomed transcendental naturalism. The writing is often tortuous. But then just as you begin to rail at the short steps of the truncated sentences (his prose walks with a rope around the ankle and a mischievous boy at the end of the rope) you reach an amazingly beautiful vista seen through a crack in the wall that long steps would have carried you hurriedly by. Again—Anderson feels too profoundly to have read widely or even well. What he takes to be only an empty tomato can whose beauty he has himself discovered may turn out to be a Greek vase wrought on the Ægean twenty centuries before. Again the significance of the little stone eludes me. I believe it to have no significance at all. In the book he has perhaps endowed lesser things with significance. In the case of the stone his power is not in evidence and the episode is marred.

There is a recent piece of trash entitled *Simon Called Peter*,[8] which seems to me utterly immoral, because the characters move in a continual labyrinth of mild sexual stimulation. Over this stimulation play the colored lights of romantic Christianity.

Now anything is immoral that consoles, stimulates or confirms a distortion. Anything that acts in place of the natural will to live is immoral. All cheap amusement becomes, at maturity, immoral—the heroin of the soul.

Many Marriages is not immoral—it is violently anti-social. But if its protagonist rested at a defiance of the fallible human institution of monogamy the book would be no more than propaganda. On the contrary, *Many Marriages* begins where *The New Machiavelli*[9] left off. It does not so much justify the position of its protagonist as it casts a curious and startling light on the entire relation between man and woman. It is the reaction of a sensitive, highly civilized man to the phenomenon of lust—but it is distinguished from the work of Dreiser, Joyce and Wells (for example) by utter lack both of a concept of society as a whole and of the necessity of defying or denying such a concept. For the purpose of the book no such background as Dublin Catholicism, middlewestern morality, or London Fabianism[10] could ever have existed. For all his washing-machine factory, the hero of *Many Marriages* comes closer than any character, not excepting Odysseus, Lucifer, Attila, Tarzan and, least of all, Conrad's Michaelis,[11] to existing in an absolute vacuum. It seems to me a rather stupendous achievement.

I do not like the man in the book. The world in which I trust, on which I seem to set my feet, appears to me to exist through a series of illusions. These illusions need and occasionally get a thorough going over ten times or so during a century.

The man whose power of compression is great enough to review this book in a thousand words does not exist. If he does he is probably writing subtitles for the movies or working for a car card[12] company.

New York Herald, 4 March 1923, Sect. 9, p. 5.

1. Poet Alfred Tennyson (1809–1892) and novelist Charles Dickens (1812–1870) were enormously popular English Victorian writers.
2. French poet, dramatist, and novelist Alfred de Musset (1810–1857) was sensationally involved with French novelist Aurore-Lucile Dupin (1804–1876), who wrote as George Sand.
3. British nurse Nightingale (1820–1910) organized army hospitals during the Crimean War.
4. William Booth (1829–1912), founder of the Salvation Army.
5. American playwright (1879–1933).
6. Franklin P. Adams's column in the *New York World* printed contributions from readers.
7. Idealistic title characters in the two-part novel (1605, 1615) by Spanish writer Miguel de Cervantes (1547–1616) and in the 1900 novel by Joseph Conrad.
8. Fitzgerald greatly disliked this 1921 novel by English writer Robert Keable (1887–1927) and mentioned it in *The Great Gatsby* (1925).
9. H. G. Wells's 1910 novel in which a public figure becomes involved in a sexual scandal.
10. English socialist movement.
11. Character in Joseph Conrad's *The Secret Agent* (1907).
12. Car cards were advertisements displayed in public transportation.

"10 Best Books I Have Read"
(Author of *This Side of Paradise,*
The Beautiful and Damned, etc.)

Samuel Butler's *Note Books.*[1] The mind and heart of my favorite Victorian.

The Philosophy of Friedrich Nietzsche (H. L. Mencken).[2] A keen, hard intelligence interpreting the Great Modern Philosopher.

A Portrait of the Artist as a Young Man (James Joyce). Because James Joyce is to be the most profound literary influence in the next fifty years.

Zuleika Dobson (Max Beerbohm). For the sheer delight of its exquisite snobbery.

The Mysterious Stranger (Mark Twain).[3] Mark Twain in his most sincere mood. A book and a startling revelation.

Nostromo (Joseph Conrad). The great novel of the past fifty years, as *Ulysses*[4] is the great novel of the future.

Vanity Fair (Thackeray). No explanation required.

The Oxford Book of English Verse. This seems to me a better collection than Palgrave's.[5]

Thais (Anatole France).[6] The great book of the man who is Wells and Shaw together.

Seventeen (Booth Tarkington). The funniest book I've ever read.—

Jersey City Evening Journal, 24 April 1923, p. 9.
Syndicated by the North American Newspaper Alliance.

---

1. *The Note-Books of Samuel Butler,* ed. Henry Festing Jones (1912).
2. (1908).
3. Ed. Albert Bigelow Paine and Frederick A. Duneka (1916).
4. 1922 novel by James Joyce.
5. *The Oxford Book of English Verse* (1921), ed. Arthur Quiller-Couch; *The Golden Treasury of the Best Songs and Lyrical Poems in the English Language* (1889), ed. Francis Turner Palgrave.
6. (1890).

"Confessions"

F. Scott Fitzgerald, the first chronicler of the flapper, in This Side of Paradise *makes this explanatory reply when I asked him what book he would rather have written than any other:*
Dear Miss Butcher:[1]

I'd rather have written Conrad's *Nostromo* than any other novel. First, because I think it is the greatest novel since *Vanity Fair* (possibly excluding *Madame Bovary*),[2] but chiefly because Nostromo, the man, intrigues me so much. Now the Nostromo who exists in life and always has existed, whether as a Roman centurion or a modern top sergeant, has often crept into fiction, but until Conrad there was no one to ponder over him. He was dismissed superficially and abruptly even by those who most admired his efficient handling of the proletariat either in crowds or as individuals. Kipling realized that this figure, with his almost autocratic disdain of weakness, is one of the most powerful props of the capitalistic system, and under various names he occurs in many of Kipling's stories of Indian life—but always as a sort of glorified servant. The literary attitude toward him has been that of an officer sitting in his club with a highball during drill.

"Well, I've got nothing to worry about. Sergt. O'Hare has the troop and——" this with a patronizing condescension—"I believe he knows just about as much about handling them as I do."

Now Conrad didn't stop there. He took this man of the people and imagined him with such a completeness that there is no use of any one else pondering over him for some time. He is one of the most important types in our civilization. In particular he's one that always made a haunting and irresistible appeal to me. So I would rather have dragged his soul from behind his astounding and inarticulate presence than written any other novel in the world.

Sincerely,
F. Scott Fitzgerald

Public letter, *Chicago Daily Tribune*, 19 May 1923, p. 9.

1. Fanny Butcher was book critic for the *Chicago Tribune*.
2. Gustave Flaubert's 1857 novel of French provincial life.

"Under Fire"

Through the Wheat.[1] By Thomas Boyd. New York:
Charles Scribner's Sons. 1923. $1.75.

Reviewed by F. Scott Fitzgerald

"I did not know how good a man I was till then. . . . I remember my
youth and the feeling that will never come back any more—the feeling that
I could last forever, outlast the sea, the earth, and all men . . . the trium-
phant conviction of strength, the heat of life in the handful of dust, the
glow in the heart that with every year grows dim, grows cold, grows small,
and expires, and expires too soon—before life itself."

So, in part, runs one of the most remarkable passages of English prose
written these thirty years—a passage from Conrad's *Youth*[2]—and since that
story I have found in nothing else even the echo of that lift and ring until I
read Thomas Boyd's *Through the Wheat.* It is the story of certain privates in
a marine regiment which, the jacket says, was rushed into action under a
bright June sunlight five years ago to stop the last thrust of the German
Army towards Paris. These men were sustained by no democratic idealism,
no patriotic desperation, and by no romance, except the romance of unknown adventure. But they were sustained by something else at once more
material and more magical, for in the only possible sense of the word they
were picked men—they were exceptionally solid specimens of a healthy
stock. No one has a greater contempt than I have for the recent hysteria
about the Nordic theory, but I suppose that the United States marines were
the best body of troops that fought in the war.

Now, young Hicks, Mr. Boyd's protagonist, is taken as an average individual in a marine regiment, put through a short period of training in France,
a trench raid, a long wait under shell fire (a wait during which, if C. E.
Montague[3] is to be believed, the average English regiment of the last year
would have been utterly demoralized), and finally ordered forward in the
face of machine gun fire through an endless field of yellow wheat. The
action is utterly real. At first the very exactitude of the detail makes one
expect no more than another piece of expert reporting, but gradually the
thing begins to take on significance and assume a definite and arresting
artistic contour. The advance goes on—one by one the soldiers have come
to know, know fragmentarily and by sudden flashes and illuminations, go
down and die, but young Hicks and the rest go on, heavy footed and blind
with sweat, through the yellow wheat. Finally, without one single recourse
to sentiment, to hysteria, or to trickery, the author strikes one clear and
unmistakable note of heroism, of tenuous and tough-minded exaltation, and

with this note vibrating sharply in the reader's consciousness the book ends.

There is a fine unity about it all which only becomes fully apparent when this note is struck. The effect is cumulative in the sheerest sense; there are no skies and stars and dawns pointed out to give significance to the insignificant or to imply a connection where there is no connection. There are no treasured-up reactions to æsthetic phenomena poured along the pages, either for sweetening purposes or to endow the innately terrible with a higher relief. The whole book is written in the light of one sharp emotion and hence it is as a work of art rather than as a textbook for patrioteer or pacifist that the book is arresting.

Already I have seen reviews which take it as propaganda for one side or the other—in both cases this is unfair. The fact that both sides claim it tends to prove the author's political disinterestedness. As Thomas Boyd has been one of the loudest in praise of *Three Soldiers* and *The Enormous Room*,[4] it is to his credit that he has not allowed any intellectualism, however justified, to corrupt the at once less thoughtful and more profound emotion of his attitude. Still less has he been influenced by the Continental reaction to the last year of war. This, too, is as it should be, for that poignant despair, neatly as our novelists have adapted it to their ends, could not have been part of the mental make-up of the Fifth and Sixth Marines. Dos Passos and Elliot Paul[5] filtered the war through an artistic intellectualism and in so doing attributed the emotions of exhausted nations to men who for the most part were neither exhausted nor emotional.

To my mind, this is not only the best combatant story of the Great War, but also the best war book since *The Red Badge of Courage*.

The Literary Review of the New York Evening Post, 26 May 1923, p. 715.

1. Fitzgerald had recommended Boyd's novel to Maxwell Perkins at Scribners.
2. (1902).
3. (1867–1928), British newspaper writer and novelist whose *Disenchantment* (1922) is a bitter account of the average soldier's experience in World War I.
4. 1922 novel by E. E. Cummings (1894–1962).
5. Fitzgerald is probably referring to *Impromptu* (1923) by Paul (1891–1958), American expatriate writer who co-founded the Paris literary magazine *Transition*.

"Censorship or Not"

Then Mr. Fitzgerald:

"The clean-book bill[1] will be one of the most immoral measures ever adopted. It will throw American art back into the junk-heap where it rested comfortably between the Civil War and the World War. The really immoral books like *Simon Called Peter* and *Mumbo Jumbo*[2] won't be touched; they'll attack Hergesheimer, Drieser, Anderson and Cabell, whom they detest because they can't understand. George Moore,[3] Hardy and Anatole France who are unintelligible to children and idiots will be supprest at once for debauching the morals of village clergymen."

The Literary Digest, 77 (23 June 1923), 31, 61.
Statements by various people about the campaign against unclean books by Justice Ford of the Supreme Court of New York State.

1. Bill sponsored in the New York State legislature; it was intended to prohibit the sale of immoral books.

2. 1923 novel by Henry Clews, Jr. (1876–1937).

3. Anglo-Irish writer (1852–1933) who was best known for his novel *Esther Waters* (1894).

"Prediction Is Made About James Joyce Novel: F. S. Fitzgerald Believes *Ulysses* Is Great Book of Future"

Will James Joyce be to the next two generations what Henry James, Nietzsche, Wells, Shaw, Mencken, Dreiser, and Conrad have been to the present generation? F. Scott Fitzgerald, the prophet and voice of the younger American smart set, says that while Conrad's *Nostromo* is the great novel of the past fifty years, *Ulysses* by James Joyce is the great novel of the future. In his list of "The Books I Have Enjoyed Most," Scott Fitzgerald places *A Portrait of the Artist as a Young Man* (Huebsch) as third from the top and avers that Joyce is to be "the most profound literary influence in the next fifty years."[1]

Whether the sons and daughters of the wild young things now who figure in Mr. Fitzgerald's brilliant pictures of the very present will actually read a great deal of Joyce we are left to guess, but the prediction which Mr. Fitzgerald makes of the intellectual temper of the new age may be a revelation to his many admirers. Fitzgerald stands today as a writer for and about the frivolous and semi-cynical. Samuel Butler, Friedrich Nietzsche, and Anatole France were the intellectual influences which molded Fitzgerald's mind. He says this in making up his list of books he enjoyed most. Ibsen[2] and the Greek and Latin classics made Joyce, in a literary way, what he is. Is Joyce in turn to be the founder of a school of writers who will interpret the life of tomorrow with the same passionate naturalism, that amazing ability to depict "the stream of consciousness," the Gargantuan satire and laughter, and that unsentimental lyric joy in the unreserved acceptance of life, which distinguish Joyce's works as unique in this seething era?

Richmond Times-Dispatch, 24 June 1923, Sect. 2, p. 5.

1. See "10 Best Books I Have Read" in this volume.
2. Henrik Ibsen (1828–1906), Norwegian realist playwright.

"In Literary New York"

F. Scott Fitzgerald Says Appearance in January of Mencken and Nathan's American Mercury Will Be Event of the Year

—Tom Boyd Writing for Scribner's Magazine.

Dear Bernard:[1] You ask me for the news from literary New York. Outside of the fact that Rebecca West and Frank Swinnerton[2] are in town, there isn't any. Tom Boyd, after being feted on all sides by admirers of his books, got off for France and is sending back short stories for *Scribner's Magazine* by every boat.

The books of the fall seem to have determined themselves as *A Lost Lady*,[3] Thomas Beer's life of Stephen Crane[4] and Elinor Wylie's[5] *Jennifer Lorn*, a remarkable period romance which just misses—but misses—being a classic. Floyd Dell's new book (*Janet March*) is a drab, dull statistic throughout. How such an intelligent, sophisticated man can go on year after year turning out such appalling novels is a question for the psychoanalysts, to whom, I understand, he resorts.

Aldous Huxley's *Antic Hay*, while a delightful book, is inferior on all counts to Van Vechten's[6] *The Blind Bow-Boy*.

But the real event of the year will, of course, be the appearance in January of *The American Mercury*.[7] *The Smart Set* without Mencken and Nathan is already on the stands, and a dreary sight is is. In their nine years' association with it those two men had a most stupendous and far reaching influence on the whole course of American writing. Their influence was not so much on the very first-rate writers, though even there it was considerable in many cases as on the cultural background. Their new venture is even more interesting. We shall see what we shall see.

You ask for news of me. There is little and that bad. My play (*The Vegetable*) opened in Atlantic City and foundered on the opening night. It did better in subsequent performances, but at present is laid up for repairs.[8]

—Scott Fitzgerald

Unlocated clipping (fall–winter 1923) in Fitzgerald's scrapbooks (Princeton University Library).

1. Bernard Vaughan, presumably a member of the *St. Paul Daily News* staff.
2. West (1892–1983) and Swinnerton (1884–1982) were English novelists.
3. Novel by Willa Cather.
4. *Stephen Crane: A Study in American Letters;* Beer (1889?–1940) was a fiction writer and historian.
5. Wylie (1885–1928) was a poet and novelist.
6. Carl Van Vechten (1880–1964) was a cultural critic and novelist.
7. After withdrawing from *The Smart Set*, H. L. Mencken and George Jean Nathan founded *The American Mercury*.
8. *The Vegetable* did not reach Broadway.

To: Maxwell Perkins
c. 10 April 1924

A few words more relative to our conversation this afternoon. While I have every hope + plan of finishing my novel in June you know how those things often come out.[1] And even if it takes me 10 times that long I cannot let it go out unless it has the very best I'm capable of in it or even as I feel sometimes, something better than I'm capable of. Much of what I wrote last summer was good but it was so interrupted that it was ragged + in approaching it from a new angle I've had to discard a lot of it—in one case 18,000 words (part of which will appear in the Mercury as a short story). It is only in the last four months that I've realized how much I've—well, almost <u>deteriorated</u> in the three years since I finished the Beautiful and Damned. The last four months of course I've worked but in the two years— over two years—before that, I produced exactly <u>one</u> play, <u>half a dozen</u> short stories and three or four articles—an average of about <u>one hundred</u> words a day. If I'd spent this time reading or travelling or doing anything—even staying healthy—it'd be different but I spent it uselessly, niether in study nor in contemplation but only in drinking and raising hell generally. If I'd written the B. + D. at the rate of 100 words a day it would have taken me <u>4 years</u> so you can imagine the moral effect the whole chasm had on me.

What I'm trying to say is just that I'll have to ask you to have patience about the book and trust me that at last, or at least for the 1st time in years, I'm doing the best I can. I've gotten in dozens of bad habits that I'm trying to get rid of

1. Laziness
2. Referring everything to Zelda—a terrible habit, nothing ought to be referred to anybody until its finished
3. Word consciousness—self doubt

   ect. ect. ect. ect.

I feel I have an enormous power in me now, more than I've ever had in a way but it works so fitfully and with so many bogeys because I've <u>talked so much</u> and not lived enough within myself to delelop the nessessary self reliance. Also I don't know anyone who has used up so [torn] sonel experience as I have at 27. Copperfield + Pendennis[2] were written at past forty while This Side of Paradise was three books + the B. + D. was two. So in my new novel I'm thrown directly on purely creative work—not trashy imaginings as in my stories but the sustained imagination of a sincere and yet radiant world. So I tread slowly and carefully + at times in considerable distress. The book will be a consciously artistic achievment + must depend on that as the 1st books did not.

If I ever win the right to any liesure again I will assuredly not waste it as I wasted this past time. Please believe me when I say that now I'm doing the best I can.

F. Scott Fitzgerald: A Life in Letters, pp. 65, 67.

1. *The Great Gatsby* was completed in summer 1924.
2. *David Copperfield* (1850) by Dickens and *Pendennis* (1850) by Thackeray.

To: Harold Ober
20 September 1924

. . . .

Considering the fact that of the eleven stories I've written this year 4 of the 7 that have been published were run 1st in their issues I think I've had hard luck with the movies. I must try some love stories with more action this time. I'm going to try to write three that'll do for Famous-Players[1] as well as for the Post. . . .

F. Scott Fitzgerald: A Life in Letters, p. 82.

1. Movie studio.

To: Maxwell Perkins
c. 10 October 1924

. . . This is to tell you about a young man named Ernest Hemmingway, who lives in Paris, (an American) writes for the transatlantic Review + has a brilliant future. Ezra Pount published a a collection of his short pieces in Paris, at some place like the Egotist Press.[1] I havn't it hear now but its remarkable + I'd look him up right away. He's the real thing.[2]

F. Scott Fitzgerald: A Life in Letters, p. 82.

1. *Three Stories & Ten Poems* (1923) was published in Paris by Robert McAlmon's Contact Editions; *in our time* (1924) was published in Paris by William Bird's Three Mountains Press as one of six volumes edited by Ezra Pound (1885–1972).
2. Hemingway (1899–1971) had signed with Boni & Liveright for publication of *In Our Time* (1925) before Perkins's letter reached him. Scribners became his publisher commencing with *The Torrents of Spring* (1926) and *The Sun Also Rises* (1926).

To: Harold Ober
25 October 1924

I am sending you today under separate cover the manuscript of my new novel <u>The Great Gatsby</u> for serialization. Whether it will serialize you will be a better judge than I. There is some pretty frank stuff in it and I wouldn't want it to be chopped as Hovey[1] chopped the <u>Beautiful + Damned</u>. Now here are my ideas:

    (1.) I think the best bet by all odds is <u>Liberty</u>. It is a love story and it is sensational. Also it is only 50,000 words long which would give them ten installments of 5000 words each, just what they're looking for. And moreover if they started it by February 1st it could be over in time for spring publication. I havn't had a book for almost three years now and I want Scribners to bring this out in April. I wish you would specify to John Wheeler[2] that it must be run through by then.

    (2.) Of course Ray Long[3] will have to have first look at it according to our contract of 1923. But I don't want him to have it (small chance of his wanting it) because in his magazines it would drag on forever + book publication would be postponed. So I'd like to ask him $25,000 for it—a prohibitive price. But it wouldn't be worth my while to give it to him for less. For <u>Liberty</u> I would take $15,000 + I'm against asking more because of a peculiar situation between John[4] + me. He told me he'd never bargain for a thing of mine again—he'd take it at the price offered or refuse it. Ring Lardner[5] told him I was annoyed at him—anyhow its a sort of personal question as you see. So I don't think I'd want to ask him more than $15,000. When I was getting $900 a story I got $7000 or a serial, so now that I'm getting $1750, $15000 for a serial seems a fair price. Especially as its very short.

    (3.) The Post I don't want to offer it to. Its not their kind of thing + I don't want to have it in there anyhow as it kills the book sale at one blow. So that's out.

    (4.) In fact I think <u>Liberty</u> is far and away the best bet—I don't see who else could squeeze it in before April. The third chapter bars it from the womens magazines and that leaves nothing except the Red Book which would drag it out till Fall.[6]

F. Scott Fitzgerald: A Life in Letters, p. 83.

1. Carl Hovey (1876–1956) was editor of *Metropolitan Magazine*, which had serialized *The Beautiful and Damned*.

2. John N. Wheeler (1886–1973), editor of *Liberty*.

3. (1878–1935), editor for magazines owned by William Randolph Hearst (1863–1951).

4. Wheeler.

5. Ring W. Lardner (1885–1933), American sports writer, humorist, and short-story writer.

6. *The Great Gatsby* was not serialized until after its April 1925 book publication; it appeared in *Famous Story Magazine* (April–August 1926).

To: Maxwell Perkins
c. 7 November 1924

. . . .

But I am confused at what you say about Gertrude Stien.[1] I thought it was one purpose of critics + publishers to educate the public up to original work. The first people who risked Conrad certainly didn't do it as a commercial venture. Did the evolution of startling work into accepted work cease twenty years ago?

. . . .

F. Scott Fitzgerald: A Life in Letters, p. 85.

1. Fitzgerald recommended that Perkins read the *Transatlantic Review* serialization of *The Making of Americans* (1925) by Gertrude Stein (1874–1946). On 18 October Perkins explained his reasons for not pursuing the expatriate American experimental writer as a Scribners author: "I am reading the Gertrude Stein as it comes out, and it fascinates me. But I doubt if the reader who had no <u>literary</u> interest, or not much, would have patience with her method, effective as it does become. Its peculiarities are much more marked than in 'The Three Lives.'" (*Dear Scott/Dear Max: The Fitzgerald-Perkins Correspondence*, edited by John Kuehl and Jackson R. Bryer [New York: Scribners, 1971], p. 79).

To: Harold Ober
March 1925

. . . .

Good stories write themselves—bad ones have to be written so this took up about three weeks.[1] And look at it. I'd rather not offer it to the Post because everybody sees the <u>Post</u> but I know its saleable and I need the money. I leave it to you.

. . . .

F. Scott Fitzgerald: A Life in Letters, p. 96.

1. "Not in the Guidebook," *Woman's Home Companion* (November 1925).

To: Maxwell Perkins
10 April 1925

The book[1] comes out today and I am overcome with fears and forebodings. Supposing women didn't like the book because it has no important woman in it, and critics didn't like it because it dealt with the rich and contained no peasants borrowed out of Tess[2] in it and set to work in Idaho? Suppose it didn't even wipe out my debt to you—why it will have to sell 20,000 copies even to do that! In fact all my confidence is gone—I wouldn't tell you this except for the fact that by the this reaches you the worst will be known. I'm sick of the book myself—I wrote it over at least five times and I still feel that what should be the strong scene (in the Hotel) is hurried and ineffective. Also the last chapter, the burial, Gatsby's father ect is faulty. Its too bad because the first five chapters and parts of the 7th and 8th are the best things I've ever done.

. . . .

Another thing—I'm convinced that Myers[3] is all right but have him be sure and keep all such trite phrases as "Surely the book of the Spring!" out of the advertiseing. That one is my pet abomination. Also to use no quotations except those of unqualified and exceptionally entheusiastic praise from emminent individuals. Such phrase as

"Should be on everyone's summer list"
Boston Transcript

"Not a dull moment . . . a thoroughly sound solid piece of work"

havn't sold a copy of any book in three years. I thought your advertising for Ring was great. I'm sorry you didn't get Wescotts new book. Several people have written me that The Apple of the Eye[4] is the best novel of the year.

. . . .

This is only a vague impression, of course, but I wondered if we could think of some way to advertise it so that people who are perhaps weary of assertive jazz and society novels might not dismiss it as "just another book like his others." I confess that today the problem baffles me—all I can think of is to say in general to avoid such phrases as "a picture of New York life" or "modern society"—though as that is exactly what the book is its hard to avoid them. The trouble is so much superficial trash has sailed under those banners. Let me know what you think

F. Scott Fitzgerald: A Life in Letters, pp. 105–106.

1. *The Great Gatsby*.
2. Thomas Hardy's *Tess of the D'Urbervilles* (1891), a novel set in rural England.
3. Wallace Meyer (1888–1971), advertising manager at Scribners.
4. By Glenway Wescott (1901–1987).

To: Maxwell Perkins
c. 24 April 1925

. . . .

In all events I have a book of good stories for the fall.[1] Now I shall write some cheap ones until I've accumulated enough for my my next novel. When that is finished and published I'll wait and see. If it will support me with no more intervals of trash I'll go on as a novelist. If not I'm going to quit, come home, go to Hollywood and learn the movie business. I can't reduce our scale of living and I can't stand this financial insecurity. Anyhow there's no point in trying to be an artist if you can't do your best. I had my chance back in 1920 to start my life on a sensible scale and I lost it and so I'll have to pay the penalty. Then perhaps at 40 I can start writing again without this constant worry and interruption.

. . . .

F. Scott Fitzgerald: A Life in Letters, p. 107.

1. *All the Sad Young Men* was published in February 1926.

Maxwell Perkins, Fitzgerald's editor at Scribners.

To: H. L. Mencken
4 May 1925

. . . .

I think the book is so far a commercial failure—at least it was two weeks after publication—hadn't reached 20,000 yet. So I rather regret (but not violently) the fact that I turned down $15,000.00 for the serial rights. However I have all the money I need and was growing rather tired of being a popular author. My trash for the Post grows worse and worse as there is less and less heart in it—strange to say my whole heart was in my first trash. I thought that the <u>Offshore Pirate</u> was quite as good as <u>Benediction</u>.[1] I never really "wrote down" until after the failure of the *Vegetable* and that was to make this book possible. I would have written down long ago if it had been profitable—I tried it unsuccessfully for the movies. People don't seem to realize that for an intelligent man writing down is about the hardest thing in the world. When people like Hughes and Stephen Whitman[2] go wrong after one tragic book it is because they never had any real egos or attitudes but only empty bellies and cross nerves. The bellies full and the nerves soothed with vanity they see life rosily and would be violently insincere in writing anything but the happy trash they do. . . .

. . . .

F. Scott Fitzgerald: A Life in Letters, p. 111.

1. "The Offshore Pirate," *The Saturday Evening Post* (29 May 1920) and "Benediction," *The Smart Set* (February 1920); both stories were collected in *Flappers and Philosophers* (1920).
2. Rupert Hughes's best-known novel was *The Thirteenth Commandment* (1916) and Stephen French Whitman's was *Predestined* (1910).

To: Maxwell Perkins
c. 22 May 1925

. . . .

. . . I think all the reviews[1] I've seen, except two, have been absolutely stupid and lowsy. Some day they'll eat grass, by God! This thing, both the effort and the result have hardened me and I think now that I'm much better than any of the young Americans <u>without exception</u>.

. . . .

F. Scott Fitzgerald: A Life in Letters, p. 113.

1. Of *The Great Gatsby*.

To: Maxwell Perkins,
c. 1 June 1925

. . . .

Now, Max, I have told you many times that you are my publisher, and permanently, as far as one can fling about the word in this too mutable world. If you like I will sign a contract with you immediately for my next three books. The idea of leaving you has never for <u>one single moment</u> entered my head.

<u>First.</u> Tho, as a younger man, I have not always been in sympathy with some of your publishing ideas, (which were evolved under the pre-movie, pre-high-literacy-rate conditions of twenty to forty years ago), the personality of you and of Mr. Scribner,[1] the tremendous squareness, courtesy, generosity and open- mindedness I have always met there and, if I may say it, the special consideration you have all had for me and my work, much more than make up the difference.

<u>Second</u> You know my own idea on the advantages of one publisher who backs you and your work. And my feeling about uniform books in the matter of house and binding.

<u>Third</u> The curious advantage to a rather radical writer in being published by what is now an ultra-conservative house.

. . . .

All this is preparatory to saying that his[2] new book sounds utterly lowsy—Shiela Kaye-Smith[3] has used the stuff about the farmer having girls instead of boys and being broken up about it. The characters you mention have every one, become stock-props in the last ten years—"Christy, the quaint old hired man" after a season in such stuff as Owen Davis' <u>Ice Bound</u>[4] must be almost ready for the burlesque circuit.

<u>History of the Simple Inarticulate Farmer and his</u>
<u>Hired Man Christy</u>
(Both guaranteed to be utterly full of the Feel of the Soil)

1st Period

1855—English Peasant discovered by Geo. Elliot in <u>Mill on the Floss</u>, <u>Silas Marner</u> ect.[5]
1888—Given intellectual interpretation by Hardy in <u>Jude</u> and <u>Tess</u>
1890—Found in France by Zola in <u>Germinal</u>[6]
1900—Crowds of Scandanavians, Hamsun, Bojer[7] ect, tear him bodily from the Russian, and after a peep at Hardy, Hamlin Garland[8] finds him in the middle west.

———————————

Most of that, however, was literature. It was something pulled by the individual out of life and only partly with the aid of models in other literatures.

2nd Period

1914—Shiela Kaye-Smith frankly imitates Hardy, produces two good books + then begins to imitate herself.

1915—Brett Young[9] discovers him in the coal country

1916—Robert Frost[10] discovers him in New England

1917—Sherwood Anderson discovers him in Ohio

1918—Willa Cather turns him Swede

1920—Eugene O'Niell puts him on the boards in _Different_ + _Beyond Horizon_[11]

1922—Ruth Suckow[12] gets in before the door closes

These people were all good second raters (except Anderson). Each of them brought something to the business—but they exhausted the ground, the type was set. All was over.

3rd Period

The Cheapskates discover him—Bad critics and novelists ect.

1923 Homer Croy writes West of the Water Tower[13]

1924 Edna Ferber turns from her flip jewish saleswoman for a strong silent earthy carrot grower and—the Great Soul of Charley Towne thrills to her passionately. Real and Earthy Struggle[14]

1924 Ice Bound by the author of Nellie the Beautiful Cloak Model[15] winsPulitzer Prize

The Able Mcgloughlins wins $10,000 prize + is forgotten the following wk.[16]

1925 The Apple of the Eye[17] pronounced a masterpiece

1926— TOM, BOYD, WRITES, NOVEL, ABOUT, INARTICULATE, FARMER WHO, IS, CLOSE, TO SOIL, AND, HIS, HIRED, MAN CHRISTY! "STRONG! VITAL! REAL!"

As a matter of fact the American peasant as "real" material scarcely exists. He is scarcely 10% of the population, isn't bound to the soil at all as the English + Russian peasants were—and, if has any sensitivity whatsoever (except a most sentimental conception of himself, which our writers persistently shut their eyes to) he is in the towns before he's twenty. Either Lewis, Lardner and myself have been badly fooled, or else using him as typical American material is simply a stubborn seeking for the static in a world that for almost a hundred years has simply not been static. Isn't it a 4th rate imagination that can find only that old property farmer in all this amazing time and land? And anything that ten people a year can do well enough to pass muster has become so easy that it isn't worth the doing.

I can not disassociate a man from his work.—That this Wescott (who is an effeminate Oxford fairy) and Tom Boyd and Burton Rascoe[18] (whose real ambition is to lock themselves into a stinking little appartment and screw each others' wives) are going to tell us mere superficial "craftsmen" like Hergeshiemer, Wharton, Tarkington and me about the Great Beautiful Appreciation they have of the Great Beautiful life of the Manure Widder—rather turns my stomach. The real people like Gertrude Stien (with whom I've talked) and Conrad (see his essay on James) have a respect for people whose materials may not touch theirs <u>at a single point</u>. But the fourth rate + highly derivative people like Tom are loud in their outcry against any subject matter that doesn't come out of the old, old bag which their betters have used and thrown away.

For example there is an impression among the thoughtless (including Tom) that Sherwood Anderson is a man of profound ideas who is "handicapped by his inarticulateness." As a matter of fact Anderson is a man of practically no ideas—<u>but he is one of the very best and finest writers in the English language today</u>. God, he can write! Tom could never get such rythms in his life as there are on the pages of <u>Winesburg, Ohio</u>—. Simple! The words on the lips of critics makes me hilarious: Anderson's style is about as simple as an engine room full of dynamoes. But Tom flatters himself that he can sit down for five months and by dressing up a few heart throbs in overalls produce literature.

It amazes me, Max, to see you with your discernment and your fine intelligence, fall for that whole complicated fake. Your chief critical flaw is to confuse mere earnestness with artistic sincerity. On two of Ring's jackets have been statements that he never wrote a dishonest word (maybe it's one jacket). But Ring and many of the very greatest artists have written thousands of words in plays, poems and novels which weren't even faintly sincere or ernest and were yet <u>artisticly sincere</u>. The latter term is *not* a synonym for plodding ernestness. Zola did not say the last word about literature; nor the first.

I append all the data on my fall book, and in closing I apologize for seeming impassioned about Tom and his work when niether the man or what he writes has ever been personally inimical to me. He is simply the scapegoat for the mood Rascoe has put me in and, tho I mean every word of it, I probably wouldn't have wasted all this paper on a book that won't sell + will be dead in a month + an imitative school that will be dead by its own weight in a year or so, if the news about Liveright hadn't come on top of the Rascoe review and ruined my disposition. Good luck to <u>Drummond</u>. I'm sure one or two critics will mistake it for profound stuff—maybe even Mencken who has a weakness in that direction. But I think you should look closer

. . . .

<u>Advertising Notes</u>
Suggested line for jacket: "Show transition from his early exuberant stories of youth which created a new type of American girl and the later and more serious mood which produced <u>The Great Gatsby</u> and marked him as one of the half dozen masters of English prose now writing in America. . . . What other writer has shown such unexpected developments, such versatility, changes of pace"

ect - ect - ect - I think that, toned down as you see fit, is the general line. Don't say "Fitzgerald has done it!" + then in the next sentence that I am an artist. People who are interested in artists aren't interested in people who have "done it." Both are O.K. but don't belong in the same ad. This is an author's quibble. All authors have one quibble.

However, you have always done well by me (Except for Black's[19] memorable excretion in the <u>Allumni Weekly</u>: do you remember "Make it a Fitzgerald Christmas!") and I leave it to you. If 100,000 copies are not sold I shall shift to Mitchell Kennerley.[20]

By the way what has become of Black? I hear he has written a very original and profound novel. It is said to be about an inarticulate farmer and his struggles with the "soil" and his sexual waverings between his inarticulate wife and an inarticulate sheep. He finally chooses his old pioneering grandmother as the most inarticulate of all but finds her in bed with none other than our old friend THE HIRED MAN CHRISTY!

CHRISTY HAD DONE IT!

[In 1962 Fitzgerald's famous letter to Perkins was sold at auction at Chrystie's (not old man Christy's) for £7000.][21]

F. Scott Fitzgerald: A Life in Letters, pp. 116–120, 122.

1. Charles Scribner II, president (1879–1928) of Charles Scribner's Sons.
2. Thomas Boyd's novel *Samuel Drummond*, published by Scribners in 1925, examines the life of an American farmer.
3. Sheila Kaye Smith (1887–1956), British regional novelist whose best-known work included *Starbrace* (1909) and *Joanna Godden* (1921).
4. 1923 play that won a Pulitzer Prize.
5. George Eliot (Mary Ann Evans, 1819–1890) published *The Mill on the Floss* in 1860 and *Silas Marner* in 1861.
6. *Germinal* was published in 1885.
7. Knut Hamsun (1859–1952) and Johan Bojer (1872–1959), Norwegian novelists.
8. (1860–1940), local-color story writer.
9. British novelist Francis Brett Young (1884–1954).
10. American poet (1874–1963).
11. *Diff'rent* and *Beyond the Horizon* by O'Neill (1888–1953) were produced in 1920.
12. Suckow (1902–1960) wrote realistic fiction about the Midwest.
13. Croy (1883–1947) was a midwestern novelist and humorist.
14. Edna Ferber (1885–1968) won the Pulitzer Prize for her novel *So Big* (1924); Charles Hanson Towne (1877–1949) was a journalist and editor.
15. Owen Davis's 1906 melodrama.
16. *The Able McLaughlins* (1923) by Margaret Wilson (1882–1973) won a Pulitzer Prize for fiction.
17. By Wescott.
18. (1892–1957), columnist and critic.
19. John Black, formerly of Scribners' advertising department.
20. (1878–1950), publisher notorious for his reluctance to pay royalties.
21. Fitzgerald's bracketed note is a joke. This letter has not been auctioned, but it would have brought $10,000 in 1962.

To: Maxwell Perkins
20 February 1926

. . . .

My God! If it should sell 10,000 copies I'd be out of debt to you for the 1st time since 1922.[1] Isn't that a disgrace, when I get $2500. for a story as my regular price. But trash doesn't come as easily as it used to and I've grown to hate the poor old debauched form itself.

. . . .

F. Scott Fitzgerald: A Life in Letters, p. 137.

1. Scribners sold some 23,000 copies of *The Great Gatsby* in 1925–1926. Fitzgerald's royalty was thirty cents per copy.

To: Harold Ober
c. 15 March 1926

This is one of the lowsiest stories I've ever written.[1] Just <u>terrible</u>! I lost interest in the middle (by the way the last part is typed triple space because I thought I could fix it—but I couldn't)

<u>Please</u>—and I mean this—don't offer it to the <u>Post</u>. I think that as things are now it would be <u>wretched</u> policy. Nor to the <u>Red Book</u>. It hasn't *one* redeeming <u>touch</u> of my usual spirit in it. I was desperate to begin a story + invented a business plot—the kind I can't handle. I'd rather have $1000, for it from some obscure place than twice that + have it seen. <u>I feel very strongly about this</u>!

Am writing two of the best stories I've ever done in my life.[2]

F. Scott Fitzgerald: A Life in Letters, p. 139.

1. "Your Way and Mine," *Woman's Home Companion* (May 1927).
2. Probably "Jacob's Ladder," *The Saturday Evening Post* (20 August 1927) and "The Love Boat," *The Saturday Evening Post* (8 October 1927).

"How to Waste Material:
A Note on My Generation"

By F. Scott Fitzgerald

Ever since Irving's[1] preoccupation with the necessity for an American background, for some square miles of cleared territory on which colorful variants might presently arise, the question of material has hampered the American writer. For one Dreiser who made a single-minded and irreproachable choice there have been a dozen like Henry James who have stupid-got with worry over the matter, and yet another dozen who, blinded by the fading tail of Walt Whitman's comet, have botched their books by the insincere compulsion to write "significantly" about America.

Insincere because it is not a compulsion found in themselves—it is "literary" in the most belittling sense. During the past seven years we have had at least half a dozen treatments of the American farmer, ranging from New England to Nebraska; at least a dozen canny books about youth, some of them with surveys of the American universities for background; more than a dozen novels reflecting various aspects of New York, Chicago, Washington, Detroit, Indianapolis, Wilmington, and Richmond; innumerable novels dealing with American politics, business, society, science, racial problems, art, literature, and moving pictures, and with Americans abroad at peace or in war; finally several novels of change and growth, tracing the swift decades for their own sweet lavender or protesting vaguely and ineffectually against the industrialization of our beautiful old American life. We have had an Arnold Bennett for every five towns[2]—surely by this time the foundations have been laid! Are we competent only to toil forever upon a never completed first floor whose specifications change from year to year?

In any case we are running through our material like spendthrifts—just as we have done before. In the Nineties there began a feverish search for any period of American history that hadn't been "used," and once found it was immediately debauched into a pretty and romantic story. These past seven years have seen the same sort of literary gold rush; and for all our boasted sincerity and sophistication, the material is being turned out raw and undigested in much the same way. One author goes to a midland farm for three months to obtain the material for an epic of the American husbandmen! Another sets off on a like errand to the Blue Ridge Mountains, a third departs with a Corona[3] for the West Indies—one is justified in the belief that what they get hold of will weigh no more than the journalistic loot brought back by Richard Harding Davis[4] and John Fox, Jr.,[5] twenty years ago.

Worse, the result will be doctored up to give it a literary flavor. The farm story will be sprayed with a faint dilution of ideas and sensory impressions from Thomas Hardy; the novel of the Jewish tenement block will be festooned with wreaths from *Ulysses* and the later Gertrude Stein; the document of dreamy youth will be prevented from fluttering entirely away by means of great and half great names—Marx, Spencer, Wells, Edward FitzGerald[6]— dropped like paper weights here and there upon the pages. Finally the novel of business will be cudgeled into being satire by the questionable but constantly reiterated implication that the author and his readers don't partake of the American commercial instinct.

And most of it—the literary beginnings of what was to have been a golden age—is as dead as if it had never been written. Scarcely one of those who put so much effort and enthusiasm, even intelligence, into it, got hold of any material at all.

To a limited extent this was the fault of two men—one of whom, H. L. Mencken, has yet done more for American letters than any man alive. What Mencken felt the absence of, what he wanted, and justly, back in 1920, got away from him, got twisted in his hand. Not because the "literary revolution" went beyond him but because his idea had always been ethical rather than æsthetic. In the history of culture no pure æsthetic idea has ever served as an offensive weapon. Mencken's invective, sharp as Swift's,[7] made its point by the use of the most forceful prose style now written in English. Immediately, instead of committing himself to an infinite series of pronouncements upon the American novel, he should have modulated his tone to the more urbane, more critical one of his early essay on Dreiser.

But perhaps it was already too late. Already he had begotten a family of hammer and tongs men—insensitive, suspicious of glamour, preoccupied exclusively with the external, the contemptible, the "national" and the drab, whose style was a debasement of his least effective manner and who, like glib children, played continually with his themes in his maternal shadow. These were the men who manufactured enthusiasm when each new mass of raw data was dumped on the literary platform—mistaking incoherence for vitality, chaos for vitality. It was the "new poetry movement" over again, only that this time its victims were worth the saving. Every week some new novel gave its author membership in "that little band who are producing a worthy American literature." As one of the charter members of that little band I am proud to state that it has now swollen to seventy or eighty members.

And through a curious misconception of his work, Sherwood Anderson must take part of the blame for this enthusiastic march up a blind alley in the dark. To this day reviewers solemnly speak of him as an inarticulate, fumbling man, bursting with ideas—when, on the contrary, he is the possessor of a brilliant and almost inimitable prose style, and of scarcely any ideas at all. Just as the prose of Joyce in the hands of, say, Waldo Frank[8] becomes insignificant and idiotic, so the Anderson admirers set up

Hergesheimer as an anti-Christ and then proceed to imitate Anderson's lapses from that difficult simplicity they are unable to understand. And here again critics support them by discovering merits in the very disorganization that is to bring their books to a timely and unregretted doom.

Now the business is over. "Wolf" has been cried too often. The public, weary of being fooled, has gone back to its Englishmen, its memoirs and its prophets. Some of the late brilliant boys are on lecture tours (a circular informs me that most of them are to speak upon "the literary revolution"!), some are writing potboilers, a few have definitely abandoned the literary life—they were never sufficiently aware that material, however closely observed, is as elusive at the moment in which it has its existence unless it is purified by an incorruptible style and by the catharsis of a passionate emotion.

Of all the work by the young men who have sprung up since 1920 one book survives—*The Enormous Room* by E. E. Cummings. It is scarcely a novel; it doesn't deal with the American scene; it was swamped in the mediocre downpour, isolated—forgotten. But it lives on, because those few who cause books to live have not been able to endure the thought of its mortality. Two other books, both about the war, complete the possible salvage from the work of the younger generation—*Through the Wheat* and *Three Soldiers*, but the former despite its fine last chapters doesn't stand up as well as *Les Croix de Bois*[9] and *The Red Badge of Courage*, while the latter is marred by its pervasive flavor of contemporary indignation. But as an augury that someone has profited by this dismal record of high hope and stale failure comes the first work of Ernest Hemingway.[10]

II

In Our Time consists of fourteen stories, short and long, with fifteen vivid miniatures interpolated between them. When I try to think of any contemporary American short stories as good as "Big Two-Hearted River," the last one in the book, only Gertrude Stein's "Melanctha," Anderson's "The Egg," and Lardner's "Golden Honeymoon" come to mind. It is the account of a boy on a fishing trip—he hikes, pitches his tent, cooks dinner, sleeps, and next morning casts for trout. Nothing more—but I read it with the most breathless unwilling interest I have experienced since Conrad first bent my reluctant eyes upon the sea.

The hero, Nick, runs through nearly all the stories, until the book takes on almost an autobiographical tint—in fact "My Old Man," one of the two in which this element seems entirely absent, is the least successful of all. Some of the stories show influences but they are invariably absorbed and transmuted, while in "My Old Man" there is an echo of Anderson's way of thinking in those sentimental "horse stories," which inaugurated his respectability and also his decline four years ago.

But with "The Doctor and the Doctor's Wife," "The End of Something," "The Three Day Blow," "Mr. and Mrs. Elliot," and "Soldier's Home," you are immediately aware of something temperamentally new. In the first of these a man is backed down by a half breed Indian after committing himself to a fight. The quality of humiliation in the story is so intense that it immediately calls up every such incident in the reader's past. Without the aid of a comment or a pointing finger one knows exactly the sharp emotion of young Nick who watches the scene.

The next two stories describe an experience at the last edge of adolescence. You are constantly aware of the continual snapping of ties that is going on around Nick. In the half stewed, immature conversation before the fire you watch the awakening of that vast unrest that descends upon the emotional type at about eighteen. Again there is not a single recourse to exposition. As in "Big Two-Hearted River," a picture—sharp, nostalgic, tense—develops before your eyes. When the picture is complete a light seems to snap out, the story is over. There is no tail, no sudden change of pace at the end to throw into relief what has gone before.

Nick leaves home penniless; you have a glimpse of him lying wounded in the street of a battered Italian town, and later of a love affair with a nurse on a hospital roof in Milan. Then in one of the best of the stories he is home again. The last glimpse of him is when his mother asks him, with all the bitter world in his heart, to kneel down beside her in the dining room in Puritan prayer.

Anyone who first looks through the short interpolated sketches will hardly fail to read the stories themselves. "The Garden at Mons" and "The Barricade" are profound essays upon the English officer, written on a postage stamp. "The King of Greece's Tea Party," "The Shooting of the Cabinet Ministers," and "The Cigar-store Robbery" particularly fascinated me, as they did when Edmund Wilson first showed them to me in an earlier pamphlet, over two years ago.[11]

Disregard the rather ill considered blurbs upon the cover.[12] It is sufficient that here is no raw food served up by the railroad restaurants of California and Wisconsin. In the best of these dishes there is not a bit to spare. And many of us who have grown weary of admonitions to "watch this man or that" have felt a sort of renewal of excitement at these stories wherein Ernest Hemingway turns a corner into the street.

The Bookman, 63 (May 1926), 262–265.

1. Washington Irving (1783–1859), American man of letters, who created Rip Van Winkle and Ichabod Crane.
2. Some of Bennett's best fiction is set in the pottery-manufacturing district of England known as the Five Towns.
3. Make of typewriter.
4. (1864–1916), American fiction writer and war correspondent.
5. American novelist (1862?–1919) who covered the Spanish-American war.
6. German political economist Karl Marx, English philosopher Herbert Spencer

(1820–1903), novelist H. G. Wells, and English poet Edward FitzGerald (1809–1883), who translated *The Rubáiyát of Omar Khayyám* (1859).

7. Anglo-Irish satirist Jonathan Swift (1667–1745), author of *Gulliver's Travels* (1726).

8. American author (1889–1967) who wrote impressionistic prose.

9. World War I novel published in 1919 by French writer Roland Dorgelès (Roland Lecavelé, 1886–1973).

10. The first Hemingway book published in the United States.

11. The interchapters were first published in the slender Three Mountains Press volume *in our time* (Paris, 1924). Fitzgerald had urged Perkins to publish Hemingway on the basis of this booklet.

12. The front of the dust jacket had blurbs from Sherwood Anderson, Donald Ogden Stewart, Edward J. O'Brien, Waldo Frank, American writer Gilbert Seldes (1893–1970), and English writer Ford Madox Ford (1873–1939).

Ernest Hemingway

To: Harold Ober
c. 3 May 1926

· · · · · · ·

I have your two letters in regard to <u>Liberty</u>. Now as to the short story business alone I would rather, without qualification, stay with the *Post* at $2500. than go to <u>Liberty</u> at $3500. Not only that but I shall probably write no short stories of any kind until next autumn.

But there is another element which might force me to leave the *Post* and that is the novel serialization. The novel is about one fourth done and will be delivered for possible serialization about January 1st.[1] It will be about 75,000 words long, divided into 12 chapters, concerning tho this is absolutely confidential such a case as that girl who shot her mother on the Pacific coast last year.[2] In other words, like <u>Gatsby</u> it is highly sensational. Not only would this bar it from the <u>Post</u> but also they are hostile, as you know, to the general cast of thought that permeates my serious work.

On the other hand <u>Liberty</u> is evidently very much in my favor at the moment. And if they would give between $25,000 and $40,000 for the serial I'd be an idiot to throw it away. In other words with say about 30,000 for the serial + assurance that Liberty will have a stable editorial policy at least till Jan 1st 1927, I'd better swing over there. Frankly I'm at sea. Perhaps it had better depend on whether they would really contract for the novel in advance. I hope to bring it home completed next December.

· · · · · · ·

F. Scott Fitzgerald: A Life in Letters, pp. 140–141.

1. *Tender Is the Night* was not published until April 1934.
2. The 1925 Dorothy Ellingson case was one of the sources for the matricide novel that developed into *Tender Is the Night*.

"Fitzgerald, Spenglerian"
by Harry Salpeter

F. Scott Fitzgerald is a Nietzschean, F. Scott Fitzgerald is a Spenglerian,[1] F. Scott Fitzgerald is in a state of cosmic despair. From within his slightly shuttered eyes, F. Scott Fitzgerald looks out upon a world which is doomed, in his sight, to destruction; from his unbearded lips comes conviction of America that is as final as the sentence is harsh. Summation of the evidence and conviction came in such a rush of words, in such a tumbling of phrase upon phrase that neither objection nor appeal was possible. It was a rush of words which only powerful feeling could dictate. Here was I interviewing the author of *This Side of Paradise*, the voice and embodiment of the jazz age, its product and its beneficiary, a popular novelist, a movie scenarist, a dweller in the gilded palaces, a master of servants, only to find F. Scott Fitzgerald, himself, shorn of these associations, forecasting doom, death and damnation to his generation, in the spirit, if not in the rhetoric, of your typical spittoon philosopher. In a pleasant corner of the Plaza[2] tea garden he sounded like an intellectual Samson prophesying the crumbling of its marble columns. He looks like a candid, serious youth. His blue eyes, fair hair and clear-cut profile, no less than his reputation, give the lie to the mind of F. Scott Fitzgerald.

I had caught Fitzgerald at the Plaza, his midway stop between Hollywood where, after much travail, he had completed a scenario for Constance Talmadge,[3] and Brandywine Hundred, Del.,[4] an address which tickles him. There he will make his home for the next two years and there he will complete his next novel. This, he said, had been vaguely suggested by the Loeb-Leopold[5] case and in the tragic moments of this novel will be mirrored some of the cosmic despair under the burden of which Fitzgerald manages, somehow, to maintain a resilient step.

And after this novel—on which he has already worked three years—is completed?

Why, what is there left to do? Go to pieces. Or write another novel. A writer is good only for writing and showing off. Then people find him out or he runs out of money and then he goes and writes another novel.

* * *

Fitzgerald has been "a hot Nietzschean" ever since he read *Thus Spake Zarathustra*.[6] To-day, Oswald Spengler's *Decline of the West*[7] is his "bed-book." What have Nietzsche and Spengler in common? "Spengler stands on the shoulders of Nietzsche and Nietzsche on those of Goethe."[8] This civilization has nothing more to produce. "We threw up our fine types in the eighteenth century, when we had Beethoven[9] and Goethe. The race had a mind then." All that there is left to do is to go into a period of universal hibernation and begin all over again at the sheep- grazing stage. He said:

> Spenglerism signals the death of this civilization. We are in a period paralleling Rome 185 years after Christ, Greece just before Alexander,[10] the Mohammedan world about 1200. There is now no mind of the race, there is now no great old man of the tribe, there are no longer any feet to sit at. People have to stage sham battles in their own minds.

> Mussolini,[11] the last slap in the face of liberalism, is an omen for America. America is ready for an Alexander, a Trajan[12] or a Constantine.[13] The idea that we're the greatest people in the world because we have the most money in the world is ridiculous. Wait until this wave of prosperity is over! Wait ten or fifteen years! Wait until the next war on the Pacific, or against some European combination! Then we shall have to fight for our race and not under the leadership of a Calvin Coolidge.[14]

> The next fifteen years will show how much resistance there is in the American race. The only thing that can make it worth while to be an American is a life and death struggle, a national testing. After that it may be possible for a man to say 'I'm an American' as a man might say 'I'm a Frenchman' or 'I'm a German,' or, until recently, when the colonies made cowards of them all, 'I'm an Englishman.' The good American is the best in the world, as an individual. But taken collectively, he is a mass product without common sense or guts or dignity.

At present writing, this descendant of the author of "The Star-Spangled Banner"[15] is not proud to be an American. "I have never said I was an American." That descendant can say: "Better that an entire Division should have been wiped out than that Otto Braun should have been killed." Braun, a German boy, at the age of nineteen or twenty, gave such evidences of genius that he was regarded as a Goethe in the budding. He was killed in the Argonne during the advance of the 77th Division.[16]

Yet the man who is not proud to be an American is an American, if descent, on one side, from landholders on grant who came in 1630 means anything. On one side, said Fitzgerald, he comes from straight 1850 potato-famine Irish[17] who prospered with the rising Middle West; and, on the other, from sometimes prosperous, sometimes indigent, but always proud, Maryland stock, who threw off, among other freaks, Philip Key, the manufacturer who made, without charge, all the buttons on the Continental uniforms, and Francis Scott Key.

* * *

We talked about the American in Paris, to which city Fitzgerald sometimes goes in quest of refuge from America.

The best of America drifts to Paris. The American in Paris is the best American. It is more fun for an intelligent person to live in an intelligent country. France has the only two things toward which we drift as we grow older—intelligence and good manners.

And why isn't it any fun to be an American?

Because it's too big to get your hands on. Because it's a woman's country. Because its very nice and its various local necessities have made it impossible for an American to have a real credo. After all, an American is condemned to saying "I don't like this." He has never had time—and I mean time, the kind of inspired hush that people make for themselves in which to want to be or to do on the scale and with all the arrogant assumptions with which great races make great dreams. There has never been an American tragedy. There have only been great failures. That is why the story of Aaron Burr—let alone that of Jefferson Davis[18]—opens up things that we who accept the United States as an established unit hardly dare to think about.

Fitzgerald is distrait. He can't call himself a liberal. Finding liberalism "mushy and ineffectual," he is compelled to turn to the Mussolini-Ludendorff[19] idea. He does and does not want Mussolini. "If you're against Mussolini you're for the cesspool that Italy was before him; if you're for Mussolini you're for Caesarism." To call one's self a Communist is no solution either. Fitzgerald's hope for the Nation lies in the birth of a hero who will be of age when America's testing comes. It is possible that an American woman may be big enough of soul to bear and nurture such a hero; it is more likely that he will come out of the immigrant class, in the guise of an east-side newsboy. "His mother will be a good woman, in the sense that Otto Braun's mother was; she knew that he was a hero. But when this American hero is born one knows that he will not be brought up by the reading of liberal magazines, nor educated by women teachers." The father, said Fitzgerald, doesn't matter. Behind Fitzgerald's pessimism there is mysticism.

New York World, 3 April 1927, 12M.

1. Reference to German historian and political philosopher Osward Spengler (1880–1936), who believed that Western civilization was in decline.
2. The Plaza Hotel in New York.
3. Fitzgerald's screenplay for actress Talmadge (1898–1973) was rejected.
4. "Ellerslie" mansion was near Wilmington, Delaware.
5. Chicagoans Richard Loeb (1905?–1936) and Nathan Leopold (1904–1971) committed an "intellectual murder" in 1924. The first version of the novel that became *Tender Is the Night* had the working title "The Boy Who Murdered His Mother."
6. Published in four parts between 1883 and 1892.

7. First published in German (1918–1922) and then published in English translations (1926–1928).

8. German poet and thinker Johann Goethe (1749–1832).

9. German composer Ludwig van Beethoven (1770–1827).

10. Alexander the Great (356–323 B.C.), King of Macedonia and conqueror of much of the Middle East.

11. Benito Mussolini (1883–1945), Italian dictator and founder of fascism.

12. (c. 53–117), Roman Emperor.

13. Constantine the Great (c. 274–337), the first Roman emperor to foster Christianity.

14. (1872–1933), the thirtieth president of the United States.

15. Fitzgerald was a second cousin, three times removed of Francis Scott Key (1779–1843).

16. *The Diary of Otto Braun*, published in English translation in 1924, was greatly admired by Fitzgerald.

17. The failure of the Irish potato crop resulted in a great wave of immigration to America.

18. Burr (1756–1836) unsuccessfully plotted to colonize the Southwest as an entity separate from the United States; Davis (1808–1889) was president of the Confederacy during the American Civil War (1861–1865).

19. Erich von Ludendorff (1865–1937), World War I German general who became a political figure.

"F. Scott Fitzgerald Is Bored by Efforts at Realism in 'Lit':

Not Flesh and Blood Characters but Petulant Phantoms Appear in Stories in March Issue.

Poetry Earns More Praise

Griswold's Sonnets Outstanding Feature of Issue— Careful Work by Barnouw and Day Is Noted"

---

by F. Scott Fitzgerald '17.

In my days stories in the *Lit*[1] were about starving artists, dying poilus, the plague in Florence and the soul of the Great Khan. They took place, chiefly, behind the moon and a thousand years ago. Now they all take place on Nassau Street,[2] no longer back than yesterday. Playing safe they are more "real," but by reason of their narrow boundaries they are desperately similar to each other.

There is the sensitive undergraduate who, perhaps because he is the author, is never given a recognizable skin; there is mention of Nassau Street and Gothic towers; without once seeing or feeling the visual world, without being fresh or tired, without being desperate or ecstatic, neither eating nor loving, and drinking only as a mannerism of the day, this petulant ghost moves through a vague semi-adventure with a girl, a parent, the faculty or another shadow labelled his roommate. Acted upon but never acting, limp and suspicious, he lacks even the normal phosphorescence of decay.

He drifts through the two best stories in this month's *Lit*—in one he barely attains a stalemate with his father, due to the latter's advantage of being flesh and blood, since he is observed, however superficially, from the outside. "Stranger" by Charles Yost is really a pretty good story, though like all tales of futility and boredom it unavoidably shares the quality of its subject—but it is intelligent, restrained and with some but not enough excellent writing.

A. Z. F. Wood's "St. George and the Dragon" is even a little better. Offended by the manner of his home town, the ghost grows angry and knocks down not a yokel but another ghost by mistake. We are left to imagine his humiliation. If the author had been a little less facile about Jim's real motives the story would have carried a great deal of conviction, for it is credible, well-written and interesting throughout.

H. M. Alexander's "Peckham's Saturday Night" is a good story. "Waking Up" by A. S. Alexander is below the author's standard. "The Old Meeting House" by H. A. Rue is Gray's "Elegy"[3] copiously watered—it might have come out of the *Lit* of forty years ago.

The poetry is better. Griswold's two sonnets show imagination and power and, I dare say, a great deal of honest toil. They are incomparably the best thing in the issue—cheering, even exciting. Erik Barnouw's lighter piece is excellent. So is Price Day's poem—it has feeling, not a few real felicities and, again, welcome signs of patience and care. Wilfred Owen's "Brass Moon" has quality—his shorter pieces are trite; we have such feeble lines as "walk solemnly single file," "piquant turned-up nose," "creep in upon the window sill" etc. "Harlem and the Ritz" by H. T. B. is trivial but I like the form of his long poem. "Defiance" by Grier Hart is fair. The remaining verse is of no interest.

To conclude: This is a dignified but on the whole unadventurous number of the oldest college magazine in America. The present reviewer's strongest reaction is his curiosity as to the fate of Mr. Yost's and Mr. Wood's phantoms. One is sure, of course, they they will in a few years refuse to go into their fathers' businesses, one hardly blames them—but what then? The American father, under the influence of his wife, will immediately yield and the ghost will carry his pale negatives out into the world. Those to whom life has been a more passionate and stirring affair than one must suppose it now is at Princeton will not envy him his hollow victory.

Review of March 1928 issue of *The Nassau Literary Magazine*, *The Daily Princetonian*, 16 March 1928, pp. 1, 3.

1. *The Nassau Literary Magazine*, the Princeton University undergraduate journal for which Fitzgerald had written during his student years.
2. The main thoroughfare in the town of Princeton.
3. A meditative poem, "Elegy in a Country Churchyard" (1750), by English writer Thomas Gray (1716–1771).

"Fitzgerald Back From Riviera; Is Working On Novel"

Describing the French Riviera as "the most fascinating amalgamation of wealth, luxury and general uselessness in the world," Scott Fitzgerald, famous and still youthful American novelist, has returned to Paris after a short sojourn in Nice. He was accompanied by his wife and little daughter, "Scottie Jr.," and will remain here until he has finished his latest book—the first in two and a half years.

"That's the why of my new novel," said Mr. Fitzgerald. "It's about the Riviera, and that's all I can say about it today."

The young author of *This Side of Paradise* and half a dozen other best-sellers didn't give the reporter a chance to ask questions. "As I said on leaving Nice," he continued, "I have nothing to say about the Hoover Administration, the *I'm Alone* case,[1] Prohibition in America, Col. Lindbergh[2] or why I live abroad."

He consented, however, to confide a bit of Riviera scandal. "The American artists' colony at Cagnes-sur-Mer[3] is having a lot of trouble with the town postmaster," he laughed. "Their cheques from home haven't been arriving fast enough, and you know what life is for Bohemians when cheques stop coming from home. Anyway, I hear they're going to have the postmaster fired for holding up their letters."

The genial Mr. Fitzgerald advised Sinclair Lewis's new novel *Dodsworth*[4] for "all Americans abroad who don't pay any attention to H. L. Mencken's criticisms."

Chicago Daily Tribune (Paris Edition), 9 April 1929, p. 8.

1. On 22 March 1929 the British schooner *I'm Alone*, an alleged rumrunner, was sunk by the U.S. Coast Guard off the coast of Louisiana.
2. Charles A. Lindbergh (1902–1974) had made the first trans-Atlantic solo flight in May 1927.
3. Town on the French Riviera.
4. Lewis's novel deals in part with an American businessman's reactions to Europe.

To: Harold Ober
c. 15 July 1929

Of course I was delighted with the news about the raise—which makes actually 900% in 10 yrs., you've made for me.[1] Probably in this case by your own entheusiasm for the story. For that I thank you also. For the enormous loans you've made me I don't even dare begin.

. . . .

F. Scott Fitzgerald: A Life in Letters, p. 168.

1. *The Saturday Evening Post* paid Fitzgerald $4,000 for "At Your Age" (17 August 1929).

To: Ernest Hemingway
9 September 1929

. . . .

. . . Here's a last flicker of the old cheap pride:—the <u>Post</u> now pay the old whore $4000. a screw. But now its because she's mastered the 40 positions—in her youth one was enough.

F. Scott Fitzgerald: A Life in Letters, p. 169.

To: Maxwell Perkins
May 1930

. . . Harold Ober wrote me that if it[1] couldn't be published this fall I should publish the Basil Lee stories,[2] but I know too well by whom reputations are made + broken to ruin myself completely by such a move—I've seen Tom Boyd, Michael Arlen[3] + too many others fall through the eternal trapdoor of trying cheat the public, no matter what their public is, with substitutes—better to let four years go by. I wrote young + I wrote a lot + the pot takes longer to fill up now but the novel, my novel, is a different matter than if I'd hurriedly finished it up a year and a half ago. If you think Callahgan hasn't completely blown himself up with this death house masterpiece[4] just wait and see the pieces fall. I don't know why I'm saying this to you who have never been anything but my most loyal and confident encourager and friend but Ober's letter annoyed me today + put me in a wretched humor. I know what I'm doing—honestly, Max. How much time between The Cabala + The Bridge of St Lois Rey, between The Genius + The American Tragedy between The Wisdom Tooth + Green Pastures.[5] I think time seems to go by quicker there in America but time put in is time eventually taken out—and whatever this thing of mine is its certainly not a mediocrity like The Woman of Andros + The Forty Second Parallel.[6] "He through" is an easy cry to raise but its safer for the critics to raise it at the evidence in print than at a long silence.

F. Scott Fitzgerald: A Life in Letters, pp. 181–182.

1. The novel that developed into *Tender Is the Night*.
2. A series of *Saturday Evening Post* stories (1928–1929) tracing Basil Duke Lee from boyhood to college.
3. British novelist (1895–1956) chiefly remembered for his best-selling 1924 novel *The Green Hat*.
4. Canadian novelist Morley Callaghan (1903–1990) was published by Scribners; Fitzgerald is referring to Callaghan's *It's Never Over* (1930).
5. *The Cabala* (1926) and *The Bridge of San Luis Rey* (1927) are by Thornton Wilder (1897–1975); *The "Genius"* (1915) and *An American Tragedy* (1925) are by Theodore Dreiser (1871–1945); and *The Wisdom Tooth* (1926) and *The Green Pastures* (1929) are by Marc Connelly (1890–1980).
6. Wilder's *The Woman of Andros* (1930) and Dos Passos's *The 42nd Parallel* (1930).

To: Harold Ober
c. 13 May 1930

. . . .

. . . I know you're losing faith in me + Max too but God knows one has to rely in the end on one's own judgement. I could have published four lowsy, half baked books in the last five years + people would have thought I was at least a worthy young man not drinking myself to pieces in the south seas—but I'd be dead as Michael Arlen, Bromfield,[1] Tom Boyd, Callaghan + the others who think they can trick the world with the hurried and the second rate. These <u>Post</u> stories in the <u>Post</u> are at least not any spot on me—they're honest and if their <u>form</u> is stereotyped people know what to expect when they pick up the <u>Post</u>. The novel is another thing—if, after four years I published the Basil Lee stories as a book I might as well get tickets for Hollywood immediately.

. . . .

(3) Costain's[2] suggestion (incidently he can go to hell). The only way I can write a decent story is to imagine no one's going to accept it + who cares. Self-consciousness about editors is <u>ruinous</u> to me. They can make their critisisms afterwards. I'm not doing to do another Josephine[3] thing until I can get that out of my head. I tore up the beginning of one. You might tell him pleasantly, of course, that I just can't work that way—Still there's no use telling him—the harms done but if he has any other ideas about writing stories please don't tell me.

. . . .

F. Scott Fitzgerald: A Life in Letters, pp. 182–183.

1. Novelist Louis Bromfield (1896–1956).
2. Thomas B. Costain (1885–1965) was a *Saturday Evening Post* editor who became a best-selling historical novelist.
3. In 1930–1931 Fitzgerald wrote a series of *Saturday Evening Post* stories with a young protagonist named Josephine Perry.

To: Maxwell Perkins
c. 1 Sept. 1930

All the world seems to end up in this flat and antiseptic smelling land—with an overlay of flowers.[1] Tom Wolfe[2] is the only man I've met here who isn't sick or hasn't sickness to deal with. You have a great find in him—what he'll do is incalculable. He has a deeper culture than Ernest and more vitality, if he is slightly less of a poet that goes with the immense surface he wants to cover. Also he lacks Ernests quality of a stick hardened in the fire—he is more susceptible to the world. John Bishop told me he needed advice about cutting ect, but after reading his book I thought that was nonsense. He strikes me as a man who should be let alone as to length, if he has to be published in five volumes.[3] I liked him enormously.

. . . .

F. Scott Fitzgerald: A Life in Letters, pp. 199–200.

1. Fitzgerald was in Switzerland, where his wife was being treated for mental illness.
2. Novelist Thomas Wolfe (1900–1938) became a Scribners author in 1929.
3. Perkins had worked closely with Wolfe on the cutting and revising of *Look Homeward, Angel* (1929).

Statement on *Huckleberry Finn*[1]

Huckleberry Finn took the first journey <u>back</u>. He was the first to look <u>back</u> at the republic from the perspective of the west. His eyes were the first eyes that ever looked at us objectively that were not eyes from overseas. There were mountains at the frontier but he wanted more than mountains to look at with his restless eyes—he wanted to find out about men and how they lived together. And because he turned back we have him forever.

F. Scott Fitzgerald

(The Matthew J. and Arlyn Bruccoli Collection of F. Scott Fitzgerald, Thomas Cooper Library, University of South Carolina.)

1. This statement was read at the banquet of the International Mark Twain Society marking the one-hundredth anniversary on 30 November 1930 of Mark Twain's birthday.

To: Maxwell Perkins
c. 30 April 1932

. . . .

. . . I'm not certain enough of Zelda's present stability of character to expose her to any superlatives. If she has a success coming she must associate it with work done in a workmanlike manner for its own sake, + part of it done fatigued and uninspired, and part of it done when even to remember the original inspiration and impetus is a psychological trick.[1]

. . . .

F. Scott Fitzgerald: A Life in Letters, p. 217.

1. Zelda Fitzgerald's only novel, *Save Me the Waltz*, was published by Scribners in 1932.

To: Bennett Cerf
29 August 1932

Of course I think Ulysses[1] should be published legally in America. In the first place time has crept up on Ulysses, and many people are under the daisies who were horrified ten years ago. In the second place compared to pornography on the newstands Ulysses is an Elsie book.[2] And in the third place people who have the patience to read Ulysses are not the kind who will slobber over a few little Rabelaisian passages.

Correspondence of F. Scott Fitzgerald, edited by Matthew J. Bruccoli and Margaret M. Duggan with the assistance of Susan Walker (New York: Random House, 1980), p. 296.

1. James Joyce's *Ulysses*, published in Paris in 1922, was banned from the United States. In 1932 Bennett Cerf and Donald Klopfer, the owners of Random House, undertook a successful effort to publish the work in America.
2. Elsie Dinsmore, the heroine of twenty-eight girls' books by Martha Farquharson Finley (1828–1909).

To: Maxwell Perkins
25 September 1933

. . . .

3. Will publication with you absolutely preclude that the book will be chosen by the Literary Guild or the Book of the Month?[1] Whatever the answer the serial[2] will serve the purpose of bringing my book to the memory and attention of my old public and of getting straight financially with you. On the other hand, it is to both our advantages to capitalize if possible such facts as that the editors of those book leagues might take a fancy to such a curious idea that the author, Fitzgerald, actually wrote a book after all these years (this is all said with the reservation that the book is good.) Please answer this as it is of importance to me to know whether I must expect my big returns from serial and possibly theatrical and picture rights or whether I have as good a chance at a book sale, launched by one of those organizations, as any other best seller.

. . . .

5. My plan, and I think it is very important, is to prevail upon the <u>Modern Library</u>, even with a subsidy, to bring out <u>Gatsby</u> a few weeks after the book publication of this novel.[3] Please don't say that anybody would possi-

bly have the psychology of saying to themselves "One of his is in the <u>Modern Library</u> therefore I will not buy another," or that the two books could be confused. The people who buy the <u>Modern Library</u> are not at all the people who buy the new books. <u>Gatsby</u>—in its present form, not actually available in sight to book buyers, will only get a scattering sale as a result of the success of this book. I feel that every time your business department has taken a short- sighted view of our community of interest in this matter, which is my reputation, there has been no profit on your part and something less than that on mine. As for example, a novel of Ernest's in the <u>Modern Library</u> and no novel of mine, a good short story of Ernest's in their collection of the Great Modern Short Stories and a purely commercial story of mine.[4] I want to do this almost as much as I want to publish this novel and will cooperate to the extent of sharing the cost.

. . . .

F. Scott Fitzgerald: A Life in Letters, pp. 236, 236.

1. *Tender Is the Night* was a June 1934 "alternate" for the Literary Guild.

2. The novel was serialized in *Scribner's Magazine* (January–April 1934).

3. *The Great Gatsby* was reprinted by the Modern Library in September 1934 without a subsidy from Fitzgerald. It did not sell well and was discontinued.

4. By 1933 both *The Sun Also Rises* and *A Farewell to Arms* were in the Modern Library. Modern Library's *Great Modern Short Stories* (1930) reprinted Fitzgerald's "At Your Age" and Hemingway's "The Three-Day Blow."

"One Hundred False Starts"

"CRACK!" Goes the pistol and off starts this entry. Sometimes he has caught it just right; more often he has jumped the gun. On these occasions, if he is lucky, he runs only a dozen yards, looks around and jogs sheepishly back to the starting place. But too frequently he makes the entire circuit of the track under the impression that he is leading the field, and reaches the finish to find he has no following. The race must be run all over again.

A little more training, take a long walk, cut out that nightcap, no meat at dinner, and stop worrying about politics—

So runs an interview with one of the champion false starters of the writing profession—myself. Opening a leather-bound waste-basket which I fatuously refer to as my "notebook," I pick out at random a small, triangular piece of wrapping paper with a cancelled stamp on one side. On the other side is written:

Boopsie Dee was cute.

Nothing more. No cue as to what was intended to follow that preposterous statement. Boopsie Dee, indeed, confronting me with this single dogmatic fact about herself. Never will I know what happened to her, where and when she picked up her revolting name, and whether her cuteness got her into much trouble.

I pick out another scrap:

Article: Unattractive Things Girls Do, to pair with counter article by woman: Unattractive Things Men Do.

No. 1. Remove glass eye at dinner table.

That's all there is on that scrap. Evidently, an idea that had dissolved into hilarity before it had fairly got under way. I try to revive it seriously. What unattractive things do girls do—I mean universally nowadays—or what unattractive things do a great majority of them do, or a strong minority? I have a few feeble ideas, but no, the notion is dead. I can only think of an article I read somewhere about a woman who divorced her husband because of the way he stalked a chop, and wondering at the time why she didn't try him out on a chop before she married him. No, that all belongs to a gilded age when people could afford to have nervous breakdowns because of the squeak in daddy's shoes.

Lines to an Old Favourite

There are hundreds of these hunches. Not all of them have to do with literature. Some are hunches about importing a troupe of Ouled Naïl danc-ers from Africa,[1] about bringing the Grand-Guignol[2] from Paris to New

York, about resuscitating football at Princeton—I have two scoring plays that will make a coach's reputation in one season—and there is a faded note "explain to D. W. Griffith[3] why costume plays are sure to come back." Also my plan for a film version of H. G. Wells's *History of the World*.[4]

These little flurries caused me no travail—they were opium eater's illusions, vanishing with the smoke of the pipe, or you know what I mean. The pleasure of thinking about them was the exact equivalent of having accomplished them. It is the six-page, ten-page, thirty-page globs of paper that grieve me professionally, like unsuccessful oil shafts; they represent my false starts.

There is, for example, one false start which I have made at least a dozen times. It is—or rather has tried to take shape as—a short story. At one time or another, I have written as many words on it as would make a presentable novel, yet the present version is only about twenty-five hundred words long and hasn't been touched for two years. Its present name—it has gone under various aliases—is The Barnaby Family.

From childhood I have had a daydream—what a word for one whose entire life is spent noting them down—about starting at scratch on a desert island and building a comparatively high state of civilization out of the materials at hand. I have always felt that Robinson Crusoe cheated when he rescued the tools from the wreck, and this applies equally to the Swiss Family Robinson,[5] the Two Little Savages,[6] and the balloon castaways of *The Mysterious Island*.[7] In my story, not only would no convenient grain of wheat, repeating rifle, 4000 H.P. Diesel engine or technocratic butler[8] be washed ashore but even my characters would be helpless city dwellers with no more wood lore than a cuckoo out of a clock.

The creation of such characters was easy, and it was easy washing them ashore:

For three long hours they were prostrated on the beach. Then Donald sat up.

"Well, here we are," he said with sleepy vagueness.

"Where?" his wife demanded eagerly.

"It couldn't be America and it couldn't be the Philippines," he said, "because we started from one and haven't got to the other."

"I'm thirsty," said the child.

Donald's eyes went quickly to the shore.

"Where's the raft?" He looked rather accusingly at Vivian. "Where's the raft?"

"It was gone when I woke up."

"It would be," he exclaimed bitterly. "Somebody might have thought of bringing the jug of water ashore. If I don't do it, nothing is done in this house—I mean this family."

All right, go on from there. Anybody—you back there in the tenth row—step up! Don't be afraid. Just go on with the story. If you get stuck, you can look up tropical fauna and flora in the encyclopedia, or call up a neighbour who has been shipwrecked.

Anyhow, that's the exact point where my story—and I still think it's a great plot—begins to creak and groan with unreality. I turn around after a while with a sense of uneasiness—how could anybody believe that rubbish about monkeys throwing coconuts?—trot back to the starting place, and I resume my crouch for days and days.

A Murder That Didn't Jell

During such days I sometimes examine a clot of pages which is headed Ideas for Possible Stories. Among others, I find the following.

Bath water in Princeton or Florida.

Plot—suicide, indulgence, hate, liver and circumstance.

Snubbing or having somebody.

Dancer who found she could fly.

Oddly enough, all these are intelligible, if not enlightening, suggestions to me. But they are all old—old. I am as apt to be stimulated by them as by my signature or the beat of my feet pacing the floor. There is one that for years has puzzled me, that is as great a mystery as Boopsie Dee.

Story: THE WINTER WAS COLD

CHARACTERS

Victoria Cuomo

Mark de Vinci

Jason Tenweather

Ambulance surgeon

Stark, a watchman

What was this about? Who were these people? I have no doubt that one of them was to be murdered or else to be a murderer. But all else about the plot I have forgotten long ago.

I turn over a little. Here is something over which I linger longer; a false start that wasn't bad, that might have been run out.

WORDS

When you consider the more expensive article and finally decide on the cheaper one, the salesman is usually thoughtful enough to make it all right for you. "You'll probably get the most wear out of this," he says consolingly, or even, "That's the one I'd choose myself."

The Trimbles were like that. They were specialists in the neat promotion of the next best into the best.

"It'll do to wear around the house," they used to say; or, "We want to wait until we can get a really nice one."

It was at this point that I decided I couldn't write about the Trimbles. They were very nice and I would have enjoyed somebody else's story of how they made out, but I couldn't get under the surface of their lives—what kept them content to make the best of things instead of changing things. So I gave them up.

There is the question of dog stories. I like dogs and would like to write at least one dog story in the style of Mr. Terhune[9] but see what happens when I take pen in hand.

DOG
THE STORY OF A LITTLE DOG

Only a newsboy with a wizened face, selling his papers on the corner. A big dog fancier, standing on the curb, laughed contemptuously and twitched up the collar of his Airedale coat. Another rich dog man gave a little bark of scorn from a passing taxicab.

But the newsboy was interested in the animal that had crept close to his feet. He was only a cur; his fuzzy coat was inherited from his mother, who had been a fashionable poodle, while in stature he resembled his father, a Great Dane. And somewhere there was a canary concerned, for a spray of yellow feathers projected from his backbone—

You see, I couldn't go on like that. Think of dog owners writing in to the editors from all over the country, protesting that I was no man for that job.

I am thirty-six years old. For eighteen years, save for a short space during the war, writing has been my chief interest in life, and I am in every sense a professional.

Yet even now when, at the recurrent cry of "Baby needs shoes," I sit down facing my sharpened pencils and block of legal-sized paper, I have a feeling of utter helplessness. I may write my story in three days or, as is more frequently the case, it may be six weeks before I have assembled anything worthy to be sent out. I can open a volume from a criminal-law library and find a thousand plots. I can go into highway and byway, parlor and kitchen, and listen to personal revelations that, at the hands of other writers, might endure forever. But all that is nothing—not even enough for a false start.

Twice-Told Tales

Mostly, we authors must repeat ourselves—that's the truth. We have two or three great and moving experiences in our lives—experiences so great and moving that it doesn't seem at the time that anyone else has been so caught up and pounded and dazzled and astonished and beaten and broken and rescued and illuminated and rewarded and humbled in just that way ever before.

Then we learn our trade, well or less well, and we tell our two or three stories—each time in a new disguise—maybe ten times, maybe a hundred, as long as people will listen.

If this were otherwise, one would have to confess to having no individuality at all. And each time I honestly believe that, because I have found a new background and a novel twist, I have really got away from the two or three fundamental tales I have to tell. But it is rather like Ed Wynn's[10] famous anecdote about the painter of boats who was begged to paint some ancestors for a client. The bargain was arranged, but with the painter's final warning that the ancestors would all turn out to look like boats.

When I face the fact that all my stories are going to have a certain family resemblance, I am taking a step toward avoiding false starts. If a friend says he's got a story for me and launches into a tale of being robbed by Brazilian pirates in a swaying straw hut on the edge of a smoking volcano in the Andes, with his fiancée bound and gagged on the roof, I can well believe there were various human emotions involved; but having successfully avoided pirates, volcanoes, and fiancées who get themselves bound and gagged on roofs, I can't feel them. Whether it's something that happened twenty years ago or only yesterday, I must start out with an emotion—one that's close to me and that I can understand.

It's an Ill Wind

Last summer I was hauled to the hospital with high fever and a tentative diagnosis of typhoid. My affairs were in no better shape than yours are, reader. There was a story I should have written to pay my current debts, and I was haunted by the fact that I hadn't made a will. If I had really had typhoid I wouldn't have worried about such things, nor made that scene at the hospital when the nurses tried to plump me into an ice bath. I didn't have either the typhoid or the bath, but I continued to rail against my luck that just at this crucial moment I should have to waste two weeks in bed, answering the baby talk of nurses and getting nothing done at all. But three days after I was discharged I had finished a story about a hospital.[11]

The material was soaking in and I didn't know it. I was profoundly moved by fear, apprehension, worry, impatience; every sense was acute, and that is the best way of accumulating material for a story. Unfortunately, it does not always come so easily. I say to myself—looking at the awful blank block of paper—"Now, here's this man Swankins that I've known and liked for ten years. I am privy to all his private affairs, and some of them are wows. I've threatened to write about him, and he says to go ahead and do my worst."

But can I? I've been in as many jams as Swankins, but I didn't look at them the same way, nor would it ever have occurred to me to extricate myself from the Chinese police or from the clutches of that woman in the way Swankins chose. I could write some fine paragraphs about Swankins, but build a story around him that would have an ounce of feeling in it—impossible.

Or into my distraught imagination wanders a girl named Elsie about whom I was almost suicidal for a month, in 1916.

"How about me?" Elsie says. "Surely you swore to a lot of emotions back there in the past. Have you forgotten?"

"No, Elsie, I haven't forgotten."

"Well, then, write a story about me. You haven't seen me for twelve years, so you don't know how fat I am now and how boring I often seem to my husband."

"No, Elsie, I ——"

"Oh, come on. Surely I must be worth a story. Why, you used to hang around saying good-bye with your face so miserable and comic that I thought I'd go crazy myself before I got rid of you. And now you're afraid even to start a story about me. Your feeling must have been pretty thin if you can't revive it for a few hours."

"No Elsie; you don't understand. I have written about you a dozen times. That funny little rabbit curl to your lip, I used in a story six years ago. The way your face all changed just when you were going to laugh—I gave that characteristic to one of the first girls I ever wrote about. The way I stayed around trying to say good night, knowing that you'd rush to the phone as soon as the front door closed behind me—all that was in a book that I wrote once upon a time."

"I see. Just because I didn't respond to you, you broke me into bits and used me up piecemeal."

"I'm afraid so, Elsie. You see, you never so much as kissed me, except that once with a kind of a shove at the same time, so there really isn't any story."

Plots without emotions, emotions without plots. So it goes sometimes. Let me suppose, however, that I have got under way; two days' work, two thousand words are finished and being typed for a first revision. And suddenly doubts overtake me.

A Jury of One

What if I'm just horsing around? What's going on in this regatta anyhow? Who could care what happens to the girl, when the sawdust is obviously leaking out of her moment by moment? How did I get the plot all tangled up? I am alone in the privacy of my faded blue room with my sick cat, the bare February branches waving at the window, an ironic paperweight that says Business is Good, a New England conscience—developed in Minnesota—and my greatest problem:

"Shall I run it out? Or shall I turn back?"

Shall I say:

"I know I had something to prove, and it may develop farther along in the story?"

Or:

"This is just bullheadedness. Better throw it away and start over."

The latter is one of the most difficult decisions that an author must make. To make it philosophically, before he has exhausted himself in a hundred-hour effort to resuscitate a corpse or disentangle innumerable wet snarls, is a test whether or not he is really a professional. There are often occasions when such a decision is doubly difficult. In the last stages of a novel, for instance, where there is no question of junking the whole, but when an entire favorite character has to be hauled out by the heels, screeching, and dragging half a dozen good scenes with him.

It is here that these confessions tie up with a general problem as well as with those peculiar to a writer. The decision as to when to quit, as to when one is merely floundering around and causing other people trouble, has to be made frequently in a lifetime. In youth we are taught the rather simple rule never to quit, because we are presumably following programs made by people wiser than ourselves. My own conclusion is that when one has embarked on a course that grows increasingly doubtful and feels the vital forces beginning to be used up, it is best to ask advice, if decent advice is within range. Columbus didn't and Lindbergh couldn't. So my statement at first seems heretical toward the idea that it is pleasantest to live with—the idea of heroism. But I make a sharp division between one's professional life, when, after the period of apprenticeship, not more than 10 per cent of advice is worth a hoot, and one's private and worldly life, when often almost anyone's judgment is better than one's own.

Once, not so long ago, when my work was hampered by so many false starts that I thought the game was up at last, and when my personal life was even more thoroughly obfuscated, I asked an old Alabama Negro:

"Uncle Bob, when things get so bad that there isn't any way out, what do you do then?"

Homely Advice But Sound

The heat from the kitchen stove stirred his white sideburns as he warmed himself. If I cynically expected a platitudinous answer, a reflection of something remembered from Uncle Remus,[12] I was disappointed.

"Mr. Fitzgerald," he said, "when things get that-away I wuks."

It was good advice. Work is almost everything. But it would be nice to be able to distinguish useful work from mere labor expended. Perhaps that is part of work itself—to find the difference. Perhaps my frequent, solitary sprints around the track are profitable. Shall I tell you about another one?

Very well. You see, I had this hunch—But in counting the pages, I find that my time is up and I must put my book of mistakes away. On the fire? No! I put it weakly back in the drawer. These old mistakes are now only toys—and expensive ones at that—give them a toy's cupboard and then hurry back into the serious business of my profession. Joseph Conrad defined it more clearly, more vividly than any man of our time:

"My task is by the power of the written word to make you hear, to make you feel—it is, before all, to make you see."[13]

It's not very difficult to run back and start over again—especially in private. What you aim at is to get in a good race or two when the crowd is in the stand.

The Saturday Evening Post, 205 (4 March 1933), 13, 65–66.

1. North African girls who performed erotic dances.

2. Paris theatre known for its horror productions.

3. Director (1875–1948) famous for his movie spectacles—*The Birth of a Nation* (1915) and *Intolerance* (1916).

4. Fitzgerald was impressed by Wells's 1920 work *The Outline of History* and later used it as the basis for the "College of One" syllabus he prepared for Sheilah Graham (d. 1988), the Hollywood columnist who was his companion during his last years.

5. Novel published in English in 1814 by Swiss writer Rudolf Wyss (1781–1830); it was a popular imitation of *Robinson Crusoe* (1719) by English novelist and pamphleteer Daniel Defoe (1660–1731).

6. *Two Little Savages; Being the Adventures of Two Boys Who Lived as Indians and What They Learned* (1903) by Ernest Thompson Seton (1860–1946).

7. Adventure story, first published in English translation in 1875, by French writer Jules Verne (1828–1905).

8. Reference to *The Admirable Crichton* (1902), a play by Sir James M. Barrie (1860–1937), in which the butler becomes the head of a shipwrecked family of English aristocrats.

9. Albert Payson Terhune (1872–1942), author of novels about collies.

10. (1886–1966), comedian known as "The Perfect Fool."

11. "One Interne," *The Saturday Evening Post* (5 November 1932).

12. Black story-teller in stories by Joel Chandler Harris (1848–1908).

13. From the Introduction to *The Nigger of the Narcissus* (1898).

"Ring"[1]

October, 1933

For a year and a half, the writer of this appreciation was Ring Lardner's most familiar companion; after that, geography made separations and our contacts were rare.[2] When my wife and I last saw him in 1931, he looked already like a man on his deathbed—it was terribly sad to see that six feet three inches of kindness stretched out ineffectual in the hospital room. His fingers trembled with a match, the tight skin on his handsome skull was marked as a mask of misery and nervous pain.

He gave a very different impression when we first saw him in 1921—he seemed to have an abundance of quiet vitality that would enable him to outlast anyone, to take himself for long spurts of work or play that would ruin any ordinary constitution. He had recently convulsed the country with the famous kitten-and- coat saga (it had to do with a world's series bet and with the impending conversion of some kittens into fur), and the evidence of the betting, a beautiful sable, was worn by his wife at the time. In those days he was interested in people, sports, bridge, music, the stage, the news-papers, the magazines, the books. But though I did not know it, the change in him had already begun—the impenetrable despair that dogged him for a dozen years to his death.

He had practically given up sleeping, save on short vacations deliber-ately consecrated to simple pleasures, most frequently golf with his friends, Grantland Rice[3] or John Wheeler. Many a night we talked over a case of Canadian ale until bright dawn, when Ring would rise and yawn: "Well, I guess the children have left for school by this time—I might as well go home."

The woes of many people haunted him—for example, the doctor's death sentence pronounced upon Tad,[4] the cartoonist (who, in fact, nearly out-lived Ring)—it was as if he believed he could and ought to do something about such things. And as he struggled to fulfill his contracts, one of which, a comic strip based on the character of "the busher,"[5] was a terror, indeed, it was obvious that he felt his work to be directionless, merely "copy." So he was inclined to turn his cosmic sense of responsibility into the channel of solving other people's problems—finding someone an introduction to a the-atrical manager, placing a friend in a job, maneuvering a man into a golf club. The effort made was often out of proportion to the situation; the truth back of it was that Ring was getting off—he was a faithful and consci-entious workman to the end, but he had stopped finding any fun in his work ten years before he died.

About that time (1922) a publisher[6] undertook to reissue his old books and collect his recent stories and this gave him a sense of existing in the literary world as well as with the public, and he got some satisfaction from the reiterated statements of Mencken and F. P. A. as to his true stature as a writer. But I don't think he cared then—it is hard to understand but I don't think he really gave a damn about anything except his personal relations with a few people. A case in point was his attitude to those imitators who lifted everything except the shirt off his back—only Hemingway has been so thoroughly frisked—it worried the imitators more than it worried Ring. His attitude was that if they got stuck in the process he'd help them over any tough place.

Throughout this period of huge earnings and an increasingly solid reputation on top and beneath, there were two ambitions more important to Ring than the work by which he will be remembered; he wanted to be a musician—sometimes he dramatized himself ironically as a thwarted composer—and he wanted to write shows. His dealings with managers would make a whole story: they were always commissioning him to do work which they promptly forgot they had ordered, and accepting librettos that they never produced. (Ring left a short ironic record of Ziegfeld.)[7] Only with the aid of the practical George Kaufman[8] did he achieve his ambition, and by then he was too far gone in illness to get a proper satisfaction from it.

The point of these paragraphs is that, whatever Ring's achievement was, it fell short of the achievement he was capable of, and this because of a cynical attitude toward his work. How far back did that attitude go?—back to his youth in a Michigan village? Certainly back to his days with the Cubs.[9] During those years, when most men of promise achieve an adult education, if only in the school of war, Ring moved in the company of a few dozen illiterates playing a boy's game. A boy's game, with no more possibilities in it than a boy could master, a game bounded by walls which kept out novelty or danger, change or adventure. This material, the observation of it under such circumstances, was the text of Ring's schooling during the most formative period of the mind. A writer can spin on about his adventures after thirty, after forty, after fifty, but the criteria by which these adventures are weighed and valued are irrevocably settled at the age of twenty-five. However deeply Ring might cut into it, his cake had exactly the diameter of Frank Chance's diamond.[10]

Here was his artistic problem, and it promised future trouble. So long as he wrote within that enclosure the result was magnificent: within it he heard and recorded the voice of a continent. But when, inevitably, he outgrew his interest in it, what was Ring left with?

He was left with his fine linguistic technique—and he was left rather helpless in those few acres. He had been formed by the very world on which his hilarious irony had released itself. He had fought his way through to knowing what people's motives are and what means they are likely to resort to in order to attain their goals. But now he had a new problem—what to do about it. He went on seeing, and the sights traveled back to the optic nerve, but no longer to be thrown off in fiction, because they were no longer sights that could be weighed and valued by the old criteria. It was never that he was completely sold on athletic virtuosity as the be-all and end-all of problems; the trouble was that he could find nothing finer. Imagine life conceived as a business of beautiful muscular organization—an arising, an effort, a good break, a sweat, a bath, a meal, a love, a sleep—imagine it achieved; then imagine trying to apply that standard to the horribly complicated mess of living, where nothing, even the greatest conceptions and workings and achievements, is else but messy, spotty, tortuous—and then one can imagine the confusion that Ring faced on coming out of the ball park.

He kept on recording but he no longer projected, and this accumulation, which he has taken with him to the grave, crippled his spirit in the latter years. It was not the fear of Niles, Michigan,[11] that hampered him—it was the habit of silence, formed in the presence of the "ivory" with which he lived and worked. Remember it was not humble ivory—Ring has demonstrated that—it was arrogant, imperative, often megalomaniacal ivory. He got the habit of silence, then the habit of repression that finally took the form of his odd little crusade in *The New Yorker* against pornographic songs.[12] He had agreed with himself to speak only a small portion of his mind.

The present writer once suggested to him that he organize some *cadre* within which he could adequately display his talents, suggesting that it should be something deeply personal, and something on which Ring could take his time, but he dismissed the idea lightly; he was a disillusioned idealist but he had served his Fates well, and no other ones could be casually created for him—"This is something that can be printed," he reasoned; "this, however, belongs with that bunch of stuff that can never be written."

He covered himself in such cases with protests of his inability to bring off anything big, but this was specious, for he was a proud man and had no reason to rate his abilities cheaply. He refused to "tell all" because in a crucial period of his life he had formed the habit of not doing it—and this he had elevated gradually into a standard of taste. It never satisfied him by a damn sight.

So one is haunted not only by a sense of personal loss but by a conviction that Ring got less percentage of himself on paper than any other American of the first flight. There is *You Know Me Al,* and there are about a dozen wonderful short stories (my God, he hadn't even saved them—the material of *How to Write Short Stories* was obtained by photographing old issues in the public library!), and there is some of the most uproarious and inspired nonsense since Lewis Carroll.[13] Most of the rest is mediocre stuff, with flashes, and I would do Ring a disservice to suggest it should be set upon an altar and worshipped, as have been the most casual relics of Mark Twain. Those three volumes should seem enough—to everyone who didn't know Ring. But I venture that no one who knew him but will agree that the personality of the man overlapped it. Proud, shy, solemn, shrewd, polite, brave, kind, merciful, honorable—with the affection these qualities aroused he created in addition a certain awe in people. His intentions, his will, once in motion, were formidable factors in dealing with him—he always did every single thing he said he would do. Frequently he was the melancholy Jaques,[14] and sad company indeed, but under any conditions a noble dignity flowed from him, so that time in his presence always seemed well spent.

On my desk, at the moment, I have the letters Ring wrote to us; here is a letter one thousand words long, here is one of two thousand words— theatrical gossip, literary shop talk, flashes of wit but not much wit, for he was feeling thin and saving the best of that for his work, anecdotes of his activities. I reprint the most typical one I can find:

"The Dutch Treat show[15] was a week ago Friday night. Grant Rice and I had reserved a table, and a table holds ten people and no more. Well, I had invited, as one guest, Jerry Kern,[16] but he telephoned at the last moment that he couldn't come. I then consulted with Grant Rice, who said he had no substitute in mind, but that it was a shame to waste our extra ticket when tickets were at a premium. So I called up Jones, and Jones said yes, and would it be all right for him to bring along a former Senator who was a pal of his and had been good to him in Washington. I said I was sorry, but our table was filled and, besides, we didn't have an extra ticket. 'Maybe I could dig up another ticket somewhere,' said Jones. 'I don't believe so,' I said, 'but anyway the point is that we haven't room at our table.' 'Well,' said Jones, 'I could have the Senator eat somewhere else and join us in time for the show.' 'Yes,' I said, 'but we have no ticket for him.' 'Well, I'll think up something,' he said. Well, what he thought up was to bring himself and the Senator and I had a hell of a time getting an extra ticket and shoving the Senator in at another table where he wasn't wanted, and later in the evening, the Senator thanked Jones and said he was the greatest fella in the world and all I got was good night.

"Well, I must close and nibble on a carrot. R.W.L."

Even in a telegram Ring could compress a lot of himself. Here is one: WHEN ARE YOU COMING BACK AND WHY PLEASE ANSWER RING LARDNER

This is not the moment to recollect Ring's convivial aspects, especially as he had, long before his death, ceased to find amusement in dissipation, or indeed in the whole range of what is called entertainment—save for his perennial interest in songs. By grace of the radio and of the many musicians who, drawn by his enormous magnetism, made pilgrimages to his bedside, he had a consolation in the last days, and he made the most of it, hilariously rewriting Cole Porter's lyrics[17] in the *New Yorker*. But it would be an evasion for the present writer not to say that when he was Ring's neighbor a decade ago, they tucked a lot under their belts in many weathers,[18] and spent many words on many men and things. At no time did I feel that I had known him enough, or that anyone knew him—it was not the feeling that there was more stuff in him and that it should come out, it was rather a qualitative difference, it was rather as though, due to some inadequacy in one's self, one had not penetrated to something unsolved, new and unsaid. That is why one wishes that Ring had written down a larger proportion of what was in his mind and heart. It would have saved him longer for us, and that in itself would be something. But I would like to know what it was, and now I will go on wishing—what did Ring want, how did he want things to be, how did he think things were?

A great and good American is dead. Let us not obscure him by the flowers, but walk up and look at that fine medallion, all abraded by sorrows that perhaps we are not equipped to understand. Ring made no enemies, because he was kind, and to many millions he gave release and delight.

The New Republic, 76 (11 October 1933), 254–255.

1. Ring W. Lardner began as a sports writer and columnist and became a respected short-story writer with the publication of *You Know Me Al: A Busher's Letters* (1916). A master of the American vernacular, Lardner was regarded as a humorist, but his fiction has bite. Fitzgerald arranged for Lardner to become one of Maxwell Perkins's authors and provided the title *How to Write Short Stories* (1924) for Lardner's first Scribners book. He was the source for Abe North in *Tender Is the Night*, written when Lardner was dying.

2. Fitzgerald and Lardner were Great Neck, Long Island, neighbors from 1922 to 1924. The Fitzgeralds did not return to the New York City area.

3. Popular sportswriter (1880–1954).

4. Thomas Aloysius Dorgan (1877–1929) signed his work TAD.

5. Lardner provided the story line and dialogue for a comic strip based on Jack Keefe, the "busher" (the brash rookie baseball player) of his *You Know Me Al* stories.

6. Maxwell Perkins of Scribners.

7. Impresario Florenz Ziegfeld (1869–1932) was the model for the villainous producer in Lardner's "A Day with Conrad Green" (1925).

8. Kaufman collaborated with Lardner on the successful play *June Moon* (1929).

9. As a young reporter Lardner had covered the Chicago Cubs.

10. First baseman Frank Chance (1877–1924) ("Tinker to Evers to Chance") became manager of the Chicago Cubs; his diamond was the baseball infield.

11. Lardner grew up in Niles.

12. Articles published in 1933.

13. Some of Lardner's nonsense humor was collected in *What of It?* (1925). Charles Lutwidge Dodgson (1832–1898) wrote *Alice's Adventures in Wonderland* (1865) under the pseudonym Lewis Carroll.

14. Character in Shakespeare's *As You Like It*.

15. Annual show put on by a New York men's club.

16. Songwriter Jerome Kern (1885–1945).

17. Cole Porter (1893–1964) wrote clever, often suggestive songs. Lardner particularly disliked Porter's "I've Got You Under My Skin," which he referred to as "a hymn to the subcutaneous."

18. Lardner and Fitzgerald were alcoholics.

To: H. L. Mencken
23 April 1934

. . . .

I would rather impress my image (even though an image the size of a nickel) upon the soul of a people than be known, except in so far as I have my natural obligation to my family—to provide for them. I would as soon be as anonymous as Rimbaud,[1] if I could feel that I had accomplished that purpose—and that is no sentimental yapping about being disinterested. It is simply that having once found the intensity of art, nothing else that can happen in life can ever again seem as important as the creative process.

. . . .

F. Scott Fitzgerald: A Life in Letters, p. 256.

1. French symbolist poet Arthur Rimbaud (1854–1891).

H. L. Mencken, "The Baltimore Anti-Christ."

Introduction to the Modern Library
Reprint of *The Great Gatsby*

To one who has spent his professional life in the world of fiction the request to "write an introduction" offers many facets of temptation. The present writer succumbs to one of them; with as much equanimity as he can muster, he will discuss the critics among us, trying to revolve as centripetally as possible about the novel which comes hereafter in this volume.

To begin with, I must say that I have no cause to grumble about the "press" of any book of mine. If Jack (who liked my last book) didn't like this one—well then John (who despised my last book) *did* like it; so it all mounts up to the same total. But I think the writers of my time were spoiled in that regard, living in generous days when there was plenty of space on the page for endless ratiocination about fiction—a space largely created by Mencken because of his disgust for what passed as criticism before he arrived and made his public. They were encouraged by his bravery and his tremendous and profound love of letters. In his case, the jackals are already tearing at what they imprudently regard as a moribund lion, but I don't think many men of my age can regard him without reverence, nor fail to regret that he got off the train. To any new effort by a new man he brought an attitude; he made many mistakes—such as his early undervaluation of Hemingway— but he came equipped; he never had to go back for his tools.

And now that he has abandoned American fiction to its own devices, there is no one to take his place. If the present writer had seriously to attend some of the efforts of political diehards to tell him the values of a métier he has practised since boyhood—well, then, babies, you can take this number out and shoot him at dawn.

But all that is less discouraging, in the last few years, than the growing cowardice of the reviewers. Underpaid and overworked, they seem not to care for books, and it has been saddening recently to see young talents in fiction expire from sheer lack of a stage to act on: West,[1] McHugh[2] and many others.

I'm circling closer to my theme song, which is: that I'd like to communicate to such of them who read this novel a healthy cynicism toward contemporary reviews. Without undue vanity one can permit oneself a suit of chain mail in any profession. Your pride is all you have, and if you let it be tampered with by a man who has a dozen prides to tamper with before lunch, you are promising yourself a lot of disappointments that a hard-boiled professional has learned to spare himself.

This novel is a case in point. Because the pages weren't loaded with big names of big things and the subject not concerned with farmers (who were the heroes of the moment), there was easy judgment exercised that had nothing to do with criticism but was simply an attempt on the part of men who had few chances of self- expression to express themselves. How anyone could take up the responsibility of being a novelist without a sharp and concise attitude about life is a puzzle to me. How a critic could assume a point of view which included twelve variant aspects of the social scene in a few hours seems something too dinosaurean to loom over the awful loneliness of a young author.

To circle nearer to this book, one woman, who could hardly have written a coherent letter in English, described it as a book that one read only as one goes to the movies around the corner.[3] That type of criticism is what a lot of young writers are being greeted with, instead of any appreciation of the world of imagination in which they (the writers) have been trying, with greater or lesser success, to live—the world that Mencken made stable in the days when he was watching over us.

Now that this book is being reissued, the author would like to say that never before did one try to keep his artistic conscience as pure as during the ten months put into doing it. Reading it over one can see how it could have been improved—yet without feeling guilty of any discrepancy from the truth, as far as I saw it; truth or rather the *equivalent* of the truth, the attempt at honesty of imagination. I had just re-read Conrad's preface to *The Nigger*, and I had recently been kidded half haywire by critics who felt that my material was such as to preclude all dealing with mature persons in a mature world. But, my God! it was my material, and it was all I had to deal with.

What I cut out of it both physically and emotionally would make another novel!

I think it is an honest book, that is to say, that one used none of one's virtuosity to get an effect, and, to boast again, one soft-pedalled the emotional side to avoid the tears leaking from the socket of the left eye, or the large false face peering around the corner of a character's head.

If there is a clear conscience, a book can survive—at least in one's feelings about it. On the contrary, if one has a guilty conscience, one reads what one wants to hear out of reviews. In addition, if one is young and willing to learn, almost all reviews have a value, even the ones that seem unfair.

The present writer has always been a "natural" for his profession, in so much that he can think of nothing he could have done as efficiently as to have lived deeply in the world of imagination. There are plenty other people constituted as he is, for giving expression to intimate explorations, the:

—Look—this is here!

—I saw this under my eyes.

—*This* is the way it was!

—No, it was like this.

"Look! Here is that drop of blood I told you about."

—"Stop everything! Here is the flash of that girl's eyes, here is the reflection that will always come back to me from the memory of her eyes.

—"If one chooses to find that face again in the non-refracting surface of a washbowl, if one chooses to make the image more obscure with a little sweat, it should be the business of the critic to recognize the intention.

—"No one felt like this before—says the young writer—but *I* felt like this; I have a pride akin to a soldier going into battle; without knowing whether there will be anybody there, to distribute medals or even to record it."

But remember, also, young man: you are not the first person who has ever been alone and alone.

F. SCOTT FITZGERALD

Baltimore, Md.
August, 1934.

"Introduction," The Great Gatsby
(New York: Modern Library, 1934), pp. vii–xi.

1. By 1934 Nathanael West (1903–1940) had published *The Dream Life of Balso Snell* (1931), *Miss Lonelyhearts* (1933), and *A Cool Million* (1934).

2. Vincent McHugh (1904–1983) published the novel *Sing Before Breakfast* in 1933.

3. Unsigned review, "F. Scott Fitzgerald's Latest a Dud," *New York World*, 12 April 1925, Sect. 3, p. 7M.

Because of low sales, the 1934 Modern Library printing
of Fitzgerald's masterpiece was withdrawn from the series.

"My Ten Favorite Plays"

F. Scott Fitzgerald, who achieved a startling success with *This Side of Paradise*, who added to his prestige with *The Great Gatsby* (which Owen Davis dramatized)[1] and whose latest (and some readers say best) novel is *Tender Is the Night*, writes from Park Avenue, town of Baltimore, listing the following as his outstanding impressions in the theater:

1—Charles Chaplin in *The Pilgrim*.[2]

2—Performance of an obscure stock company actor in Gillette's *Secret Service*[3] about 1906.

3—My own performance in a magicians' show at the age of nine.

4—Greta Garbo in her first big role.[4]

5—E. H. Sothern as Lord Dundreary in *Our American Cousin*.[5]

6—George M. Cohan in *The Little Millionaire*.[6]

7—Ina Claire in *The Quaker Girl*.

8—The Theatre Guild actress who played the stage role in *Grand Hotel* that Joan Crawford played in the movies. I've seen her twice and I think she's one of the greatest actresses in the world.[7]

9—Ernest Truex's face when he was carrying through bravely in a flop of my own that opened cold in Atlantic City.[8]

10—David W. Griffith's face as I imagine it during the filming of *The Birth of a Nation* when he was "forging in the smithy of his soul"[9] all the future possibilities of the camera.

New York Sun, 10 September 1934, p. 19.

1. Davis wrote a stage adaptation of *The Great Gatsby*, which was produced on Broadway in 1926.

2. Chaplin made *The Pilgrim* in 1923.

3. Actor-playwright William Gillette (1855–1937) wrote his play *Secret Service* in 1895.

4. Garbo (1905–1990) had her first American film successes as Elena in *The Temptress* (1926) and as Anna Karenina in *Love* (1927).

5. Sothern (1859–1933) appeared in the 1908 production of *Our American Cousin*. President Abraham Lincoln was watching a performance of this play, written in 1858 by Tom Taylor (1817–1880), when he was assassinated in April 1865.

6. Cohan (1878–1942) both wrote and starred in *The Little Millionaire* (1911).

7. Hortense Alden (1903–1978) appeared in the 1930 stage version of *Grand Hotel*, written by Vicki Baum (1896–1960).

8. Truex (1889–1973) appeared in Fitzgerald's *The Vegetable*.

9. Fitzgerald is quoting from the final lines of Joyce's *A Portrait of the Artist as a Young Man*.

"Fitzgerald's Letter of Recommendation for Nathanael West's Guggenheim Fellowship Application"[1]

TO THE TRUSTEES OF THE GUGGENHEIM FELLOWSHIP

Dear Sirs:

Today Nathanael West[2] asked me for a letter of reference on behalf of his application for a Guggenheim fellowship.

—and, in the same post, came a consignment of a reprint by the Modern Library of a novel of mine, THE GREAT GATSBY, which had a new preface that included the statement that I thought young writers in America were being harmed now for the lack of a public, and I had mentioned specifically Nathanael West.

I don't know on what basis the Guggenheim fellowships are given but I know some of the people who have profited by them, and, while many of the men have been chosen worthily and well, such as Thomas Wolfe and Allan Tate,[3] there have been others who have been sent to Europe who have not been worth their salt, and who—in the eventuality—have proved nothing.

I have sometimes felt that you have put especial emphasis on poetry while I think that the most living literary form in America at the moment is prose fiction. In my opinion Nathanael West is a potential leader in the field of prose fiction. He seems to me entirely equipped to go over on the fellowship.[4]

With best wishes to the custodians of the great idea.

Sincerely yours,
F. Scott Fitzgerald
1307 Park Avenue
Baltimore, Maryland
September 25, 1934

Jay Martin, "Fitzgerald Recommends Nathanael West for a Guggenheim," *Fitzgerald/Hemingway Annual 1971*, edited by Matthew J. Bruccoli and C. E. Frazer Clark, Jr. (Washington, D.C.: NCR/Microcard Editions, 1971), 302–304.

1. The Guggenheim Foundation (established 1925) provides grants for artists and scholars.
2. Fitzgerald and West had not met; West asked Fitzgerald for a recommendation on the basis of his favorable comment in the introduction to the Modern Library edition of *The Great Gatsby*.
3. Novelist Thomas Wolfe and poet Allen Tate (1899–1979).
4. West did not receive a Guggenheim grant.

To: Maxwell Perkins
11 March 1935

. . . .

. . . It has become increasingly plain to me that the very excellent organization of a long book or the finest perceptions and judgment in time of revision do not go well with liquor. A short story can be written on a bottle, but for a novel you need the mental speed that enables you to keep the whole pattern in your head and ruthlessly sacrifice the sideshows as Ernest did in "A Farewell to Arms." If a mind is slowed up ever so little it lives in the individual part of a book rather than in a book as a whole; memory is dulled. I would give anything if I hadn't had to write Part III of "Tender is the Night" entirely on stimulant. If I had one more crack at it cold sober I believe it might have made a great difference. Even Ernest commented on sections that were needlessly included and as an artist he is as near as I know for a final reference. . . .

. . . .

F. Scott Fitzgerald: A Life in Letters, pp. 277–278.

To: Harold Ober
c. 2 July 1935

. . . .

There is no use <u>of me</u> trying to rush things. Even in years like '24, '28, '29, '30 all devoted to short stories I could not turn out more than 8–9 top price stories a year. It simply is impossible—all my stories are concieved like novels, require a special emotion, a special experience—so that my readers, if such there be, know that each time it'll be something new, not in form but in substance (it'd be far better for me if I could do pattern stories but the pencil just goes dead on me. I wish I could think of a line of stories like the Josephine or Basil ones which could go faster + pay $3000. But no luck yet. If I ever get out of debt I want to try a second play. It's just possible I could knock them cold if I let go the vulgar side of my talent.)

. . . .

F. Scott Fitzgerald: A Life in Letters, p. 284.

To: Harold Ober
31 December 1935

I'd have gone to Hollywood a year ago last spring. I don't think I could do it now but I might. Especially if there was no choice. Twice I have worked out there on other people's stories—on an "original" with John Considine[1] telling me the plot twice a week and on the Katherine Brush story[2]—it simply fails to use what qualities I have. I don't blame you for lecturing me since I have seriously inconvenienced you, but it would be hard to change my temperament in middle-life. No single man with a serious literary reputation has made good there. If I could form a partnership with some technical expert it might be done. (That's very different from having a supervisor who couldn't fit either the technical or creative role but is simply a weigher of completed values.) I'd need a man who knew the game, knew the people, but would help me tell and sell my story—<u>not his</u>. This man would be hard to find, because a <u>smart</u> technician doesn't want or need a partner, and an uninspired one is inclined to have a dread of ever touching tops. I could work best with a woman, because they haven't any false pride about yielding a point. I could have worked with old Bess Meredith[3] if we hadn't been in constant committees of five. I'm afraid unless some such break occurs I'd be no good in the industry.

. . . .

F. Scott Fitzgerald: A Life in Letters, p. 294.

1. John W. Considine, Jr. (1898–1961), United Artists producer for whom Fitzgerald wrote the rejected screenplay "Lipstick" in 1927.
2. Katharine Brush (1902–1952) was author of *Red-Headed Woman* (1931), which Fitzgerald adapted for M-G-M in 1931; his screenplay was not used.
3. Bess Meredyth (1890?–1952) was a silent-screen actress who became a successful screenwriter.

To: Adelaide Neall,[1]
5 June 1936

    I appreciated your interest yesterday. I think that if one cares about a metiér (sp.) it is almost necessary to learn it over again every few years. Somewhere about the middle of "Tender is the Night" I seemed to have lost my touch on the short story—by touch I mean the exact balance, how much plot, how much character, how much background you can crowd into a limited number of words. It is a nice adjustment and essentially depends upon the enthusiasm with which you approach a given subject. In the last two years I've only too often realized that many of my stories were built rather than written.

. . . .

F. Scott Fitzgerald: A Life in Letters, p. 301.

1. A fiction editor at *The Saturday Evening Post*.

Poster for the 24 June 1933 issue of the magazine.

"Author's House"

I have seen numerous photographs and read many accounts of the houses of Joan Crawford, Virginia Bruce and Claudette Colbert,[1] usually with the hostess done up from behind with a bib explaining how on God's earth to make a Hollywood soufflée or open a can of soup without removing the appendix in the same motion. But it has been a long time since I have seen a picture of an author's house and it occurs to me to supply the deficiency.

Of course I must begin with an apology for writing about authors at all. In the days of the old *Smart Set* Mencken and Nathan had a rejection slip which notified the aspirant that they would not consider stories about painters, musicians and authors—perhaps because these classes are supposed to express themselves fully in their own work and are not a subject for portraiture. And having made the timorous bow I proceed with the portrait.

Rather than leave a somber effect at the end we begin at the bottom, in a dark damp unmodernized cellar. As your host's pale yellow flashlight moves slowly around through the spiderwebs, past old boxes and barrels and empty bottles and parts of old machines you feel a little uneasy.

"Not a bad cellar—as cellars go," the author says. "You can't see it very well and I can't either—it's mostly forgotten."

"What do you mean?"

"It's everything I've forgotten—all the complicated dark mixture of my youth and infancy that made me a fiction writer instead of a fireman or a soldier.

"You see fiction is a trick of the mind and heart composed of as many separate emotions as a magician uses in executing a pass or a palm. When you've learned it you forget it and leave it down here."

"When did you learn it?"

"Oh every time I begin I have to learn it all over again in a way. But the intangibles are down here. Why I chose this God awful metier of sedentary days and sleepless nights and endless dissatisfaction. Why I would choose it again. All that's down here and I'm just as glad I can't look at it too closely. See that dark corner?"

"Yes."

"Well, three months before I was born my mother lost her other two children and I think that came first of all though I don't know how it worked exactly. I think I started then to be a writer."

Your eyes fall on another corner and you give a start of alarm.

"What's that?" you demand.

"That?" The author tries to change the subject, moving around so as to obscure your view of the too recent mound of dirt in the corner that has made you think of certain things in police reports.

But you insist.

"That is where it is buried," he says.

"What's buried?"

"That's where I buried my love after—" he hesitates.

"After you *killed* her?"

"After I killed *it*."

"I don't understand what you mean."

The author does not look at the pile of earth.

"That is where I buried my first childish love of myself, my belief that I would never die like other people, and that I wasn't the son of my parents but a son of a king, a king who ruled the whole world."

He breaks off.

"But let's get out of here. We'll go upstairs."

In the living room the author's eye is immediately caught by a scene outside the window. The visitor looks—he sees some children playing football on the lawn next door.

"There is another reason why I became an author."

"How's that?"

"Well, I used to play football in a school and there was a coach who didn't like me for a damn. Well, our school was going to play a game up on the Hudson, and I had been substituting for our climax runner who had been hurt the week before. I had a good day substituting for him so now that he was well and had taken his old place I was moved into what might be called the position of blocking back. I wasn't adapted to it, perhaps because there was less glory and less stimulation. It was cold, too, and I don't stand cold, so instead of doing my job I got thinking how grey the skies were. When the coach took me out of the game he said briefly:

"'We simply can't depend on you.'

"I could only answer, 'Yes, sir.'

"That was as far as I could explain to him literally what happened—and it's taken me years to figure it out for my own benefit. I had been playing listlessly. We had the other team licked by a couple of touchdowns, and it suddenly occurred to me that I might as well let the opposing end—who hadn't so far made a single tackle—catch a forward pass, but at the last moment I came to life and realized that I couldn't let him catch the pass, but that at least I wouldn't intercept it, so I just knocked it down.

"That was the point where I was taken out of the game. I remember the desolate ride in the bus back to the train and the desolate ride back to school with everybody thinking I had been yellow on the occasion, when actually I was just distracted and sorry for that opposing end. That's the truth. I've been afraid plenty of times but that wasn't one of the times. The point is it inspired me to write a poem for the school paper which made me as big a hit with my father as if I had become a football hero. So when I went home that Christmas vacation it was in my mind that if you weren't able to function in action you might at least be able to tell about it, because you felt the same intensity—it was a back door way out of facing reality."

They go into a dining room now. The author walks through it in haste and a certain aversion.

"Don't you enjoy food?" the visitor asks.

"Food—yes! But not the miserable mixture of fruit juices and milk and whole-wheat bread I live on now."

"Are you dyspeptic?"

"Dyspeptic! I'm simply ruined."

"How so?"

"Well, in the middle west in those days children started life with fried food and waffles and that led into endless malted milks and bacon buns in college and then a little later I jumped to meals at Foyot's and the Castelli dei Caesari and the Escargot[2] and every spice merchant in France and Italy. And under the name of alcohol—Clarets and Burgundys, Chateau Yquems and Champagnes, Pilsener and Dago Red, prohibition Scotch and Alabama white mule.[3] It was very good while it lasted but I didn't see what pap lay at the end." He shivered, "Let's forget it—it isn't dinner time. Now this—" he says opening a door, "is my study."

A secretary is typing there or rather in a little alcove adjoining. As they come in she hands the author some letters. His eye falls on the envelope of the first one, his face takes on an expectant smile and he says to the visitor:

"This is the sequel to something that was rather funny. Let me tell you the first part before I open this. Well, about two weeks ago I got a letter under cover from *The Saturday Evening Post*, addressed not to me but to

Thomas Kracklin,
Saturday Evening post
Philadelphia
pennsylvania Pa

On the envelope were several notations evidently by the *Post's* mail department.

> *Not known here*
> *Try a story series in 1930 files*
> *Think this is character in story by X in 1927 files*

"This last person had guessed it, for Thomas Kracklin was indeed a character in some stories of mine. Here's what the letter said:

> Mr. Kracklin I wonder if you are any kin to mine because my name was Kracklin an I had a brother an he did not see us much any more we was worried about him an I thought when I read your story that you was that Kracklin an I thought if I wrote you I would find out yours truly Mrs. Kracklin Lee.

"The address was a small town in Michigan. The letter amused me and was so different from any that I had received for a long time that I made up an answer to it. It went something like this:

My dear Mrs. Kracklin Lee:

I am indeed your long lost brother. I am now in the Baltimore Penitentiary awaiting execution by hanging. If I get out I will be glad to come to visit you. I think you would find me all right except I cannot be irritated as I sometimes kill people if the coffee is cold. But I think I won't be much trouble except for that but I will be pretty poor when I get out of the penitentiary and will be glad if you can take care of me—unless they string me up next Thursday. Write me care of my lawyer.

"Here I gave my name and then signed the letter 'Sincerely, Thomas Kracklin.' This is undoubtedly the answer."

The author opened the envelope—there were two letters inside. The first was addressed to him by his real name.

Dear Sir I hope my brother has not been hung an I thank you for sending his letter I am a poor woman an have no potatoes this day an can just buy the stamp but I hope my brother has not been hung an if not I would like to see him an will you give him this letter yours truly Mrs. Kracklin Lee.

This was the second letter:

Dear Brother I have not got much but if you get off you can come back here an I could not promise to suply you with much but maybe we could get along cannot really promise anythin but I hope you will get off an wish you the very best always your sister Mrs. Kracklin Lee.

When he had finished reading the author said:

"Now isn't it fun to be so damn smart! Miss Palmer, please write a letter saying her brother's been reprieved and gone to China and put five dollars in the envelope."

"But it's too late," he continued as he and his visitor went upstairs. "You can pay a little money but what can you do for meddling with a human heart? A writer's temperament is continually making him do things he can never repair.

"This is my bedroom. I write a good deal lying down and when there are too many children around, but in summer it's hot up here in the day-time and my hand sticks to the paper."

The visitor moved a fold of cloth to perch himself on the side of a chair but the author warned him quickly:

"Don't touch that! It's just the way somebody left it."

"Oh I beg your pardon."

"Oh it's all right—it was a long long time ago. Sit here for a moment and rest yourself and then we'll go on up."

"Up?"

"Up to the attic. This is a big house you see—on the old-fashioned side."

The attic was the attic of Victorian fiction. It was pleasant, with beams of late light slanting in on piles and piles of magazines and pamphlets and children's school books and college year books and "little" magazines from Paris and ballet programs and the old *Dial* and *Mercury* and *L'Illustration*[4] unbound and the *St. Nicholas*[5] and the journal of the Maryland Historical Society, and piles of maps and guide books from the Golden Gate to Bou Saada. There were files bulging with letters, one marked "letters from my grandfather to my grandmother" and several dozen scrap books and clipping books and photograph books and albums and "baby books" and great envelopes full of unfiled items. . . .

"This is the loot," the author said grimly. "This is what one has instead of a bank balance."

"Are you satisfied?"

"No. But it's nice here sometimes in the late afternoon. This is a sort of a library in its way, you see—the library of a life. And nothing is as depressing as a library if you stay long in it. Unless of course you stay there all the time because then you adjust yourself and become a little crazy. Part of you gets dead. Come on let's go up."

"Where?"

"Up to the cupola—the turret, the watch-tower, whatever you want to call it. I'll lead the way."

It is small up there and full of baked silent heat until the author opens two of the glass sides that surround it and the twilight wind blows through. As far as your eye can see there is a river winding between green lawns and trees and purple buildings and red slums blended in by a merciful dusk. Even as they stand there the wind increases until it is a gale whistling around the tower and blowing birds past them.

"I lived up here once," the author said after a moment.

"Here? For a long time?"

"No. For just a little while when I was young."

"It must have been rather cramped."

"I didn't notice it."

"Would you like to try it again?"

"No. And I couldn't if I wanted to."

He shivered slightly and closed the windows. As they went downstairs the visitor said, half apologetically:

"It's really just like all houses, isn't it?"

The author nodded.

"I didn't think it was when I built it, but in the end I suppose it's just like other houses after all."

Esquire, 6 (July 1936), 40, 108.

1. Movie actresses.
2. Gourmet restaurants in Paris and Rome.
3. Moonshine corn whiskey.
4. French magazine.
5. Children's magazine.

"Afternoon of an Author"[1]

When he woke up he felt better than he had for many weeks, a fact that became plain to him negatively—he did not feel ill. He leaned for a moment against the door frame between his bedroom and bath till he could be sure he was not dizzy. Not a bit, not even when he stooped for a slipper under the bed.

It was a bright April morning, he had no idea what time because his clock was long unwound but as he went back through the apartment to the kitchen he saw that his daughter had breakfasted and departed and that the mail was in, so it was after nine.

"I think I'll go out today," he said to the maid.

"Do you good—it's a lovely day." She was from New Orleans, with the features and coloring of an Arab.

"I want two eggs like yesterday and toast, orange juice and tea."

He lingered for a moment in his daughter's end of the apartment and read his mail. It was an annoying mail with nothing cheerful in it—mostly bills and advertisements with the diurnal Oklahoma school boy and his gaping autograph album. Sam Goldwyn[2] might do a ballet picture with Spessiwitza[3] and might not—it would all have to wait till Mr. Goldwyn got back from Europe when he might have half a dozen new ideas. Paramount wanted a release on a poem that had appeared in one of the author's books, as they didn't know whether it was an original or quoted.[4] Maybe they were going to get a title from it. Anyhow he had no more equity in that property—he had sold the silent rights many years ago and the sound rights last year.

"Never any luck with movies," he said to himself. "Stick to your last, boy."

He looked out the window during breakfast at the students changing classes on the college campus across the way.

"Twenty years ago I was changing classes," he said to the maid. She laughed her débutante's laugh.

"I'll need a check," she said, "if you're going out."

"Oh, I'm not going out yet. I've got two or three hours' work. I meant late this afternoon."

"Going for a drive?"

"I wouldn't drive that old junk—I'd sell it for fifty dollars. I'm going on the top of a bus."

After breakfast he lay down for fifteen minutes. Then he went into the study and began to work.

The problem was a magazine story that had become so thin in the middle that it was about to blow away. The plot was like climbing endless stairs, he had no element of surprise in reserve, and the characters who started so bravely day-before-yesterday couldn't have qualified for a newspaper serial.

"Yes, I certainly need to get out," he thought. "I'd like to drive down the Shenandoah Valley, or go to Norfolk on the boat."

But both of these ideas were impractical—they took time and energy and he had not much of either—what there was must be conserved for work. He went through the manuscript underlining good phrases in red crayon and after tucking these into a file slowly tore up the rest of the story and dropped it in the waste- basket. Then he walked the room and smoked, occasionally talking to himself.

"Wee-l, let's see—"

"Nau-ow, the next thing—would be—"

"Now let's see, now—"

After awhile he sat down thinking:

"I'm just stale—I shouldn't have touched a pencil for two days."

He looked through the heading "Story Ideas" in his notebook until the maid came to tell him his secretary was on the phone—part time secretary since he had been ill.

"Not a thing," he said. "I just tore up everything I'd written. It wasn't worth a damn. I'm going out this afternoon."

"Good for you. It's a fine day."

"Better come up tomorrow afternoon—there's a lot of mail and bills."

He shaved, and then as a precaution rested five minutes before he dressed. It was exciting to be going out—he hoped the elevator boys wouldn't say they were glad to see him up and he decided to go down the back elevator where they did not know him. He put on his best suit with the coat and trousers that didn't match. He had bought only two suits in six years but they were the very best suits—the coat alone of this one had cost a hundred and ten dollars. As he must have a destination—it wasn't good to go places without a destination—he put a tube of shampoo ointment in his pocket for his barber to use, and also a small phial of luminol.[5]

"The perfect neurotic," he said, regarding himself in the mirror. "By-product of an idea, slag of a dream."

II

He went into the kitchen and said good-by to the maid as if he were going to Little America.[6] Once in the war he had commandeered an engine on sheer bluff and had it driven from New York to Washington to keep from being A.W.O.L.[7] Now he stood carefully on the street corner waiting for the light to change, while young people hurried past him with a fine disregard for traffic. On the bus corner under the trees it was green and cool and he thought of Stonewall Jackson's last words: "Let us cross over the river and rest under the shade of the trees."[8] Those Civil War leaders seemed to have realized very suddenly how tired they were—Lee shriveling into another man, Grant with his desperate memoir-writing at the end.[9]

The bus was all he expected—only one other man on the roof and the green branches ticking against each window through whole blocks. They would probably have to trim those branches and it seemed a pity. There was so much to look at—he tried to define the color of one line of houses and could only think of an old opera cloak of his mother's that was full of tints and yet was of no tint—a mere reflector of light. Somewhere church bells were playing "Venite Adoremus"[10] and he wondered why, because Christmas was eight months off. He didn't like bells but it had been very moving when they played "Maryland, My Maryland" at the governor's funeral.

On the college football field men were working with rollers and a title occurred to him: "Turf-keeper" or else "The Grass Grows," something about a man working on turf for years and bringing up his son to go to college and play football there. Then the son dying in youth and the man's going to work in the cemetery and putting turf over his son instead of under his feet. It would be the kind of piece that is often placed in anthologies, but not his sort of thing—it was sheer swollen antithesis, as formalized as a popular magazine story and easier to write. Many people, however, would consider it excellent because it was melancholy, had digging in it and was simple to understand.

The bus went past a pale Athenian railroad station brought to life by the blue shirted redcaps out in front. The street narrowed as the business section began and there were suddenly brightly dressed girls, all very beautiful—he thought he had never seen such beautiful girls. There were men too but they all looked rather silly, like himself in the mirror, and there were old undecorative women, and presently, too, there were plain and unpleasant faces among the girls; but in general they were lovely, dressed in real colors all the way from six to thirty, no plans or struggles in their faces, only a state of sweet suspension, provocative and serene. He loved life terribly for a minute, not wanting to give it up at all. He thought perhaps he had made a mistake in coming out so soon.

He got off the bus, holding carefully to all the railings and walked a block to the hotel barbershop. He passed a sporting goods store and looked in the window unmoved except by a first baseman's glove which was already dark in the pocket. Next to that was a haberdasher's and here he stood for quite a while looking at the deep shade of shirts and the ones of checker and plaid. Ten years ago on the summer Riviera the author and some others had bought dark blue workmen's shirts, and probably that had started that style. The checkered shirts were nice looking, bright as uniforms and he wished he were twenty and going to a beach club all dolled up like a Turner sunset[11] or Guido Reni's dawn.[12]

The barbershop was large, shining and scented—it had been several months since the author had come downtown on such a mission and he found that his familiar barber was laid up with arthritis; however, he explained to another man how to use the ointment, refused a newspaper and sat, rather happy and sensually content at the strong fingers on his scalp, while a pleasant mingled memory of all the barbershops he had ever known flowed through his mind.

Once he had written a story about a barber.[13] Back in 1929 the proprietor of his favorite shop in the city where he was then living had made a fortune of $300,000 on tips from a local industrialist and was about to retire. The author had no stake in the market, in fact, was about to sail for Europe for a few years with such accumulation as he had, and that autumn hearing how the barber had lost all his fortune he was prompted to write a story, thoroughly disguised in every way yet hinging on the fact of a barber rising in the world and then tumbling; he heard, nevertheless, that the story had been identified in the city and caused some hard feelings.

The shampoo ended. When he came out into the hall an orchestra had started to play in the cocktail room across the way and he stood for a moment in the door listening. So long since he had danced, perhaps two evenings in five years, yet a review of his last book had mentioned him as being fond of night clubs; the same review had also spoken of him as being indefatigable. Something in the sound of the word in his mind broke him momentarily and feeling tears of weakness behind his eyes he turned away. It was like in the beginning fifteen years ago when they said he had "fatal facility," and he labored like a slave over every sentence so as not to be like that.

"I'm getting bitter again," he said to himself. "That's no good, no good— I've got to go home."

The bus was a long time coming but he didn't like taxis and he still hoped that something would occur to him on that upper- deck passing through the green leaves of the boulevard. When it came finally he had some trouble climbing the steps but it was worth it for the first thing he saw was a pair of high school kids, a boy and a girl, sitting without any self-consciousness on the high pedestal of the Lafayette statue, their attention fast upon each other. Their isolation moved him and he knew he would get something out of it professionally, if only in contrast to the growing seclusion of his life and the increasing necessity of picking over an already well-picked past. He needed reforestation and he was well aware of it, and he hoped the soil would stand one more growth. It had never been the very best soil for he had had an early weakness for showing off instead of listening and observing.

Here was the apartment house—he glanced up at his own windows on the top floor before he went in.

"The residence of the successful writer," he said to himself. "I wonder what marvelous books he's tearing off up there. It must be great to have a gift like that—just sit down with pencil and paper. Work when you want— go where you please."

His child wasn't home yet but the maid came out of the kitchen and said: "Did you have a nice time?"

"Perfect," he said. "I went roller skating and bowled and played around with Man Mountain Dean[14] and finished up in a Turkish Bath. Any telegrams?"

"Not a thing."

"Bring me a glass of milk, will you?"

He went through the dining room and turned into his study, struck blind for a moment with the glow of his two thousand books in the late sunshine. He was quite tired—he would lie down for ten minutes and then see if he could get started on an idea in the two hours before dinner.

Esquire, 6 (August 1936), 40, 108.

1. Play on the title of *Prelude to the Afternoon of a Faun* (1894) by French composer Claude Debussy (1862–1918).

2. (1882–1974), movie producer.

3. Ballerina Olga Spessivtzewa (1895–1991). In March 1936 Fitzgerald wrote a scenario for a ballet movie.

4. The epigraph to *The Great Gatsby* was written by Fitzgerald but attributed to Thomas Parke D'Invilliers in the book.

5. A sedative.

6. In the Antarctic.

7. Fitzgerald repeated this claim elsewhere.

8. Hemingway took the title for *Across the River and Into the Trees* (1950) from these words of the Confederate general (1824–1863).

9. The Confederate commander-in-chief Robert E. Lee (1807–1870) became president of Washington College (later Washington & Lee University); the Union commander-in-chief Ulysses S. Grant (1822–1885) served two terms as president of the United States and, at the end of his life, wrote his *Personal Memoirs* (1885–1886).

10. From the Latin carol known in English as "O Come, All Ye Faithful."

11. British landscape artist J. M. W. Turner (1775–1851).

12. Italian artist Reni (1575–1642), who painted *Aurora* (1613).

13. "A Change of Class," *The Saturday Evening Post* (26 September 1931).

14. Professional wrestler.

To: Scottie Fitzgerald
20 October 1936

. . . .

Don't be a bit discouraged about your story not being tops.[1] At the same time, I am not going to encourage you about it, because, after all, if you want to get into the big time, you have to have your own fences to jump and learn from experience. Nobody ever became a writer just by wanting to be one. If you have anything to say, anything you feel nobody has ever said before, you have got to feel it so desperately that you will find some way to say it that nobody has ever found before, so that the thing you have to say and the way of saying it blend as one matter—as indissolubly as if they were conceived together.

Let me preach again for a moment: I mean that what you have felt and thought will by itself invent a new style, so that when people talk about style they are always a little astonished at the newness of it, because they think that it is only style that they are talking about, when what they are talking about is the attempt to express a new idea with such force that it will have the originality of the thought. It is an awfully lonesome business, and as you know, I never wanted you to go into it, but if you are going into it at all I want you to go into it knowing the sort of things that took me years to learn.

. . . .

F. Scott Fitzgerald: A Life in Letters, pp. 313–314.

1. Fifteen-year-old Scottie Fitzgerald was attempting to write commercial fiction.

To: Scottie Fitzgerald
July 1937

. . . .

I want to profit by these two experiences[1]—I must be very tactful but keep my hand on the wheel from the start—find out the key man among the bosses + the most malleable among the collaborators—then fight the rest tooth + nail until, in fact or in effect, I'm alone on the picture. That's the only way I can do my best work. Given a break I can make them double this contract in less than two years. . . .

F. Scott Fitzgerald: A Life in Letters, p. 331.

1. Fitzgerald, on his way to Hollywood for his third and final time, recalls his earlier unsuccessful stays there in 1927 and 1931. His June 1937 M-G-M contract was for six months at $1,000 per week. In January 1938 his contract was renewed for one year at $1,250 per week.

Fitzgerald and Scottie in Baltimore, circa 1934.

"Early Success"

October, 1937

Seventeen years ago this month I quit work or, if you prefer, I retired from business. I was through—let the Street Railway Advertising Company carry along under its own power. I retired, not on my profits, but on my liabilities, which included debts, despair, and a broken engagement and crept home to St. Paul to "finish a novel."

That novel, begun in a training camp late in the war, was my ace in the hole. I had put it aside when I got a job in New York, but I was as constantly aware of it as of the shoe with cardboard in the sole, during all one desolate spring. It was like the fox and goose and the bag of beans. If I stopped working to finish the novel, I lost the girl.

So I struggled on in a business I detested and all the confidence I had garnered at Princeton and in a haughty career as the army's worst aide-de-camp melted gradually away. Lost and forgotten, I walked quickly from certain places—from the pawn shop where one left the field glasses, from prosperous friends whom one met when wearing the suit from before the war—from restaurants after tipping with the last nickel, from busy cheerful offices that were saving the jobs for their own boys from the war.

Even having a first story accepted had not proved very exciting. Dutch Mount and I sat across from each other in a car-card slogan advertising office, and the same mail brought each of us an acceptance from the same magazine—the old *Smart Set.*

"My check was thirty—how much was yours?"

"Thirty-five."

The real blight, however, was that my story had been written in college two years before, and a dozen new ones hadn't even drawn a personal letter. The implication was that I was on the down-grade at twenty-two. I spent the thirty dollars on a magenta feather fan for a girl in Alabama.

My friends who were not in love or who had waiting arrangements with "sensible" girls, braced themselves patiently for a long pull. Not I—I was in love with a whirlwind and I must spin a net big enough to catch it out of my head, a head full of trickling nickels and sliding dimes, the incessant music box of the poor. It couldn't be done like that, so when the girl threw me over I went home and finished my novel. And then, suddenly, everything changed, and this article is about that first wild wind of success and the delicious mist it brings with it. It is a short and precious time—for when the mist rises in a few weeks, or a few months, one finds that the very best is over.

It began to happen in the autumn of 1919 when I was an empty bucket, so mentally blunted with the summer's writing that I'd taken a job repairing car roofs at the Northern Pacific shops. Then the postman rang, and that day I quit work and ran along the streets, stopping automobiles to tell friends and acquaintances about it—my novel *This Side of Paradise* was accepted for publication. That week the postman rang and rang, and I paid off my terrible small debts, bought a suit, and woke up every morning with a world of ineffable toploftiness and promise.

While I waited for the novel to appear, the metamorphosis of amateur into professional began to take place—a sort of stitching together of your whole life into a pattern of work, so that the end of one job is automatically the beginning of another. I had been an amateur before; in October, when I strolled with a girl among the stones of a southern graveyard, I was a professional and my enchantment with certain things that she felt and said was already paced by an anxiety to set them down in a story—it was called "The Ice Palace" and it was published later. Similarly, during Christmas week in St. Paul, there was a night when I had stayed home from two dances to work on a story. Three friends called up during the evening to tell me I had missed some rare doings: a well-known man-about-town had disguised himself as a camel and, with a taxi-driver as the rear half, managed to attend the wrong party. Aghast with myself for not being there, I spent the next day trying to collect the fragments of the story.

"Well, all I can say is it was funny when it happened." "No, I don't know where he got the taxi-man." "You'd have to know him well to understand how funny it was."

In despair I said:

"Well, I can't seem to find out exactly what happened but I'm going to write about it as if it was ten times funnier than anything you've said." So I wrote it, in twenty-two consecutive hours, and wrote it "funny," simply because I was so emphatically told it was funny. "The Camel's Back"[1] was published and still crops up in the humorous anthologies.

With the end of the winter set in another pleasant pumped- dry period, and, while I took a little time off, a fresh picture of life in America began to form before my eyes. The uncertainties of 1919 were over—there seemed little doubt about what was going to happen—America was going on the greatest, gaudiest spree in history and there was going to be plenty to tell about it. The whole golden boom was in the air—its splendid generosities, its outrageous corruptions and the tortuous death struggle of the old America in prohibition. All the stories that came into my head had a touch of disaster in them—the lovely young creatures in my novels went to ruin, the diamond mountains of my short stories blew up, my millionaires were as beautiful and damned as Thomas Hardy's peasants. In life these things hadn't happened yet, but I was pretty sure living wasn't the reckless, careless business these people thought—this generation just younger than me.

For my point of vantage was the dividing line between the two generations, and there I sat—somewhat self-consciously. When my first big mail came in—hundreds and hundreds of letters on a story about a girl who bobbed her hair—it seemed rather absurd that they should come to me about it. On the other hand, for a shy man it was nice to be somebody except oneself again: to be "the Author" as one had been "the Lieutenant." Of course one wasn't really an author any more than one had been an army officer, but nobody seemed to guess behind the false face.

All in three days I got married and the presses were pounding out *This Side of Paradise* like they pound out extras in the movies.

With its publication I had reached a stage of manic depressive insanity. Rage and bliss alternated hour by hour. A lot of people thought it was a fake, and perhaps it was, and a lot of others thought it was a lie, which it was not. In a daze I gave out an interview[2]—I told what a great writer I was and how I'd achieved the heights. Heywood Broun, who was on my trail, simply quoted it with the comment that I seemed to be a very self-satisfied young man, and for some days I was notably poor company. I invited him to lunch and in a kindly way told him that it was too bad he had let his life slide away without accomplishing anything. He had just turned thirty and it was about then that I wrote a line which certain people will not let me forget: "She was a faded but still lovely woman of twenty- seven."[3]

In a daze I told the Scribner Company that I didn't expect my novel to sell more than twenty thousand copies and when the laughter died away I was told that a sale of five thousand was excellent for a first novel. I think it was a week after publication that it passed the twenty thousand mark, but I took myself so seriously that I didn't even think it was funny.

These weeks in the clouds ended abruptly a week later when Princeton turned on the book—not undergraduate Princeton but the black mass of faculty and alumni. There was a kind but reproachful letter from President Hibben,[4] and a room full of classmates who suddenly turned on me with condemnation. We had been part of a rather gay party staged conspicuously in Harvey Firestone's car of robin's-egg blue, and in the course of it I got an accidental black eye trying to stop a fight. This was magnified into an orgy and in spite of a delegation of undergraduates who went to the board of Governors, I was suspended from my club for a couple of months. The *Alumni Weekly* got after my book and only Dean Gauss[5] had a good word to say for me. The unctuousness and hypocrisy of the proceedings was exasperating and for seven years I didn't go to Princeton. Then a magazine asked me for an article[6] about it and when I started to write it, I found I really loved the place and that the experience of one week was a small item in the total budget. But on that day in 1920 most of the joy went out of my success.

But one was now a professional—and the new world couldn't possibly be presented without bumping the old out of the way. One gradually developed a protective hardness against both praise and blame. Too often people liked your things for the wrong reasons or people liked them whose dislike would be a compliment. No decent career was ever founded on a public and one learned to go ahead without precedents and without fear. Counting the bag, I found that in 1919 I had made $800 by writing, that in 1920 I had made $18,000, stories, picture rights and book. My story price had gone from $30 to $1,000. That's a small price to what was paid later in the Boom, but what it sounded like to me couldn't be exaggerated.

The dream had been early realized and the realization carried with it a certain bonus and a certain burden. Premature success gives one an almost mystical conception of destiny as opposed to will power—at its worst the Napoleonic delusion. The man who arrives young believes that he exercises his will because his star is shining. The man who only asserts himself at thirty has a balanced idea of what will power and fate have each contributed, the one who gets there at forty is liable to put the emphasis on will alone. This comes out when the storms strike your craft.

The compensation of a very early success is a conviction that life is a romantic matter. In the best sense one stays young. When the primary objects of love and money could be taken for granted and a shaky eminence had lost its fascination, I had fair years to waste, years that I can't honestly regret, in seeking the eternal Carnival by the Sea. Once in the middle twenties I was driving along the High Corniche Road through the twilight with the whole French Riviera twinkling on the sea below. As far ahead as I could see was Monte Carlo, and though it was out of season and there were no Grand Dukes left to gamble and E. Phillips Oppenheim[7] was a fat industrious man in my hotel, who lived in a bathrobe—the very name was so incorrigibly enchanting that I could only stop the car and like the Chinese whisper: "Ah me! Ah me!" It was not Monte Carlo I was looking at. It was back into the mind of the young man with cardboard soles who had walked the streets of New York. I was him again—for an instant I had the good fortune to share his dreams, I who had no more dreams of my own. And there are still times when I creep up on him, surprise him on an autumn morning in New York or a spring night in Carolina when it is so quiet that you can hear a dog barking in the next county. But never again as during that all too short period when he and I were one person, when the fulfilled future and the wistful past were mingled in a single gorgeous moment—when life was literally a dream.

American Cavalcade, 1 (October 1937), 74–79.

1. *The Saturday Evening Post* (24 April 1920).
2. See "Self-Interview" (7 May 1920) in this volume.
3. Fitzgerald is possibly referring to the last section of "Winter Dreams" (*Metropolitan Magazine*, December 1922) in which the male protagonist is told that Judy Jones, the "great beauty" whom he has loved, is now twenty-seven, married, and "faded."
4. John Grier Hibben (1861–1933), president of Princeton University, wrote Fitzgerald objecting to the presentation of Princeton in *This Side of Paradise*; see *Correspondence*, pp. 58–59, for Hibbens's letter, and *F. Scott Fitzgerald: A Life in Letters*, pp. 37, 40, for Fitzgerald's reply.
5. Dean Christian Gauss (1878–1951) of Princeton was the only member of the faculty with whom Fitzgerald formed a lasting friendship.
6. "Princeton," *College Humor* (December 1927).
7. English author (1866–1946) of best-selling spy novels.

"Financing Finnegan"[1]

Finnegan and I have the same literary agent to sell our writings for us—but though I'd often been in Mr. Cannon's office just before and just after Finnegan's visits, I had never met him. Likewise we had the same publisher and often when I arrived there Finnegan had just departed. I gathered from a thoughtful sighing way in which they spoke of him—

"Ah—Finnegan—"

"Oh yes, Finnegan was here."

—that the distinguished author's visit had been not uneventful. Certain remarks implied that he had taken something with him when he went—manuscripts, I supposed, one of those great successful novels of his. He had taken "it" off for a final revision, a last draft, of which he was rumored to make ten in order to achieve that facile flow, that ready wit, which distinguished his work. I discovered only gradually that most of Finnegan's visits had to do with money.

"I'm sorry you're leaving," Mr. Cannon would tell me, "Finnegan will be here tomorrow." Then after a thoughtful pause, "I'll probably have to spend some time with him."

I don't know what note in his voice reminded me of a talk with a nervous bank president when Dillinger[2] was reported in the vicinity. His eyes looked out into the distance and he spoke as to himself:

"Of course he may be bringing a manuscript. He has a novel he's working on, you know. And a play too."

He spoke as though he were talking about some interesting but remote events of the cinquecento; but his eyes became more hopeful as he added: "Or maybe a short story."

"He's very versatile, isn't he?" I said.

"Oh yes," Mr. Cannon perked up. "He can do anything—anything when he puts his mind to it. There's never been such a talent."

"I haven't seen much of his work lately."

"Oh, but he's working hard. Some of the magazines have stories of his that they're holding."

"Holding for what?"

"Oh, for a more appropriate time—an upswing. They like to think they have something of Finnegan's."

His was indeed a name with ingots in it. His career had started brilliantly and if it had not kept up to its first exalted level, at least it started brilliantly all over again every few years. He was the perennial man of promise in American letters—what he could actually do with words was astounding, they glowed and coruscated—he wrote sentences, paragraphs, chapters that were masterpieces of fine weaving and spinning. It was only when I met some poor devil of a screen writer who had been trying to make a logical story out of one of his books that I realized he had his enemies.

"It's all beautiful when you read it," this man said disgustedly, "but when you write it down plain it's like a week in the nut-house."

From Mr. Cannon's office I went over to my publishers on Fifth Avenue and there too I learned in no time that Finnegan was expected tomorrow.

Indeed he had thrown such a long shadow before him that the luncheon where I expected to discuss my own work was largely devoted to Finnegan. Again I had the feeling that my host, Mr. George Jaggers, was talking not to me but to himself.

"Finnegan's a great writer," he said.

"Undoubtedly."

"And he's really quite all right, you know."

As I hadn't questioned the fact I inquired whether there was any doubt about it.

"Oh no," he said hurriedly. "It's just that he's had such a run of hard luck lately——"

I shook my head sympathetically. "I know. That diving into a half-empty pool was a tough break."

"Oh, it wasn't half-empty. It was full of water. Full to the brim. You ought to hear Finnegan on the subject—he makes a side-splitting story of it. It seems he was in a run-down condition and just diving from the side of the pool, you know—" Mr. Jaggers pointed his knife and fork at the table, "and he saw some young girls diving from the fifteen-foot board. He says he thought of his lost youth and went up to do the same and made a beautiful swan dive—but his shoulder broke while he was still in the air."[3] He looked at me rather anxiously. "Haven't you heard of cases like that—a ball player throwing his arm out of joint?"

I couldn't think of any orthopedic parallels at the moment.

"And then," he continued dreamily, "Finnegan had to write on the ceiling."

"On the ceiling?"

"Practically. He didn't give up writing—he has plenty of guts, that fellow, though you may not believe it. He had some sort of arrangement built that was suspended from the ceiling and he lay on his back and wrote in the air."

I had to grant that it was a courageous arrangement.

"Did it affect his work?" I inquired. "Did you have to read his stories backward—like Chinese?"

"They were rather confused for a while," he admitted, "but he's all right now. I got several letters from him that sounded more like the old Finnegan—full of life and hope and plans for the future——"

The faraway look came into his face and I turned the discussion to affairs closer to my heart. Only when we were back in his office did the subject recur—and I blush as I write this because it includes confessing something I seldom do—reading another man's telegram. It happened because Mr. Jaggers was intercepted in the hall and when I went into his office and sat down it was stretched out open before me:

WITH FIFTY I COULD AT LEAST PAY TYPIST AND GET HAIRCUT AND PENCILS LIFE HAS BECOME IMPOSSIBLE AND I EXIST ON DREAM OF GOOD NEWS DESPERATELY FINNEGAN

I couldn't believe my eyes—fifty dollars, and I happened to know that Finnegan's price for short stories was somewhere around three thousand. George Jaggers found me still staring dazedly at the telegram. After he read it he stared at me with stricken eyes.

"I don't see how I can conscientiously do it," he said.

I started and glanced around to make sure I was in the prosperous publishing office in New York. Then I understood—I had misread the telegram. Finnegan was asking for fifty thousand as an advance—a demand that would have staggered any publisher no matter who the writer was.

"Only last week," said Mr. Jaggers disconsolately, "I sent him a hundred dollars. It puts my department in the red every season, so I don't dare tell my partners any more. I take it out of my own pocket—give up a suit and a pair of shoes."

"You mean Finnegan's broke?"

"Broke!" He looked at me and laughed soundlessly—in fact I didn't exactly like the way that he laughed. My brother had a nervous—but that is afield from this story. After a minute he pulled himself together. "You won't say anything about this, will you? The truth is Finnegan's been in a slump, he's had blow after blow in the past few years, but now he's snapping out of it and I know we'll get back every cent we've—" He tried to think of a word but "given him" slipped out. This time it was he who was eager to change the subject.

Don't let me give the impression that Finnegan's affairs absorbed me during a whole week in New York—it was inevitable, though, that being much in the offices of my agent and my publisher, I happened in on a lot. For instance, two days later, using the telephone in Mr. Cannon's office, I was accidentally switched in on a conversation he was having with George Jaggers. It was only partly eavesdropping, you see, because I could only hear one end of the conversation and that isn't as bad as hearing it all.

"But I got the impression he was in good health . . . he did say something about his heart a few months ago but I understood it got well . . . yes, and he talked about some operation he wanted to have—I think he said it was cancer. . . . Well, I felt like telling him I had a little operation up my sleeve too, that I'd have had by now if I could afford it. . . . No, I didn't say it. He seemed in such good spirits that it would have been a shame to bring him down. He's starting a story today, he read me some of it on the phone. . . .

". . . I did give him twenty-five because he didn't have a cent in his pocket . . .

oh, yes—I'm sure he'll be all right now. He sounds as if he means business."

I understood it all now. The two men had entered into a silent conspiracy to cheer each other up about Finnegan. Their investment in him, in his future, had reached a sum so considerable that Finnegan belonged to them. They could not bear to hear a word against him—even from themselves.

II

I spoke my mind to Mr. Cannon. "If this Finnegan is a four- flusher you can't go on indefinitely giving him money. If he's through he's through and there's nothing to be done about it. It's absurd that you should put off an operation when Finnegan's out somewhere diving into half-empty swimming pools."

"It was full," said Mr. Cannon patiently—"full to the brim."

"Well, full or empty the man sounds like a nuisance to me."

"Look here," said Cannon, "I've got a talk to Hollywood due on the wire. Meanwhile you might glance over that." He threw a manuscript into my lap. "Maybe it'll help you understand. He brought it in yesterday."

It was a short story. I began it in a mood of disgust but before I'd read five minutes I was completely immersed in it, utterly charmed, utterly convinced and wishing to God I could write like that. When Cannon finished his phone call I kept him waiting while I finished it and when I did there were tears in these hard old professional eyes. Any magazine in the country would have run it first in any issue.

But then nobody had ever denied that Finnegan could write.

III

Months passed before I went again to New York, and then, so far as the offices of my agent and my publisher were concerned, I descended upon a quieter, more stable world. There was at last time to talk about my own conscientious if uninspired literary pursuits, to visit Mr. Cannon in the country and to kill summer evenings with George Jaggers where the vertical New York starlight falls like lingering lightning into restaurant gardens. Finnegan might have been at the North Pole—and as a matter of fact he was. He had quite a group with him, including three Bryn Mawr anthropologists, and it sounded as if he might collect a lot of material there. They were going to stay several months, and if the thing had somehow the ring of a promising little house party about it, that was probably due to my jealous, cynical disposition.

"We're all just delighted," said Cannon. "It's a God-send for him. He was fed up and he needed just this—this—"

"Ice and snow," I supplied.

"Yes, ice and snow. The last thing he said was characteristic of him. Whatever he writes is going to be pure white—it's going to have a blinding glare about it."

"I can imagine it will. But tell me—who's financing it? Last time I was here I gathered the man was insolvent."

"Oh, he was really very decent about that. He owed me some money and I believe he owed George Jaggers a little too—" He "believed," the old hypocrite. He knew damn well— "so before he left he made most of his life insurance over to us. That's in case he doesn't come back—those trips are dangerous of course."

"I should think so," I said—"especially with three anthropologists."

"So Jaggers and I are absolutely covered in case anything happens—it's as simple as that."

"Did the life-insurance company finance the trip?"

He fidgeted perceptibly.

"Oh, no. In fact when they learned the reason for the assignments they were a little upset. George Jaggers and I felt that when he had a specific plan like this with a specific book at the end of it, we were justified in backing him a little further."

"I don't see it," I said flatly.

"You don't?" The old harassed look came back into his eyes. "Well, I'll admit we hesitated. In principle I know it's wrong. I used to advance authors small sums from time to time, but lately I've made a rule against it—and kept it. It's only been waived once in the last two years and that was for a woman who was having a bad struggle—Margaret Trahill, do you know her? She was an old girl of Finnegan's, by the way."

"Remember I don't even know Finnegan."

"That's right. You must meet him when he comes back—if he does come back. You'd like him—he's utterly charming."

Again I departed from New York, to imaginative North Poles of my own, while the year rolled through summer and fall. When the first snap of November was in the air, I thought of the Finnegan expedition with a sort of shiver and any envy of the man departed. He was probably earning any loot, literary or anthropological, he might bring back. Then, when I hadn't been back in New York three days, I read in the paper that he and some other members of his party had walked off into a snowstorm when the food supply gave out, and the Arctic had claimed another sacrifice.

I was sorry for him, but practical enough to be glad that Cannon and Jaggers were well protected. Of course, with Finnegan scarcely cold—if such a simile is not too harrowing—they did not talk about it but I gathered that the insurance companies had waived *habeas corpus* or whatever it is in their lingo, and it seemed quite sure that they would collect.

His son, a fine looking young fellow, came into George Jaggers's office while I was there and from him I could guess at Finnegan's charm—a shy frankness together with an impression of a very quiet brave battle going on inside of him that he couldn't quite bring himself to talk about—but that showed as heat lightning in his work.

"The boy writes well too," said George after he had gone. "He's brought in some remarkable poems. He's not ready to step into his father's shoes, but there's a definite promise."

"Can I see one of his things?"

"Certainly—here's one he left just as he went out."

George took a paper from his desk, opened it and cleared his throat. Then he squinted and bent over a little in his chair.

"*Dear Mr. Jaggers,*" he began, "*I didn't like to ask you this in person—*" Jaggers stopped, his eyes reading ahead rapidly.

"How much does he want?" I inquired.

He sighed.

"He gave me the impression that this was some of his work," he said in a pained voice.

"But it is," I consoled him. "Of course he isn't quite ready to step into his father's shoes."

I was sorry afterwards to have said this, for after all Finnegan had paid his debts, and it was nice to be alive now that better times were back and books were no longer rated as unnecessary luxuries. Many authors I knew who had skimped along during the depression were now making long-deferred trips or paying off mortgages or turning out the more finished kind of work that can only be done with a certain leisure and security. I had just got a thousand dollars advance for a venture in Hollywood and was going to fly out with all the verve of the old days when there was chicken feed in every pot. Going in to say good-by to Cannon and collect the money, it was nice to find he too was profiting—wanted me to go along and see a motor boat he was buying.

But some last-minute stuff came up to delay him and I grew impatient and decided to skip it. Getting no response to a knock on the door of his sanctum, I opened it anyhow.

The inner office seemed in some confusion. Mr. Cannon was on several telephones at once and dictating something about an insurance company to a stenographer. One secretary was getting hurriedly into her hat and coat as upon an errand and another was counting bills from her purse.

"It'll be only a minute," said Cannon, "it's just a little office riot—you never saw us like this."

"Is it Finnegan's insurance?" I couldn't help asking. "Isn't it any good?"

"His insurance—oh, perfectly all right, perfectly. This is just a matter of trying to raise a few hundred in a hurry. The banks are closed and we're all contributing."

"I've got that money you just gave me," I said. "I don't need all of it to get to the coast." I peeled off a couple of hundred. "Will this be enough?"

"That'll be fine—it just saves us. Never mind, Miss Carlsen. Mrs. Mapes, you needn't go now."

"I think I'll be running along," I said.

"Just wait two minutes," he urged. "I've only got to take care of this wire. It's really splendid news. Bucks you up."

It was a cablegram from Oslo, Norway—before I began to read I was full of a premonition.

AM MIRACULOUSLY SAFE HERE BUT DETAINED BY AUTHORITIES PLEASE WIRE PASSAGE MONEY FOR FOUR PEOPLE AND TWO HUNDRED EXTRA I AM BRINGING BACK PLENTY GREETINGS FROM THE DEAD. FINNEGAN

"Yes, that's splendid," I agreed. "He'll have a story to tell now."

"Won't he though," said Cannon. "Miss Carlsen, will you wire the parents of those girls—and you'd better inform Mr. Jaggers."

As we walked along the street a few minutes later, I saw that Mr. Cannon, as if stunned by the wonder of this news, had fallen into a brown study, and I did not disturb him, for after all I did not know Finnegan and could not whole-heartedly share his joy. His mood of silence continued until we arrived at the door of the motor boat show. Just under the sign he stopped and stared upward, as if aware for the first time where we were going.

"Oh, my," he said, stepping back. "There's no use going in here now. I thought we were going to get a drink."

We did. Mr. Cannon was still a little vague, a little under the spell of the vast surprise—he fumbled so long for the money to pay his round that I insisted it was on me.

I think he was in a daze during that whole time because, though he is a man of the most punctilious accuracy, the two hundred I handed him in his office has never shown to my credit in the statements he has sent me. I imagine, though, that some day I will surely get it because some day Finnegan will click again and I know that people will clamor to read what he writes. Recently I've taken it upon myself to investigate some of the stories about him and I've found that they're mostly as false as the half-empty pool. That pool was full to the brim.

So far there's only been a short story about the polar expedition, a love story. Perhaps it wasn't as big a subject as he expected. But the movies are interested in him—if they can get a good long look at him first and I have every reason to think that he will come through. He'd better.

Esquire, 9 (January 1938), 41, 180, 182, 184.

1. This story is a private joke for the amusement of Fitzgerald's agent Harold Ober (Cannon) and his Scribners editor Maxwell Perkins (Jaggers).

2. Bank robber John Dillinger (1902?–1934).

3. This accident happened to Fitzgerald in July 1936.

To: Maxwell Perkins
23 April 1938

. . . .

I still feel in the dark about Tom Wolfe,[1] rather frightened for him; I cannot quite see him going it alone, but neither can I see your sacrificing yourself in that constant struggle. What a time you've had with your sons, Max—Ernest gone to Spain,[2] me gone to Hollywood, Tom Wolfe reverting to an artistic hill-billy.

. . . .

F. Scott Fitzgerald: A Life in Letters, p. 360.

1. Wolfe had left Charles Scribner's Sons.
2. Hemingway was reporting on the Spanish Civil War.

To: Scottie Fitzgerald
7 July 1938

. . . .

When I was your age I lived with a great dream. The dream grew and I learned how to speak of it and make people listen. Then the dream divided one day when I decided to marry your mother after all, even though I knew she was spoiled and meant no good to me. I was sorry immediately I had married her, but being patient in those days, made the best of it and got to love her in another way. You came along and for a long time we made quite a lot of happiness out of our lives. But I was a man divided—she wanted me to work too much for <u>her</u> and not enough for my dream. She realized too late that work was dignity and the only dignity and tried to atone for it by working herself but it was too late and she broke and is broken forever.

. . . .

F. Scott Fitzgerald: A Life in Letters, p. 363.

To: Scottie Fitzgerald
Winter 1939

. . . .

Sorry you got the impression that I'm quitting the movies[1]—they are always there—I'm doing a two weeks rewrite for Paramount at the moment after finishing a short story. But I'm convinced that maybe they're not going to make me Czar of the Industry right away, as I thought 10 months ago. It's all right Baby—life has humbled me—Czar or not we'll survive. I am even willing to compromise for Assistant Czar!

Seriously, I expect to dip in and out of the pictures for the rest of my natural life, but it is not very soul-satisfying because it is a business of telling stories fit for children and this is only interesting up to a point. It is the greatest of all human mediums of communication and it is a pity that the censorship had to come along + do this, but there we are. Only—I will never again sign a contract which binds me to tell none other than children's stories for a year and a half!

. . . .

F. Scott Fitzgerald: A Life in Letters, p. 384.

1. Fitzgerald's M-G-M contract had elapsed after eighteen months.

To: Kenneth Littauer[1]
late July? 1939

Here's another Hollywood story.[2] It is absolutely true to Hollywood as I see it. Asking you to read it I want to get two things clear. First, that it isn't particularly likely that I'll write a great many more stories about young love. I was tagged with that by my first writings up to 1925. Since then I have written stories about young love. They have been done with increasing difficulty and increasing insincerity. I would either be a miracle man or a hack if I could go on turning out an identical product for three decades.

I know that is what's expected of me, but in that direction the well is pretty dry and I think I am much wiser in not trying to strain for it but rather to open up a new well, a new vein. You see, I not only announced the birth of my young illusions in "This Side of Paradise" but pretty much the death of them in some of my last <u>Post</u> stories like "Babylon Revisited." Lorrimer seemed to understand this in a way. Nevertheless, an overwhelming number of editors continue to associate me with an absorbing interest in young girls—an interest that at my age would probably land me behind the bars.

. . . .

F. Scott Fitzgerald: A Life in Letters, p. 402.

1. Fiction editor at *Collier's*.
2. Probably "Last Kiss," declined by Littauer in 1939 but published—after Fitzgerald's death—by *Collier's* in its 16 April 1949 issue and awarded a $1,000 bonus as the best story in that issue.

To: Scottie Fitzgerald
31 October 1939

. . . .

Anyhow I am alive again—getting by that October did something—with all its strains and necessities and humiliations and struggles. I don't drink. I am not a great man, but sometimes I think the impersonal and objective quality of my talent and the sacrifices of it, in pieces, to preserve its essential value has some sort of epic grandeur. Anyhow after hours I nurse myself with delusions of that sort.

. . . .

F. Scott Fitzgerald: A Life in Letters, p. 419.

To: Zelda Fitzgerald
19 March 1940

. . . .

Nothing has developed here. I write these "Pat Hobby" stories[1]—and wait. I have a new idea now—a comedy series which will get me back into the big magazines—but my God I am a forgotten man. <u>Gatsby</u> had to be taken out of the Modern Library because it didn't sell, which was a blow.

F. Scott Fitzgerald: A Life in Letters, p. 439.

1. A series of stories that Fitzgerald wrote for *Esquire* about a Hollywood hack writer.

To: Scottie Fitzgerald
11 April 1940

. . . I go to cinema work tomorrow on a sort of half-pay, half "spec" (speculation) business on my own story <u>Babylon Revisited</u>.[1] Which is to say Columbia advances me living money while I work and if it goes over in installments with the producer, the company, the releasing people, I get an increasing sum. At bottom we eat—at top the deal is very promising.

. . . .

F. Scott Fitzgerald: A Life in Letters, p. 439.

1. Producer Lester Cowan (1907–1990) hired Fitzgerald to write a screen adaptation of his 1931 story "Babylon Revisited." The screenplay was not produced although it has been published: *Babylon Revisited: The Screenplay*, with an introduction by Budd Schulberg (New York: Carroll & Graf, 1993).

To: Zelda Fitzgerald
18 May 1940

It's hard to explain about the Saturday Evening Post matter. It isn't that I haven't tried, but the trouble with them goes back to the time of Lorimer's retirement in 1935. I wrote them three stories that year and sent them about three others which they didn't like. The last story they bought they published last in the issue and my friend, Adelaide Neil on the staff, implied to me that they didn't want to pay that big price for stories unless they could use them in the beginning of the issue. . . .

As you should know from your own attempts, high priced commercial writing for the magazines is a very definite trick. The rather special things that I brought to it, the intelligence and the good writing and even the radicalism all appealed to old Lorimer who had been a writer himself and liked style. The man who runs the magazine now[1] is an up and coming young Republican who gives not a damn about literature and who publishes almost nothing except escape stories about the brave frontiersmen, etc., or fishing, or football captains—nothing that would even faintly shock or disturb the reactionary bourgeois. Well, I simply can't do it and, as I say, I've tried not once but twenty times.

As soon as I feel I am writing to a cheap specification my pen freezes and my talent vanishes over the hill and I honestly don't blame them for not taking the things that I've offered to them from time to time in the past three or four years. An explanation of their new attitude is that you no longer have a chance of selling a story with an unhappy ending (in the old days many of mine <u>did</u> have unhappy endings—if you remember.) In fact the standard of writing from the best movies, like Rebecca,[2] is, believe it or not, much higher at present than that in the commercial magazines such as Colliers and the Post.

. . . .

F. Scott Fitzgerald: A Life in Letters, pp. 443–444.

1. Wesley Winans Stout (1890–1971).
2. *Rebecca*, the 1940 movie produced by David O. Selznick (1902–1965) and directed by Alfred Hitchcock (1899–1980), was based on the 1938 novel by English writer Daphne du Maurier (1907–1989).

To: Maxwell Perkins
20 May 1940

. . . .

Professionally, I know, the next move must come from me. Would the 25 cent press keep <u>Gatsby</u> in the public eye—or <u>is the book unpopular</u>. Has it <u>had</u> its chance? Would a popular reissue in that series with a preface <u>not</u> by me but by one of its admirers—I can maybe pick one—make it a favorite with class rooms, profs, lovers of English prose—anybody. But to die, so completely and unjustly after having given so much. Even now there is little published in American fiction that doesn't slightly bare my stamp—in a <u>small</u> way I was an original. . . .

. . . .

F. Scott Fitzgerald: A Life in Letters, p. 445.

To: Scottie Fitzgerald
12 June 1940

. . . .

What little I've accomplished has been by the most laborious and up-hill work, and I wish now I'd <u>never</u> relaxed or looked back—but said at the end of <u>The Great Gatsby</u>: "I've found my line—from now on this comes first. This is my immediate duty—without this I am nothing. . . ."

. . . .

F. Scott Fitzgerald: A Life in Letters, p. 451.

To: Zelda Fitzgerald
23 October 1940

. . . .

It's odd that my old talent for the short story vanished. It was partly that times changed, editors changed, but part of it was tied up somehow with you and me—the happy ending. Of course every third story had some other ending but essentially I got my public with stories of young love. I must have had a powerful imagination to project it so far and so often into the past.

. . . .

F. Scott Fitzgerald: A Life in Letters, pp. 467, 469.

Dust-jacket statement for Budd Schulberg's *What Makes Sammy Run?*[1]

December 13, 1940

Dear Bennett Cerf:

I told Budd I was going to write you a word about his novel with permission to quote if you wanted. I read it through in one night. It is a grand book, utterly fearless and with a great deal of beauty side by side with the most bitter satire. Such things <u>are</u> in Hollywood—and Budd reports them with fine detachment. Except for its freshness and the inevitable challenge of a new and strong personality it doesn't read like a first novel at all.

It is full of excellent little vignettes—the "extra girl" or whatever she is and her attitude on love, and the diverse yet identical attitude of the two principal women on Sammy. Especially toward the end it gets the feeling of Hollywood with extraordinary vividness. Altogether I congratulate you on publishing this fine book and I hope it has all the success it deserves.

Sincerely,

(Signed) F. Scott Fitzgerald

What Makes Sammy Run? (New York: Random House, 1941).

1. Schulberg (b. 1914) and Fitzgerald had worked together on the screenplay for *Winter Carnival* in 1939, an experience that provided the material for Schulberg's novel about Fitzgerald, *The Disenchanted* (1950). *What Makes Sammy Run?* was published in 1941.

To: Scottie Fitzgerald
undated

... There is as yet no honesty[1]—the reader will say "so what?" But when in a freak moment you will want to give the low- down, not the scandal, not the merely <u>reported</u> but the <u>profound</u> essence of what happened at a prom or after it, perhaps that honesty will come to you—and then you will understand how it is possible to make even a forlorn Laplander <u>feel</u> the importance of a trip to Cartier's!

> *The Letters of F. Scott Fitzgerald,* edited by Andrew Turnbull
> (New York: Scribners, 1963), p. 101.

1. Fitzgerald was critiquing a story by Scottie.

Excerpts from Notebooks

431 "I can't pay you much," said the editor to the author, "but I can give you some good publicity."

"I can't pay you much," said the advertiser to the editor, "but I can give you some beautiful ads."

447 It grows harder to write because there is much less weather than when I was a boy and practically no men and women at all.

737 Angered by a hundred rejection slips he wrote an extroadinarily good story and sold it privately to twenty different magazines. Within a single fortnight it was thrust twenty times upon the public. The headstone was contributed by the Author's League.

845 This is the first of six original stories written for the Screen.[1] They will not be offered to magazines. This is not because, in any sense, they are inferior products but because the magazines expect from this author descriptive and "mental" values rather than dramatic values. Also the lengths.

885 I have asked a lot of my emotions—one hundred and twenty stories, The price was high, right up with Kipling,[2] because there was one little drop of something not blood, not a tear, not my seed, but me more intimately than these, in every story, it was the extra I had. Now it has gone and I am just like you now.

Once the phial was full—here is the bottle it came in.

Hold on there's a drop left there. . . No, it was just the way the light fell

But your voice on the telephone. If I hadn't abused words so what you said might have meant something. But one hundred and twenty stories

905 He had once been a pederast and he had perfected a trick of writing about all his affairs as if his boy friends had been girls, thus achieving feminine types of a certain spurious originality. (See Proust, Cocteau and Noel Coward.)[3]

1002 As to Ernest[4] as a boy—reckless, adventurous, etc. Yet it is undeniable that the dark was peopled for him. His bravery and acquired characteristics.

1010   Boy from the Tropics
That wonderful book, <u>Soldiers of Fortune</u>[5] was a "gross representation." He was least objectionable when he talked about what they did to Igarottes and how there were natives in the backhills of Luzon who had tails of real fur.

1011 <u>Charles Brackett's Book</u>[6]
It was wonderful. I couldn't lay it down, was impelled on the contrary to hurry through it. In fact I finished it six and a half minutes while getting shaved in the Continental Hotel. It is what we call a book written at a fine pace as for the high spots there are so many that it is difficult to pick them but I could select.

1018 In a transition from say:
> <u>fight or action interest</u>
>> to
>
> love and woman interest

The transition <u>cannot</u> be abrupt. The man must be <u>before</u> or <u>after</u> an event to be interested in women; that is, if he <u>is</u> a man and not a weakwad.
Fault in transition in Musa Dag book.[7] After battle right to Julia. Sometimes clumsy. Better an interval. You cannot tie two so different masculine emotions by the same thread.

1019 Nevertheless value of Ernest's feeling about the pure heart when writing—in other words the comparatively pure heart, the "house in order."

1021 T.S.P.[8] A Romance and a Reading List
Sun also Rises.[9] A Romance and a Guide Book

1022 The only reason the artist's judgment is better is because his reason, if it is really for his work, is his opinion on the various top swayings of men and ideas is less disinterested than any other people's reason for unlike the philosophers he can at any point discountenance the whole method of his reasoning unlike the scientist he can claim being closer to nature. He reverts again and again to martyr and clown. Not apropos consider Shaw and The Bohemian Mrs. Swann and Co.[10]

1025 Books are like brothers. I am an only child. Gatsby my imaginary eldest brother, Amory my younger, Anthony my worry. Dick my comparatively good brother but all of them far from home.[11] When I have the courage to put the old white light on the home of my heart, then—

1029 I can never remember the times when I wrote anything—This Side of Paradise time or Beautiful and Damned and Gatsby time for instance. Lived in story.

1034 Just as Stendahl's portrait of a Byronic man made <u>Le Rouge et Noir</u> so couldn't <u>my</u> portrait of Ernest as Phillipe make the real modern man.[12]

1035 But there was one consolation:

They could never use any of Mr. Hemingway's four letter words, because that was for fourth class and fourth class has been abolished—

(The first class was allowed to cheat a little on the matter.)

But on the other hand they could never use any two letter words like
NO. They <u>had</u> to use three letter words like YES!

1037 There never was a good biography of a good novelist. There couldn't
be. He is too many people if he's any good.

1040 And such condescension toward the creative life—Tolstoi caught the
sense of the Napoleonic wars out in the street from the man in the street;
his comments on fiction which would make any old 1864 copy of Leslie's[13]
more humanly valuable than <u>The Red Badge of Courage</u>—the idealization
of all that passes through his empty mind; his hatred of all people who
formed the world in which he lives—a political Oscar Wilde peddling in the
provinces the plums he took from our pudding; his role of Jesus cursing. You
can see him going from prize fight to first night to baseball game—maybe
even to women—trying to put back into movement the very things Lenin
regretted that he might have destroyed—gracelessness and ugliness for its own
sake. Gentlemen, proletarians—for a prize skunk I give you Mr. Forsite.[14]

1041 D. H. Lawrence[15] great attempt to synthesize animal and emotional—
things he left out. Essential pre-Marxian. Just as I am essentially Marxian.

1042 She[16] had written a book about optimism called Wake up and Dream
which had the beautiful rusty glow of a convenient half- truth—a book that
left out illness and death, war, insanity, and all measure of achievement,
with titillating comfortability. She had also written a wretched novel and a
subsequent volume telling her friends how to write fiction, so she was on
her way to being a prophet in the great American Tradition.

1043 When Whitman said "Oh Pioneers"[17] he said all.

1045 Didn't Hemmingway say this in effect:

If Tom Wolfe ever learns to separate what he gets from books from
what he gets from life he will be an original. All you can get from books is
rhythm and technique. He's half-grown artistically—this is truer than what
Ernest said about him. But when I've criticized him (several times in talk)
I've felt bad afterwards. Putting sharp weapons in the hands of his inferiors.

1046 Reporting the extreme things as if they were the average things will
start you on the art of fiction.

1049 Conrad's secret theory examined.

He knew that things do transpire about people. Therefore he wrote the
truth and transposed it to parallel to give that quality, adding confusion

however to his structure. Nevertheless there is in his scheme a desire to imitate life which is in all the big shots. Have I such an idea in the composition of this book?

1051 Gene Stratton-Porter.[18] What a cheap old harpy she was. If Frank Norris had written one more chapter to the Octupus[19] she'd have had one more novel.

1059 Art invariably grows out of a period when in general the artist admires his own nation and wants to win its approval. This fact is not altered by the circumstances that his work may take the form of satire for satire is the subtle flattery of a certain minority in a nation. The greatest artists grow out of these periods as the tall head of the crop. They may seem not to be affected but they are.

1060 Great art is the contempt of a great man for small art.

1061 Tarkington:[20] I have a horror of going into a personal debauch and coming out of it devitalized with no interest except an acute observation of the behavior of colored people, children and dogs.

1062 The queer slanting effect of the substantive, the future imperfect, a matter of intuition or ear to O'Hara, is unknown to careful writers like Bunny and John.[21]

1064 I thought Waldo Frank was just the pen name that a whole lot of other writers used for symposiums.

1065 When the first rate author wants an exquisite heroine or a lovely morning, he finds that all the superlatives have been worn shoddy by his inferiors. It should be a rule that bad writers must start with plain heroines and ordinary mornings, and, if they are able, work up to something better.

1066 Man reads good reviews of his book so many times that he begins finally to remodel his style on them and use their rhythms.

1071 The two basic stories of all times are Cinderella and Jack the Giant Killer—the charm of women and the courage of men. The 19th century glorified the merchant's cowardly son. Now a reaction.

1072 Taking things hard—from Genevra[22] to Joe Mank—[23]: That's stamp that goes into my books so that people can read it blind like brail.

1175   BURLESQUE ON MOTHER PITCHER
     IN DOS-PASSOS MANNER:[24]

Continentals starving for want of coal finally get some but can't digest it because it's hard coal. After the war—hollow victory—they lost Montreal and it's wet. Profiteers in daguerreotypes. Everybody tired of Yankee Doodle. Men seasick crossing the Delaware. Rammed her petticoat down cannon, she was restrained. British walked away with hands over their eyes.

1177 Ernest Hemingway, while careful to avoid cliches in his work, fairly revels in them in his private life, his favorite being Parbleu ("So what?") French, and "Yes, We Have No Bananas."[25] Contrary to popular opinion he is not as tall as Thomas Wolfe, standing only six feet five in his health belt. He is naturally clumsy with his body, but shooting from a blind or from adequate cover, makes a fine figure of a man. We are happy to announce that his work will appear in future exclusively on United States postage stamps.

1179 The Barnyard boys[26]
     or Fund on the Soil
     George Barnyard
     Thomas   "
     Glenway "
     Lladeslas " , their uncle
     Knute   " , their father
     Burton Smalltown, the hired man
     Chambers, a city dude
     Ruth Kitchen
     Martha Kitchen
     Willa Kitchen, their mother
     Little Edna, an orphan
     Margaret Kitchen
    It was winter, summer, spring, anything you like, and the Barnyard Boys were merrily at work getting together epics of the American soil in time for the next publishing season. All day long they dug around in the great Hardy fields taking what would come in handy in the next winter (or spring, summer the seasons follow one another tearing up growths of by the roots)
     How Hanson you are looking cried the fan
     Chambers dress 1903
     There is no such thing as willing to be honest—like blind man willing to see

1275 My sometimes reading my own books for advice. How much I know sometimes—how little at others.

1283 Like a bad play where there is nothing to do but pick out the actors that look most like real people and watch them until, like amateurs, their true existance has become speculatively interesting

1296 To record one must be unwary

1340 The easiest way to get a reputation is to go outside the fold, shout around for a few years as a violent atheist or a dangerous radical, and then crawl back to shelter. The fatted calf is killed for Spargo, Papini, Chesterton, and Henry Arthur Jones.[27] There is a bigger temporary premium put on losing your nerve in this regard than in any other.

1357 There is this to be said for the Happy Ending: that the healthy man goes from love to love.

1373 Justification of happy ending. My father and Oscar Wilde born in the same year. One ruined at 40—one "happy" at 70. So Becky and Amelia[28] are in fact <u>true</u>.

1395 Scenario hacks having removed all life from a story substituting the stink of life—a fart, a loose joke, a dirty jeer. How they do it.

1600 <u>A Preface</u>:
    Acknowledgements, who have verified references for me or made valuable suggestions, oceanography etc., Garbo, Beebe or mythology, etiquette, lost cooking Mrs. Rorer, exploration, Hemmingway bullfighting, communism, Dos Passos, cannibalism, my own early works for necking (or petting), Amelia Earhart air currents, John J. Pershing military science, the Badaeker guides to Provence, China also curators Smithsonian Cardinal Vatican; also Universities Paris, etc., Guttengen Hydrogen, Oxygen, Tuskeegee, fresh water and Springfield Y.M.C.A. and college of electors at Washington, use of library, editors of Encyclopedia, Mr. Charles Scribner for the use of a pencil sharpener; proofs Hem., corrections Joyce Shaw. Stravinski scoring of certain passages. To Picasso for etching, Brancusi for wood pulp, Stalin U.S.S.R. Stenography for faithfully and uncomplainingly typing the entire ms. Last and least to my wife, daughter, aunts, who put at my disposal letters, wills, portraits, photographs, documents, stamp books, post card collections, laundry marks, cigar bands, report cards, diplomas, pardons, trials, convictions, accusations, leases and unpaid bills, stamp collections and Confederate money. The idea if I'm going to begin all over again at 37. Buy book if your name in it. Bibliography. I'am indebted by Mayor Walker of Cannes. The book is without index. On England and on the Continent—but enough have shown their friendship, and I feel that they have written this book just as much as I have. (or: they have all been willing collaborators, etc.)[29]

1601 There are many places here and there and up and down the world, which like O'Henry's "Five Stories Cities,"[30] suggest that one has only to go there to see something happen, but his illusion persists largely in those without the opportunity to travel. There can be a simply unimaginable dullness in a Montana cow country saloon, in Chinatown or Limehouse—perhaps because we expect so much; this applies also to a glamorous and youthful ball after one has reached a certain age, or a gondola in Venice if one hasn't; or to Hollywood teas if one is invited or to the real haunts of the underworld if one is not; or to a Paris cafe or a lonely road at night, or a park bench at dawn—it is best to stop here and rest a moment on the park bench, using it both for a seat and for an example.

1758 The episodic book, (Dos P. + Romaine[31] etc.) may be wonderful, but the fact remains that it is episodic, and and such definition implies a limitation. You are with the character until the author gets tired of him—then you leave him for a while. In the true novel, you have to stay with the character all the time, and you acquire a sort of second wind about him, a depth of realization.

1765 In a short story, you have only so much money to buy just one costume. Not the parts of many. One mistake in the shoes or tie, and you're gone.

1791 Houses of 1925 overflowing with the first editions of Joseph Hergersheimer[32] and colored toilet paper.

1819 Ernest would always give a helping hand to a man on a ledge a little higher up.

1826 In thirty-four and thirty-five the party line[33] crept into everything except the Sears Roebuck Catalogue.

1829 Max Perkins didn't want to leave himself lying around.

1844 The pulp writer—that superficial hysteria which he substitutes for emotion.

1868 Bald Hemingway characters.

1888 Hope of Heaven.[34] He didn't bite off anything to chew on. He just began chewing with nothing in his mouth.

1889 My plan about the reissue of Paradise with changed names. (For those under Thirty Six.)[35]

1893 Fastest typist isn't best secretary. Swinburne. Trick golfer with watch, lightening calculator, kicker, et. Faulkner and Wolfe[36] are those.

1900 Sid Perleman[37] is effete—new style. He has the manner of Gerald Murphy[38] and almost always an exquisite tact in prose that borders on the precieuse. I feel that he and I (as with John O'Hara and the football-glamor-confession complex) have some early undisclosed experience in common so that at this point in our lives we find each other peculiarly sympathetic. We do not need to talk.

Sheilah noted his strange grace doing his interpretation of "Slythy"[39] in the Charade the other night.

I like his brother-in-law West.[40] I wonder if he's long- winded as a defense mechanism. I think that when I am that's why. I don't want to be liked or to teach or to interest. That is my way of saying "Don't like me—I want to go back into my dream."

I know Nat through his books which are morbid as hell, doomed to the underworld of literature. But literature. He reminds me of someone. That heaviness. But in the other person it could be got used to—in Nat it has no flashes except what I see in his eyes, in his foolish passion for that tough and stupid child Mc _ _ _ _ _ _.[41] Sid knows what I know so well that it would be blasphemy to put it in conversation.

1901 John O'Hara is in a perpetual state of just having discovered that it's a lousy world. Medium is always as if the blow had struck him half an hour before and he's still dulled by the effect. Nunally J_ _ _[42] says that he's like an idiot to whom someone has given a wonderful graflex camera and he goes around with it not knowing what to snap.

1918 People like Ernest and me were very sensitive once and saw so much that it agonized us to give pain. People like Ernest and me love to make people very happy, caring desperately about their happiness. And then people like Ernest and me had reactions and punished people for being stupid, etc., etc. People like Ernest and me----

1932 How to Read[43] is the biggest fake since Van Loon Art.[44] Now that Mencken has retired the boys who really hate books and pictures are creeping out of their sinecures again and trying to make them into specimens for dissection.

1947 Advice to young writers—Read Tolstoi, Marx and D. H. Lawrence and then read Tolstoi Marx and D. H. Lawrence.

1951 To describe an apparently dastardly character like the turn coat in Janice Meredith[45] and then show he is the real hero of the whole thing, the most politically progressive and class conscious. This is really a grand idea; a series including this and Philippe[46] might be built around it. It is the recalitrant peasant in Phillipe who splits from him in disgust + is the father of peasants.

1965 Masterpieces of American Poetry by Mark Van Doren.[47] He opened it to his astonishment upon a group of eight poems by Mark Van Doren. Rising from his couch he scissored these out and put them in the Johnny but finding Mr. Van Doren's selections as uninspired as the impertinence, he laid the book away. Life was difficult. Thsi ubiquitous feeb or was it his brother actually influenced American sales through the Book of the Month Club.

1966 Miss X who gets around a lot says all the good writers think that Van Doren—the one who put his own poems in an anthology—is an ignorant man. And that the artists spit blood about Van Loon's History of the Arts with his own illustrations. The Dutch are condescending. He does not think much of the Book of the Month., etc.

1973 As a novelist I reach out to the end of all man's variance, all man's villainy—as a man I do not go that far. I cannot claim honor—but even the knights of the Holy Grail were only striving for it, as I remember.

1974 Native Son[48]—A well written penny dreadful with the apparent moral that it is good thing for the cause when a feeble minded negro runs amuck.

1979 Ideas on Fear as being removed as well as profit motive. We know the latter can—but the former. Some day when the psycho-an are forgotten E.H.[49] will be read for his great studies into fear.

1982 Biography is the falsest of the arts. That is because there were no Keatzians before Keats, no Lincolnians before Lincoln.

2001 I am the last of the novelists for a long time now.

2017   A FABLE FOR TED PARAMORE[50]
by
F. Scott Fitzgerald

A great city set in a valley, desired a cathedral. They sent for an eminent architect who designed one distinguished by a great central tower. No sooner was it begun, however, than critics arose who objected to the tower calling it useless, ornamental, illogical, and what not—destroyed his plan and commissioning another architect to build a cathedral of great blocks and masses. It was very beautiful and Grecian in its purity but no one ever loved the cathedral of that city as they did those of Rome and Sienna and the great Duomo of Florence.

After thirty years wondering why, the citizens dug up the plans of the first architect (since grown famous) and built from it. From the first Mass the cathedral seized the imagination of the multitude and fools said it was because the tower pointed heavenward, etc., but one young realist decided to dig up the artist, now an old man, and ask him why.

The artist was too old to remember, he said—and he added "I doubt if I ever knew. But I knew I was right."

"How did you know if you don't know your reasons?"

"Because I felt good that day," answered the architect, "and if I feel good I have a reason for what I do even if I don't know the reason." So the realist went away unanswered.

On that same day a young boy going to Mass with his mother quickened his step as he crossed the cathedral square.
"Oh I like our new cathedral so much better than the old," he said.
"But the academy thinks it's not nearly so beautiful."
"But it's because of the mountains," said the little boy. "Before we had the tower I could see the mountains and they made everything seem little when you went inside the Church. Now you can't see the mountains so God inside is more important."

That was what the architect had envisioned without thinking when he accidentally raised his forfinger against the sky fifty years before.

2031 There's no such thing as a "minor" character in Dostoevski.[51]

2032 The girl must be humble; there is a lack of humility in Wolfe, Saroyan,[52] Schlessinger[53] that I find as depressing as O'Hara's glooms.

2038 The purpose of a fiction story is to create passionate curiosity and then to gratify it unexpectedly, orgasmically. Isn't that what we expect from all contacts?

2039 Tender[54] is less interesting toward the climax because of the absence of conversation. The eye flies for it and skips essential stuff for they don't want their characters resolved in dessication and analysis but like me in action that results from the previous. All the more reason for _emotional_ planning.

2058 In Fisher's Mormon Book[55] there are interesting questions of tempo _contrary_ to the dramatic assumptions or at least uneasy to answer in dramatic terms. For example: at the end we get the brave men yeilding—how does Fisher show the background of that to unbelievers. I _know_ it is true— but there is lack of art. On the other hand, in dramatic inevitability such as a Kauffman[56] scenario or an expert picture there is too much inevitability.

2066 It is so to speak Ernest's 'Tale of Two Cities' though the comparison isn't apt. I mean it is a thoroughly superficial book which has all the profundity of Rebecca.[57]

2068 I want to write scenes that are frightening and inimitable. I don't want to be as intelligible to my contemporaries as Ernest who as Gertrude Stein said, is bound for the Museums.[58] I am sure I am far enough ahead to have some small immortality if I can keep well.

2070 Action is character.

The Notebooks of F. Scott Fitzgerald, edited by Matthew J. Bruccoli (New York: Harcourt Brace Jovanovich/Bruccoli Clark, 1978).

1. These screen stories have not been identified and were probably not written.
2. Kipling was a prolific short-story writer and poet.
3. Marcel Proust (1871–1922), French novelist; Jean Cocteau (1889–1963), French poet, dramatist, and fiction writer; Noel Coward (1899–1973), English actor, playwright, and songwriter.
4. Hemingway.
5. (1897), novel by Richard Harding Davis.
6. Charles Brackett (1892–1969) became a highly successful writer-producer in Hollywood.
7. *The Forty Days of Musa Dagh* (1934) by Austrian novelist Franz Werfel (1890–1945).
8. *This Side of Paradise*, Fitzgerald's first novel.
9. *The Sun Also Rises*, Hemingway's first novel.
10. Newspaper writer Rita Swann, whom Fitzgerald knew in Baltimore during 1932–1935.
11. Amory Blaine in *This Side of Paradise*; Anthony Patch in *The Beautiful and Damned*; Dick Diver in *Tender Is the Night*.
12. Stendhal (Henri Beyle, 1783–1842) published *Le Rouge et le Noir*, which featured a Byronic hero Julien Sorel, in 1831. In 1934 and 1935 Fitzgerald wrote four stories set in ninth-century France for what he planned as a novel titled "The Count of Darkness." The hero of these stories, Philippe, was loosely based on Hemingway.
13. Frank Leslie (1821–1880) was founder of mass-circulation newspapers and magazines, including *Frank Leslie's Illustrated Newspaper* begun in 1855.
14. Editor Kyle Crichton (1896–1960) reviewed books for radical periodicals under the pseudonym Robert Forsythe.
15. (1885–1930), English writer who was the author of *Lady Chatterley's Lover* (1928) and other novels exploring sexual drives.
16. Dorothea Brande wrote *Wake Up and Live!* in 1936; her other works include *Becoming a Writer* (1934), *Most Beautiful Lady* (1935), *Letters to Philippa* (1937), and *My Invincible Aunt* (1938).
17. Walt Whitman's poem "Pioneers! O Pioneers!" was first collected in the 1871 fifth edition of *Leaves of Grass*.
18. Gene Stratton Porter (1863–1924) was a popular sentimental novelist chiefly remembered for *Freckles* (1904) and *A Girl of the Limberlost* (1909).
19. *The Octopus* was published in 1901.
20. Tarkington was a recovering alcoholic.
21. John O'Hara (1905–1970), Edmund Wilson, and John Peale Bishop.
22. Ginevra King, Fitzgerald's romantic interest during his college years.
23. Screenwriter, director, and producer Joseph Mankiewicz (1909–1993), who produced

the only movie, *Three Comrades* (1938), for which Fitzgerald received screen credit.

24. Molly Pitcher (c. 1744–1832) was a heroine of the Battle of Monmouth during the Revolutionary War. Fitzgerald is parodying Dos Passos's *U.S.A.* biographies.

25. 1922 popular song; music and lyrics by Frank Silver and Irving Cohn.

26. Fitzgerald's burlesque on the back-to-the-soil novel contains references to Norwegian novelist Knut Hamsun, American novelists Glenway Wescott and Robert W. Chambers, and critic Burton Rascoe. It also alludes to fiction writers Thomas Boyd, Ruth Suckow, Willa Cather, Edna Ferber, Margaret Wilson, and Thomas Hardy. Harry Hansen was book reviewer for the *Chicago Daily News* and, later, literary editor for the *New York World-Telegram*. See Fitzgerald's letter to Perkins (c. 1 June 1925) in this volume.

27. American socialist John Spargo (1876–1966); Italian philosopher and Catholic convert Giovanni Papini (1881–1956); English Catholic writer G. K. Chesterton (1874–1936); and English social-problem dramatist Sir Henry Arthur Jones (1851–1929).

28. The shrewd, manipulative Becky Sharp and the gentle, long-suffering Amelia Sedley, female protagonists of Thackeray's *Vanity Fair.*

29. For another version of this parody acknowledgment list see the frontispiece in *Reader's Companion to F. Scott Fitzgerald's Tender Is the Night* by Matthew J. Bruccoli with Judith S. Baughman (Columbia: University of South Carolina Press, 1996).

30. In his short story "A Municipal Report" (*Hampton's*, November 1909), O. Henry refutes Frank Norris's claim that only three American cities provide story material.

31. John Dos Passos and French writer Jules Romains (1885–1972) both wrote multi-volume novels.

32. Hergesheimer's novels included *The Three Black Pennys* (1917), *Java* (1919), and *Linda Condon* (1919).

33. Doctrines enforced by the Communist Party.

34. 1938 novel by John O'Hara.

35. Fitzgerald's plan was not acted on.

36. American novelists William Faulkner (1897–1962) and Thomas Wolfe.

37. Humorist S. J. Perelman (1904–1979) and Fitzgerald were friends in California.

38. The Fitzgeralds formed a close friendship with American expatriates Gerald (1888–1964) and Sara Murphy (1883–1975) on the French Riviera. *Tender Is the Night* is dedicated to the Murphys.

39. Word taken from the first lines of "Jabberwocky" (1871), nonsense poem by Lewis Carroll: "'Twas brillig, and the slithy toves / Did gyre and gimble in the wabe."

40. Nathanael West was the brother of Perelman's wife.

41. West was married to Eileen McKenney, the subject of Ruth McKenney's *My Sister Eileen* (1938). West and McKenney were killed in an automobile accident on 22 December 1940, the day after Fitzgerald's fatal heart attack.

42. Screenwriter Nunnally Johnson (1897–1997).

43. *How to Read a Book* (1940) by philosopher Mortimer Adler (b. 1902).

44. *The Arts* (1937) by historian Hendrik Willem Van Loon (1882–1944).

45. *Janice Meredith: A Story of the American Revolution* (1899) by Paul Leicester Ford (1865–1902).

46. The hero of Fitzgerald's unsuccessful "Count of Darkness" stories.

47. *Masterpieces of American Poets* (1936) was edited by Columbia University profes-

sor Mark Van Doren (1894–1972). His brother Carl Van Doren (1885–1950), also a professor at Columbia, was an influential historian.

48. 1940 novel by Richard Wright (1908–1960).

49. Hemingway.

50. When E. E. Paramore (1895?–1956) was assigned to Fitzgerald as a collaborator on the screenplay for *Three Comrades* in 1937, the two writers disagreed about their responsibilities.

51. Fyodor Mikhaylovich Dostoyevski (1821–1881), Russian novelist known for his psychologically complex characters.

52. Fiction writer and playwright William Saroyan (1908–1981).

53. Proletarian novelist Tess Slesinger (1905–1945).

54. *Tender Is the Night.*

55. Vardis Fisher (1895–1968) wrote several novels using Mormon material. Fitzgerald was probably referring to *Children of God* (1939).

56. Playwright George S. Kaufman.

57. Fitzgerald is commenting on Hemingway's *For Whom the Bell Tolls* (1940), which he compares to Dickens's historical novel *A Tale of Two Cities* (1859) and Du Maurier's popular 1938 romance *Rebecca.*

58. In *The Autobiography of Alice B. Toklas* (1933).

Index

179, 188n. 11

Becoming a Writer (Brande), 188n. 16

Beerbohm, Max, 46, 52n. 7, 59, 60, 86

Beer, Thomas, 14, 92

Beethoven, Ludwig van, 112, 114n. 9

Beginning of Wisdom, The (Benét), 44n. 5

Being Respectable (Flandrau), 81–82

"Benediction" (Fitzgerald), 99

Benét, Stephen Vincent, 43, 44n. 5

Bennett, Arnold, 53, 54n. 3, 105, 108n. 2

Benson, Arthur C., 23, 24n. 4

Benson, E. F., 23, 24n. 4

Benson, E. W., 24n. 4

Benson, Robert Hugh, 23, 24n. 4

"Bernice Bobs Her Hair" (Fitzgerald), 31

Bessemer, Henry, 25

Best Short Stories (ed. O'Brien), 72n. 4

Best Times: An Informal Memoir, The (Dos Passos), 22n. 20

Beyond the Horizon (O'Neill), 101, 103n. 11

Biggers, Earl Derr, 14

"Big Two-Hearted River" (Hemingway), 107, 108

Bird, William, 94

Birth of a Nation, The (Griffith), 132, 142

Bishop, John Peale, 78, 121, 181, 188n. 21

Bismarck, Otto Von, 25

Bjornstad, Alfred William, 40n. 8

Black, John, 103

Blasco Ibáñez, Vincente, 43, 44n. 10, 50n. 7

Blind Bow-Boy, The (Van Vechten), 92

Bojer, Johan, 100, 103n. 7

Bookman, The, 46, 54, 58, 65, 108

Book of Burlesques, A (Mencken), 46

Book of Prefaces, A (Mencken), 45, 47n. 4

Bookseller and Stationer, 78

Booth, William, 83, 85n. 4

Boston, Mass., 27

Boston Transcript, 97

Boyd, Thomas, 18, 43, 44n. 1, 62, 77n. 1, 78, 88–89, 92, 101, 102, 103n. 2, 119, 120, 189n. 26

Boyd, Woodward (Peggy), 76–77, 82

Boy Grew Older, The (Broun), 79–80

Brackett, Charles, 179, 188n. 6

Brancusi, Constantin, 183

Brande, Dorothea, 188n. 16

Brandywine Hundred, Del., 111

Brass, A Novel of Marriage (Norris), 53– 54

"Brass Moon" (Owen), 116

Braun, Otto, 112, 113, 114n. 16

Brentano's Book Chat, 52

Bridge of San Luis Rey, The (Wilder), 119

Bright Shawl, The (Hergesheimer), 77

Bromfield, Louis, 18, 120

Bronx, N.Y., 53

Brooke, Rupert, 38, 40n. 6, 73

Brooklyn Eagle, The, 78

Broun, Heywood, 34, 35n. 5, 60, 61n. 7, 79–80

Browning, Robert, 35n. 3

Bruccoli, Arlyn, 122

Bruccoli, Matthew J., 21n. 1, 22n. 18, 30, 122, 123, 143, 188, 189n. 29

Bruce, Virginia, 147

Brush, Catherine, 145

Bryer, Jackson R., 21n. 5, 22n. 21, 96n. 1

Bryn Mawr, 166

Bunyan, John, 82n. 4

Burr, Aaron, 113, 114n. 18

Burt, Struthers, 14

Butcher, Fanny, 87

Butler, Samuel, 34, 35n. 5, 58, 83, 86, 91

Byrne, Donn, 14

Byron, George Gordon, Lord, 28n. 3

Cabala, The (Wilder), 119

Cabell, James Branch, 31, 32n. 8, 43, 44n. 7, 90

Caesar, Julius, 40

Cagnes-sur-Mer, France, 117

Callaghan, Morley, 18, 119n. 4, 120

"Camel's Back, The" (Fitzgerald), 75, 160

Candide (Voltaire), 47n. 2

Cannes, France, 183

Capua, Italy, 52n. 10

Carroll, Lewis (Charles Lutwidge

Whitman, Walt, 41, 42n. 2, 105, 180,
 188n. 17
Whom God Hath Joined (Bennett), 53
Wilde, Oscar, 34, 35n. 6, 83, 180, 183
Wilder, Thornton, 119n. 5
Wilmington, Del., 105, 113n. 4
Wilson, Edmund, 12, 21n. 3, 22n. 22,
 58, 108, 181, 188n. 21
Wilson, Harry Leon, 14
Wilson, Margaret, 103n. 16, 189n. 26
Wilson, Woodrow, 45
Winesburg, Ohio (Anderson), 70n. 16, 102
Winter Carnival, 176
"Winter Dreams" (Fitzgerald), 18,
 162n. 3
Wisdom Tooth, The (Connelly), 119
Wodehouse, P. G., 14
Wolfe, Thomas, 14, 20, 121, 143, 170,
 180, 182, 184, 187, 189n. 36
Woman of Andros, The (Wilder), 119
Woman's Home Companion, 31, 96n. 1, 104

Wood, A. Z. F., 115, 116
Wright, Richard, 190n. 48
Wylie, Elinor, 92
Wynn, Ed, 129
Wyss, Rudolf, 132n. 5

Yale University, 80n. 8, 81
Yeats, William Butler, 25, 26n. 2
"Yes, We Have No Bananas" (Silver
 and Cohn), 182
Yost, Charles, 115, 116
You Know Me Al: A Busher's Letters
 (Lardner), 135, 137n. 1
Young, Francis Brett, 101, 103n. 9
"Your Way and Mine" (Fitzgerald), 104
Youth (Conrad), 88
Youth's Encounter (Mackenzie), 23, 52

Ziegfeld, Florenz, 134, 137n. 7
Zola, Emile, 53, 54n. 1, 100, 102
Zuleika Dobson (Beerbohm), 52, 59, 86